NEW GEOGRAPHIES

NEW GEOGRAPHIES 07

GEOGRAPHIES OF INFORMATION

edited by ALI FARD & TARANEH MESHKANI

New Geographies 07
Geographies of Information

Editors
Ali Fard & Taraneh Meshkani

Editorial Board
Daniel Daou, Daniel Ibañez,
Nikos Katsikis, Pablo Pérez Ramos

Founding Editors
Gareth Doherty, Rania Ghosn, El Hadi Jazairy,
Antonio Petrov, Stephen Ramos, Neyran Turan

Advisory Board
Eve Blau, Neil Brenner, Sonja Duempelmann,
Mohsen Mostafavi, Antoine Picon, Hashim
Sarkis, Charles Waldheim, James Wescoat

Editorial Advisor
Melissa Vaughn

Text Editor
Nancy Eklund Later

Proofreader
Rebecca McNamara

Graphic Designer
Chelsea Spencer

Design Labs Administrator
Edna Van Saun

Cover illustration from Twitter data
provided by Merlyna Lim

New Geographies is the journal of Design, Agency, and Territory founded, edited, and produced by doctoral candidates in the New Geographies Lab at the Harvard University Graduate School of Design. *New Geographies* presents the geographic as a design paradigm that links physical, representational, and political attributes of space and articulates a synthetic scalar practice. Through critical essays and projects, the journal seeks to position design's agency amid concerns about infrastructure, technology, ecology, and globalization.

New Geographies 07: Geographies of Information has been made possible by grants from the Graham Foundation for Advanced Studies in the Fine Arts and the Aga Khan Program at the Harvard University Graduate School of Design.

All attempts have been made to trace and acknowledge the sources of images. Regarding any omissions or errors, please contact:

New Geographies Lab
Harvard University Graduate School of Design
48 Quincy Street
Cambridge, MA 02138

Harvard University
Graduate School of Design

New Geographies 07
Geographies of Information

Geographies of Information

Ali Fard &
Taraneh Meshkani

Digital information and data flows permeate every aspect of our society. Global networks of communication form the backbone of commerce, education, and entertainment. The ubiquity of mobile devices, RFID tags, Wi-Fi hotspots, and online platforms has shifted our understanding of the fundamental qualities of physical space—distance, time, presence—and extended our digital footprint beyond the common spaces of home and office. The speed at which bits of information travel has enabled an almost-real-time engagement with massive amounts of information and facilitated new forms of communication, transforming the traditional broadcasting culture of previous technologies into many-to-many and interactive forms of communication.

Within this context, design extensively avails itself of the technological bounty of advanced digital tools such as CAD and CAM. Yet beyond the tools, the fluidity of digital information and the seemingly immaterial nature of communication dominate most discussions. Looking past the immaterial and fluid characteristics of global networks of information and communication to ground these networks spatially has proven to be a challenge. This has been partly due to the increasing complexity of the imbrications of digital networks and physical environments, which have for the most part escaped the attention of purist analyses of either space or technology. The enmeshing of physical environments and digital data networks of monitoring, surveillance, and control brings with it a dramatic rescaling and a destabilization of older hierarchies of scale. Furthermore, the links between urban space and cyberspace have

created a myriad of sociocultural practices and political processes that have reoriented our understanding of both physical and virtual spaces. How do information and communication technologies (ICTs) materialize at local, regional, or global scales? How does one define a contemporary geography of information? Will this geography be limited to the reach of Wi-Fi networks that percolate through cafes, offices, and public spaces of our cities, or can it also be read in the physical imprints of communication that extend far beyond the urban nucleus of cities, blanketing the globe in thick layers of wires and electronic signals? What new spatial conceptions emerge as the rapid deployment of ICTs challenges our perception of the spaces and places traditionally associated with the dissemination of information and public social interactions? Further contributing to the difficulty of grounding information and communications networks is the revolutionary ideology embedded in ICTs, which has tended to ignore the evolution of these technologies and their social and political relationships over the span of at least the past century. How does one contextualize the ever-expanding histories, forms, processes, and practices influencing the multiple geographies of information?

Understanding the contemporary networks of information and communication as inherently geographic, *Geographies of Information* attempts to realign design's relationship to ICTs by expounding the multiscalar complexities and contextual intricacies underlying their various footprints.[01]

For designers and urbanists, the friction between the fluidity of information flows and their materialization at various scales and within diverse geographies has roots in historical discussions stemming back to the military projects of World War II.[02] With the rise of cybernetics and the study of control systems in the years following the war, the influence of electronic communication technologies and their networks began to permeate the spatial disciplines as major conceptual drivers.[03] Under the heavy influence of the theoretical discourse of Marshall McLuhan and Buckminster Fuller, from the 1950s on, architecture embraced electronic communication and computers and eagerly anticipated their potential effect on cities and urban environments.[04]

Fascinated with the processing power of computers and the connective fabric of communication networks, architectural practices of the 1960s began to imagine the city as a giant computer or communication system. Cedric Price and Archigram in the United Kingdom, Superstudio and Archizoom in Italy, and the Metabolists in Japan emerged among the radical voices who believed that the new wave of electronically mediated ICTs would bring about a dramatic shift in the concept of the urban. Freed from the fixity and materiality of traditional urbanism, the city was now able to move, expand, and disperse.[05] Although the shift toward urban software gained great traction within the architectural discourse of the time, it was precisely software's dialectical relationship to the hardware that underlined almost every radical project of the 1960s.

During the next three decades, the influence of these ideas on architecture and other spatial fields was such that notions of urban transcendence—in which electronic technologies of communication would somehow replace or surmount the physicality of cities—permeated much of the discussion around ICTs and space.[06] Within this discussion, a lack of critical perspective on ICT-mediated shifts away from urban form and places often encouraged a concomitant belief that more democratic, egalitarian, decentralized, and ecologically sensitive societies would necessarily emerge as a result.[07] Having evolved from the spatial ideologies of cities and technology from the 1960s, these theories implied, in some way or another, an end to the city as we knew it.[08] More recent studies have shown, however, that although some urban exchange has been replaced by digital communication, processes of metropolitanization have granted a renewed importance to highly concentrated cities such as New York and London as command and control nodes within the global networks of production, consumption, and logistics.[09] Not only have cities not disappeared but, in fact, they have grown; and the resulting urban spaces are highly fragmented and of unequal infrastructural development and accessibility.[10]

While the incorporation of ICTs within every aspect of modern society has introduced new dynamism and hypermobility to capital, space, and social interaction, the fluidity of global networks of communication is continually materialized in the very physical infrastructure of connectivity. For influential scholars of spatial political economy, this spatial fixity lies at the core of capitalism's thirst for geographic and territorial expansion.[11] The investment into pipes, wires, cables, roads, ports, airports, and railways that underlie and connect moments of agglomeration grounds these infrastructural networks in the very space and time they are trying to overcome. Their fixity essentially embeds these networks in the social, political, and environmental processes of the localities in which they are placed.

Such material embeddedness generates urban metabolic linkages between ICTs and the "grounded" infrastructures (water, electricity, transportation) that form the basis of their local spatial production. In the case of data centers, the quintessential building typology of the information age, access to inexpensive sources of energy is required to feed the power-hungry servers and equipment.[12] The availability of immediate sources of water is also essential, as the equipment needs to be kept cool. The installation, expansion, and servicing of data centers require reliable access to transportation infrastructure. Local tax incentives and inexpensive land prices round out some of the basic prerequisites of tech company investment in a community. Physical geography, local politics, infrastructural accessibility, and location in relation to major markets of information consumption and production each play an essential role in where and when networks of information and communication hit ground. The process is inherently geographic, essentially linking ICT networks to the larger environmental systems and sociopolitical relationships that govern processes of energy generation, land use planning, water management, and capital production.

These underlying sociopolitical relations, however, are often concealed by the buried conduits of global communication and the invisible electronic signals of information—in other words, by the physical absence of ICTs in our everyday lives. Relegated to the underground and the atmosphere, tucked in the sleepy corners of the developed world, and secured behind concrete and defensive urban design, the "hidden form" of information has to a large extent escaped the critical gaze of scholars and designers alike. As Maria Kaika and Erik Swyngedouw suggest, urban infrastructure's move out of sight during the twentieth century greatly contributed to an occult reading of the social relations and power mechanisms coded in and manifested though these urban networks and the flows that run through their pipes, cables, conduits, and electronic signals.[13] This tendency of urban infrastructural networks to remain out of sight is only interrupted by accidents, disasters, or systematic failures, which bring them back into the scope of our spatial consciousness. Disruptions not only make the hidden form of infrastructural networks visible, they also contribute to the continual regeneration of these networks and expose how they regulate the livelihoods of those dependent upon them.[14] The bursting of the dot-com bubble, the many cables cuts in the middle of oceans, damage from satellite debris, loss of signal messages, destruction of essential regional and national communication networks from terrorist attacks, winter storms, earthquakes, and floods are all examples of the sudden rematerialization of the global networks of information brought about by disruption.

With cities constantly at risk—of terrorist attacks, natural disasters, the spread of disease, infrastructural failure, public upheaval—the paradigms of urban security and resilience have greatly shifted the focus of urban management and planning. Expanding on Ulrich Beck's arguments in his book *Risk Society*, urban health is now judged by how well a city responds to risk.[15] Furthermore, demographic change (often caused by migration or the aging of a population), the densification and overpopulation of city centers, problems related to sprawl, the overconsumption of energy, environmental hazards, sustainability concerns, and the exacerbation of inequality are now among the growing concerns of cities and urban environments. Within this context, large technology corporations have emerged as the flag-bearers of urban risk mitigation. Paralleling the enthusiastic response of planners to techno-scientific management of urban environments through advanced military technology after World War II, cities have for the most part embraced the promise of high technology to respond to risk and alleviate the myriad of urban problems they face.[16] From established cities such as Rio de Janeiro to new developments such as Songdo, in South Korea, new urban technology is employed to do it all—from alleviating traffic jams to responding to a crime.

Tech companies such as IBM, Cisco, Siemens, and Google have identified cities as an emerging market and have invested heavily in developing urban technology, contributing to the construction of an ideology of digitally mediated urban intelligence often referred to as the "smart city." While these corporate players partner with governments to monitor and manage urban infrastructure and services, they have for the most part adopted a neoliberal ideology, believing that the market can better manage and more efficiently deal with urban problems than can governments. Public intellectuals and others have responded, however, by decrying the depoliticization of cities and the privatization of urban infrastructures.[17] Smart city projects tend to be utopian in nature and deal with urban problems in a techno-scientific manner. The premise of most of these corporate plans is based solely on smart technologies and data optimization, and they often neglect the role of spatial form or citizen agency in finding urban solutions.[18]

It is important to note that whereas smart city ideologies have met with increasing criticism, not all urban technologies are viewed negatively. As opposed (and perhaps in response) to the top-down approach of IT corporations, many bottom-up open-source platforms have emerged (like SeeClickFix) that enable citizens to find solutions to their local infrastructure problems. Wide adoption of digital technology has also broadened accessibility and participation, contributing to the empowerment of individuals and improving transparency and accountability within traditional power structures. Successful new social movements and civic protests—the Arab Spring, Iran's Green Movement, the Euromaidan protests of Ukraine, the Occupy Movement, the 2014 Hong Kong protests—coordinated in part by digital "liberation technologies" and social media, provide positive examples of sociopolitical transformation through the use of ICTs.[19] Posts on social media networks like Twitter and Facebook, uploaded videos of protests by citizen journalists on YouTube, messaging on mobile technologies, and broadcasts by news networks from the main sites of contestation not only helped mobilize people and resources but also transformed the nature of public urban spaces during the recent uprisings. The Habermasian notion of the public sphere as a constellation of communicative and deliberative spaces that link citizens to states has become increasingly relevant in these protests, even though postmodern critiques of the public sphere still remain valid.[20] In addition to the physical spaces of interaction (coffeehouses and salons), the means of communication and information circulation (newspapers, books, pamphlets) have proven critical to the notion of the public sphere. In this regard social media platforms can be considered as not only the extension of the public spaces of streets, squares, parks, or libraries but also a new spatial condition facilitating interaction and communication.

Like physical space, however, digital media platforms are influenced by rules and regulations of access, control, use, and private versus public ownership. And although many believe that access to information and new communication technologies has empowered citizens and helped resolve a myriad of social justice issues, others are mistrustful of the way ICTs can be used as instruments of surveillance to monitor our daily lives.[21] These technologies are frequently used as means of control, secrecy, surveillance, and censorship at many levels of governance and society. This realization has precipitated a shift away from theories of surveillance and control through bureaucratic institutions or panoptic supervision and policing, toward theories involving real-time methods of surveillance that require neither the spatial rigidity of subjects nor their direct observation.[22] New digital surveillance technologies are, in many instances, different from traditional surveillance techniques in the way they deal with space. These technologies track bodies, vehicles, objects, and events in real time. They automate data collection and monitor space at vast geographic scales. Yet, as Stephen Graham and David Wood suggest, the conditions created by digital surveillance technologies have been affected by the processes of liberalization and privatization of public space.[23] The proliferation of closed-circuit television (CCTV) cameras exemplifies this condition: deployed as technical aids to detecting and preventing crime, vandalism, and even terrorism throughout the public and private realms, CCTVs have raised concerns regarding the end of privacy and the functioning of public space as an arena for social and political interaction and deliberation.

Furthermore, the new means of analyzing, modeling, and mapping urban data through data-mining algorithms or models for predictive analysis have given rise to "dataveillance." The data collection enabled by new geo-located technologies (GPS, mobile phones, social networks, crowdsourcing applications, remote sensing by satellites or drones, airborne RFID tags, credit cards) creates new urban knowledge and supports dynamic new urban models—models vastly different from the conventional, structured, census-based ones of the past. Even though these new dynamic processes of data analysis grant us more control over the performance of urban systems and of the ways in which we challenge the social and economic problems of cities, they also increasingly influence the politics of data and the violation of privacy rights. The National Security Agency's recent surveillance activities involving email communication metadata and phone tapping underscore the downside of centralized "big data" collection and analysis.

The most prevalent readings of ICT networks are plagued by conceptual dualities. By focusing on various binary conditions related to the materiality (physical or virtual), manifestation (hardware or software systems), scales of operation (global or local), or relational characteristics (social or technological) of ICTs, these analyses have been unable to fully articulate the spatial complexities of these technologies. Contemporary ICTs are inherently hybrid constructions that challenge the rigid distinctions and dichotomies between society and technological networks, macro and micro scales, human and nonhuman actors. Most importantly, the emphasis on virtuality, to the exclusion of the physical realm, often leads to a downplaying of the material conditions and physical spatialities inherent to the hypermobility of ICTs. The construction of cyberspace is dependent upon the nondigital, from its various material conditions, capital fixities, and infrastructural requirements to more symbolic means of understanding these spatialities. Hence, a hybrid reading of ICTs and their spatial constructions will better ground them within the social, cultural, technological, and political processes of the contemporary societal condition.

Geographies of Information suggests emphasizing the impure, messy, and dynamic characteristics of our contemporary society as a more productive way of studying the hybridities that support the construction of the networked materialities and social-technical relationships of information and communication networks. This volume thus presents a new set of frameworks that refrain from generalizations prevalent in modern scientific thought to highlight the complexity of socio-technical constructions, processes, and practices that form the spaces of information and communication.

A number of contributions in this volume investigate the historical origins of early communication networks and analyze the significance of geographic context and spatial form in their generation [Papanikolaou / Varnelis]. Other historical contributions explore the military and state origins of networked urban technologies of information and communication and the processes and practices that emerge from these initiatives as critical moments within the ICTs' development [Light / Kotsioris]. Following this historical contextualization, other contributions highlight the recent rise of big data and predictive analytics. They offer critical perspective on how these technologies have transformed our perception of urban intelligence, and their influence on how urban environments are imagined, monitored, and organized [Kitchin / Shepard]. Whereas some contributors look into questions of infrastructural sustainability and the productive convergence of information technologies with other infrastructural

Opposite: Grounded geographies of information.

DEW Line Station
Hall Beach, NU, Canada

Facebook Data Centers
Prineville, OR

60 Hudson Ave. (Western Union Building)
Manhattan, NY

Tahrir Square
Cairo, Egypt

NSA Utah Data Center
Bluffdale, Utah

Songdo International Business District
Songdo, South Korea

networks [Orfanos, Marinou, Sagia & Pollalis], others critique various smart city notions, including the privatization of services and infrastructures by corporate players, inequality of access and cost, the creation of generic spaces, and the emergence of new modes of surveillance and control [Picon / Greenfield / Steenson / Kitchin].

Other essays aim to underline the linkage of new ICTs and their spatialities to the social, cultural, and political processes of contemporary societies. Authors investigate fundamental conceptions of the embeddedness of information in localities, bottom-up versus top-down management of urban spaces, computational scarcity, inequality of access to information, and the emergence of new models of geographic distribution of information [McCullough / Blanchette / M. Graham / Bratton]. The influence of ICTs on the public sphere and on the political process, facilitated by social media and encouraged by new forms of activism, emerge as important aspects of these investigations [Lim / Blanchfield].

Attempting to ground these processes and practices, another group of contributions looks into the imprints and physical footprints of information technologies. These contributions examine the incipient geographies of ICTs, their building typologies and relationships to site conditions, operational scale, energy needs, and environmental requirements [S. Graham / Hallak / White]. In parallel with these investigations of ICTs' spatial manifestations, other essays and projects examine historical and emerging methods of computational mapping, along with platforms and technologies for data-driven spatial modeling and data visualization [Wilson / Pirokka, Ellis & Del Tredici].

Geographies of Information is framed as a response to the immaterial, frictionless, acontextual, and nonspatial ideologies that continue to surround contemporary networks of information and communication. Hence, this volume examines the forms, imprints, places, and territories in which the dynamism and fluidity of contemporary networks of information become crystallized. It brings together a collection of works by scholars, designers, artists, and journalists to form a spatially grounded and nuanced account of the hybrid conditions that ICTs generate, the scales at which they operate, and the processes and practices by which this production of space manifests in both advanced and emerging economies.

01. The geographic approach to design and urbanism has been at the core of the *New Geographies* project since its inception at the Harvard University Graduate School of Design by Hashim Sarkis and a group of Doctor of Design candidates. This volume is the second in a three-part series investigating the formal, spatial, and material imprints of contemporary processes of urbanization.

02. Jennifer S. Light, *From Warfare to Welfare: Defense Intellectuals and Urban Problems in Cold War America* (Baltimore: Johns Hopkins University Press, 2003).

03. The study of patterns in nature and human organizations initiated by cybernetics gained greater prominence in the architectural discourse of the time, prompting a disciplinary concern for the invisible connective networks of communication. See Reinhold Martin, *The Organizational Complex: Architecture, Media, and Corporate Space* (Cambridge, MA: MIT Press, 2003).

04. For an engaging account of network thinking and its adoption in architecture, see Mark Wigley, "Network Fever," *Grey Room* 4 (Summer 2001): 83–122.

05. See Melvin M. Webber, "Order in Diversity: Community without Propinquity," in *Cities and Space: The Future Use of Urban Land*, ed. Lowdon Wingo (Baltimore: John Hopkins University Press, 1963), 23; and Mark Wigley, "Resisting the City," in *Transurbanism*, ed. Arjen Mulder (Rotterdam: V2_Publishing/NAi Publishing, 2002), 103–21.

06. See Mark Wigley, "Resisting the City"; and Stephen Graham, *The Cybercities Reader* (London: Routledge, 2004).

07. Graham, *Cybercities Reader*, 8.

08. William Mitchell, for example, hypothesized that advances in digital communications networks and information technologies would eventually replace much of the physical circulation in cities. Advancing the longstanding concept of digital tools as extensions of the human body, Mitchell believed that many of the urban exchanges would eventually be rendered redundant by digital ICTs. William J. Mitchell, *City of Bits: Space, Place, and the Infobahn* (Cambridge, MA: MIT Press, 1995).

09. See Manuel Castells, *The Informational City: Information Technology, Economic Restructuring and the Urban-Regional Process* (Oxford: Blackwell, 1989); and Saskia Sassen, *The Global City* (Princeton, NJ: Princeton University Press, 1991).

10. Stephen Graham and Simon Marvin, *Splintering Urbanism: Networked Infrastructures, Technological Mobilities and the Urban Condition* (London: Routledge, 2001).

11. As David Harvey has suggested, global capitalism has a tendency—in fact, a need—to transcend the constraints of space and time through spatial fixity. See David Harvey, "Globalization and the 'Spatial Fix,'" *Geographische Revue* 3, no. 2 (2001): 23–30.

12. A recently published report by Greenpeace estimates that a single data center can consume the equivalent amount of electricity as nearly 180,000 homes. Based on current projections, the demand for electricity for the global IT sector is set to increase to an amount greater than the total combined electricity demands of France, Germany, Canada, and Brazil. See Gary Cook, "How Clean is Your Cloud?," Greenpeace, April 2012, http://www.greenpeace.org/international/Global/international/publications/climate/2012/iCoal/HowCleanisYourCloud.pdf.

13. Erik Swyngedouw and Maria Kaika, "Fetishizing the Modern City: The Phantasmagoria of Urban Technological Networks," *International Journal of Urban and Regional Research* 24, no. 1 (March 2000): 120–38.

14. See Stephen Graham, ed., *Disrupted Cities: When Infrastructure Fails* (New York: Routledge, 2010).

15. Ulrich Beck, *Risk Society: Towards a New Modernity*, trans. Mark Ritter (London: Sage Publications, 1992).

16. Light, *From Warfare to Welfare*.

17. See, for example, Rob Kitchin, "The Real-Time City? Big Data and Smart Urbanism," *GeoJournal* 79 (2014): 1–14; Adam Greenfield, *Against the Smart City* (New York: Do projects, 2013); and Richard Sennett, "No One Likes a City That's Too Smart," *Guardian*, December 4, 2012.

18. Alberto Vanolo, "Smartmentality: The Smart City as Disciplinary Strategy," *Urban Studies* 51, no. 5 (2014): 883–98.

19. Larry Diamond and Marc F. Plattner, eds., *Liberation Technology: Social Media and the Struggle for Democracy* (Baltimore: Johns Hopkins University Press, 2012); and Manuel Castells, *Networks of Outrage and Hope: Social Movements in the Internet Age* (Cambridge, UK: Polity Press, 2012).

20. See Jürgen Habermas, *The Structural Transformation of the Public Sphere: An Inquiry into a Category of Bourgeois Society*, trans. Thomas Burger, with Frederick Lawrence (Cambridge, MA: MIT Press, 1991).

21. Evgeny Morozov, *The Net Delusion: The Dark Side of Internet Freedom* (New York: Public Affairs, 2011).

22. See, for example, Michel Foucault, *Discipline and Punish: The Birth of the Prison*, trans. Alan Sheridan (New York: Vintage Books, 1995); Gilles Deleuze, "Postscript on the Societies of Control," *October* 59 (Winter 1992): 3–7; David Lyon, *Surveillance Society: Monitoring Everyday Life* (Buckingham, UK: Open University, 2001); and Oscar H. Gandy Jr., *The Panoptic Sort: A Political Economy of Personal Information* (Boulder, CO: Westview Press, 1993).

23. Stephen Graham and David Wood, "Digitizing Surveillance: Categorization, Space, Inequality," *Critical Social Policy* 23, no. 2 (May 2003): 227–48, esp. 229.

Image Credits
009: Images from Google Earth, with annotation by the authors.

011

Must Media Mean Remoteness?

Malcolm McCullough

Question: Instead of mapping the passive traces of informational flux, what would it mean to turn the inquiry around to ask, How does the physical situation actively guide information acts in the first place?

As architects, installation artists, and interaction designers well know, action creates context. Place is not just GPS coordinates; the geography of the city cannot be reduced to handheld wayshowing systems. Space is not just a preexisting void; it emerges both architecturally and perceptually. Generally, the more that action has created a space, the more that space becomes necessary to that activity. So it is not such a good idea to do anything anytime anyplace. Almost any cultural practice is situated, and as design researchers are aware, people do not follow rules so much as they play situations.[01] Although that seems obvious enough for interpersonal patterns of space, in, say, the theater, a dinner party, or a political demonstration, it is also often true in the use of technology. Ever since information technology moved beyond the desktop, and especially now as many more mobile apps navigate, annotate, and even operate their physical surroundings, the cultural challenge of information technology has become an exercise in situated actions.

The time seems right to reevaluate such insights, as lately almost everyone seems obsessed with smartphones. So please recite: Not everything happens on your handheld! Nor on distant servers! Don't let the Cloud keep your thoughts for you! There are situated technologies, too. Information accumulates differently in some places than in others, and of course the physical circumstances of this layering and embedding can themselves

inform. However influential the flows of data, the situations of life must nevertheless channel them—and often generate them. Now, in some design circles, these arguments have been around for twenty years, since back when the obsession with portals onto remote resources still imagined a coherent world on the far end: they called it "cyberspace." (Doesn't that word sound so 1990s?) Yet many an assumption of remoteness remains. Although life has hardly vanished through the looking glass into some disembodied otherworld, and although cities still get built and rents continue to rise, the prevailing notion of information has remained one of signals sent from afar.[02] Must this always be so?

An inquiry into informational geographies thus invites a new take on a question that likewise dates back to the 1990s: "Must media mean remoteness?"[03] Well, that depends on what you mean by "media." It depends on openness to multiple scales and interpretations of "geographies." It suggests more user-centric notions of grounding, locality, or situation. And it asks how embodied participation can recognize or generate information in the first place, and not just receive or reflect it from afar.

Instances

Consider three cases, at the scale of the street, the building, and the room, offered as a counterpoint to the more usual "zooming out" of when architects do geography. Although in each of these instances, one might ask how the circumstances of engagement create a mental or social configuration, let us leave it to another essay to chart how the spatial frequencies and aggregations of

An information technology application not normally thought of as "media": Bixi bike share, Toronto.

such instances form a larger geography. The point here is simply to ask whether proximity might have a role in any geography of information.

Since street level has become the most important site, scale, and platform of recent information technology—that is, mobile and embedded technology—let's start there. But let's not start with the augmented reality app: instead, consider a case that has been so telling for so many different urban agendas lately—the bike share station. A bicycle is something recognizable to almost anyone. To ride one involves some of the most distinctly embodied and tacit knowledge of everyday modern life. So it seems safe to say that a bicycle does not seem like "media." Yet now there is an app for it: more in the kiosk than the bicycle itself but nevertheless identified with the bicycle itself, here is a new layer of information network in local urban geography. It is certainly not a medium to sit down to or tap messages across, however. Although it involves a small screen (as so many things do lately), the kiosk is a walk-up, touchable interface, whose main action is the physical release of a bike from the rack. The handheld finds it and then perhaps provides a passcode. The bicycle itself is tagged and perhaps tracked. Although the transaction itself does communicate elsewhere (to log the trip, for instance, and charge a credit card), the act of a rental, made knowable by the presence of things, may not feel like a portal onto someplace else. In what by now has become a familiar trope among interaction designers, here is an instance where the information layer feels like just one more component or material of everyday things.[04]

As ever, the most successful technologies are the ones that disappear into everyday life. Information technology is embodied and embedded in the object that preceded it and whose use generates information rather than receiving it. Physically going for a ride, then, creates an information shadow, not only of the rental transaction and staging logistics but also perhaps of incidental conditions such as air or noise pollution documented along the way, or of clusters of other riders (for safety in numbers) found over the course of the journey. These physical circumstances make the mobility more vivid, and the territory more mentally mappable, and may generate data. Yes, the fact that the bike shares are networked may well be what is most practically useful about them; yet the network reflects the situation of mobility in this city, more than those reflecting any intrinsic logic of this particular information system. And yes, a larger geography does emerge, because the bike share network becomes one among many other networks in an urban mobility repertoire, and that ultimately alters both individual mental models and aggregate city form. But the argument here is one of proximity, of embodied objects as services, in cities that have failed to disappear into cyberspace, and where the interesting information technologies instead disappear into familiar things.

For a second instance, consider such embedding at the scale of a building. Here the most telling cases tend to be purposefully configured sites of specialized action. Although similar effects occur amid dwelling, socialization, and travel, usually the most distinct configurations are for work: the social learning spaces of a university, a hotel conference room, a courtroom, or perhaps a healthcare clinic. Consider the latter, as interaction designers and organizational scientists quite often do. While perhaps full of remarkable instruments, a clinic is also a technology and a functional type in itself, full of situations for doing this and not that, informed by this and not that data. So although not explicitly an "algorithm," as the word might mean in other disciplines, there is implicit information in what architects have conventionally called "program." And increasingly, there are embedded data systems. The clinic provides a familiar array of stations and rooms for the exchange of data—indeed, for the harvesting of data—and this works exactly because not all the data goes everywhere. Not only for reasons of privacy but also for usability, particular stations represent particular scopes of information. Like the bike share, a given site may make a particular technological transaction (for example, an X-ray), amid a general urban network (the medical-industrial complex), more understandable and accessible to a user's spatial mental model. Although all the medical information in that larger system is conceivably available anywhere throughout it, the point is nearly the opposite: everything in its place. Of course a clinic is far more complex than a bike share, for it is an institutionalized site of professional practice, whose layout embodies an understanding of what has worked in the past, and which helps participants make sense of a new situation. This illustrates how purposeful groups and their individually skilled members "act their way into understanding." Dynamic, emergent, often retrospective, "sensemaking" explains the play of many situations.[05]

And lest a medical clinic seem too arbitrary an example, note the same for, say, an artist's studio (where a visitor must not move any of the tools), or a household kitchen, which is not just for cooking but also about it. The venues, props, annotations, enclosures, and configurations that support particular activities not only put interactivity in place (and exclude irrelevant considerations) but also often represent, allow, and cue that action. Despite how much is possible online today, and despite how thoughtlessly people introduce sensors, screens, instructions, and feeds anywhere and everywhere, a great deal of life remains about showing up, knowing the protocols, and making sense of what is going on at the moment. Even in the use of remote portal technologies like laptops and phones, there is said to be a texture to communications.[06] Like the previous case of the bike share, such contexts both reshape mental models individually and aggregate into distinct urban patterns socially. Without necessarily sending or receiving any remote data, proximal configuration itself informs, and so may be an element of informational geographies.

Then let's make a third instance an unspecialized, more eponymous one: a renovated rental space in an old warehouse district; one where something more than "location, location, location" makes the high rent seem worthwhile. This might be an issue of atmosphere: operable windows, admitting interesting sounds and not just noise outside; a fascinating quality of its light that changes from season to season or across the course of the day. It might also involve materials and spatial configurations, in which at least some eccentricities contribute to the pleasure of living there. For instance, it might have an architectural form and type that outlasts changing functions. Contrary to the prevailing wisdom that occupants do not want to notice such things (and contrary also to high-tech dreams of infinite actuation, where space becomes just anything on demand), it is the fixed circumstances of this situation that appeal. Part of that appeal is in grounding the experience amid whatever overconsumption of remote information feeds might occur there, as if without the former only more of the latter might happen. Here, more so than in generic built space, an appreciated presence of surroundings may at least sometimes supplant usual distractions. A space need not be arranged so programmatically as a clinic for particular feeds to be appropriate in some spots and not others. If used for dwelling, this might mean no electronics in the bedroom, for instance. While the occupants might just call this mindfulness, here is a hyperlocal geography of information practices.

(at work...)

Deliberating (places for thinking)

Presenting (places for speaking to groups)

Collaborating (places for working within groups)

Dealing (places for negotiating)

Documenting (places for reference resources)

Officiating (places for institutions to serve their constituencies)

Crafting (places for skilled practice)

Associating (places where businesses form ecologies)

Learning (places for experiments and explanations)

Cultivating (places for stewardship)

Watching (places for monitoring)

(on the town...)

Eating, drinking, talking (places for socializing)

Gathering (places to meet)

Cruising (places for seeing and being seen)

Belonging (places for insiders)

Shopping (places for recreational retailing)

Sporting (places for embodied play)

Attending (places for cultural productions)

Commemorating (places for ritual)

(at home...)

Sheltering (places with comfortable climate)

Recharging (places for maintaining the body)

Idling (restful places for watching the world go by)

Confining (places to be held in)

Servicing (places with local support networks)

Metering (places where services flow incrementally)

(on the road...)

Gazing/touring (places to visit)

Hoteling (places to be at home away from home)

Adventuring (places for embodied challenge)

Driving (car as place)

Walking (places at human scale)

"A typology of situated interactions" as listed long ago in *Digital Ground* (2004).

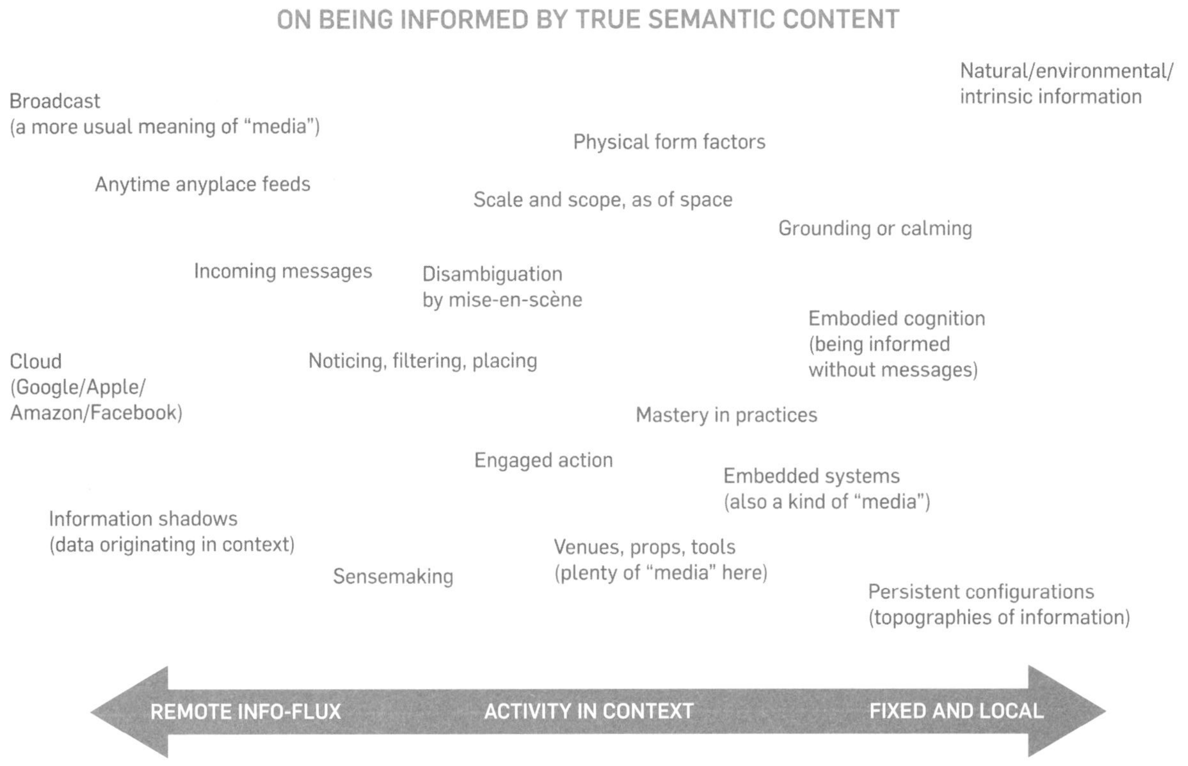

Broadcast
(a more usual meaning of "media")

Natural/environmental/
intrinsic information

Physical form factors

Anytime anyplace feeds

Scale and scope, as of space

Grounding or calming

Incoming messages

Disambiguation
by mise-en-scène

Embodied cognition
(being informed
without messages)

Cloud
(Google/Apple/
Amazon/Facebook)

Noticing, filtering, placing

Mastery in practices

Engaged action

Embedded systems
(also a kind of "media")

Information shadows
(data originating in context)

Venues, props, tools
(plenty of "media" here)

Sensemaking

Persistent configurations
(topographies of information)

REMOTE INFO-FLUX   ACTIVITY IN CONTEXT   FIXED AND LOCAL

How many other instances come to mind? Fifteen years since ambient information or pervasive computing first supplanted cyberspace as an architectural technofuture, it still helps to question senseless disconnection from context. This seems timely now as everything human beings do somewhere gets done while also texting, as if now that remote feeds *can* go anywhere, anytime, then they *should*. To question such obsessions is one main editorial premise of this volume: "NG07 is framed as a response to the immaterial, friction-less, acontextual, and non-spatial ideologies that continue to surround contemporary information and communication technologies."[07] So instead of mapping, even building, evocative crystallizations of some imagined higher-dimensional flux, at least sometimes architects and urbanists might want to emphasize tangible situations as the source and not the sink, and imagine the geography of information as something hyperlocal, and not always remote. For of course, life has both.

Terms

So, no: "media" should not always mean remoteness. Whatever the word "media" means at the moment (and remember that meaning often does depend on context), at least sometimes, increasingly, "media" might mean mediation by information technologies that have been embodied, embedded, or situated in objects at hand. Media can annotate and activate what is right here. Other, more usual meanings of the word, often based on the conventions of broadcast culture, may of course remain more prevalent, but as that culture loses its monopoly, and ever more volume of other information technology arises in ever more form factors of use, blending into the local landscapes of ever more patterns of life, it may help to rethink informational geographies sometimes. So it may help to extend notions of "media" to include the tangible, ambient, local, nonvisual, embodied, and situated. This surely beats thinking of "media" as flat-screen TVs everywhere!

So with the benefit of these examples above, I turn now to some useful terms. To say that form informs, as action creates context, may seem easy enough in recent design culture. Again, many of the ideas in this essay have been around for twenty years or more. But now amid a smartphone-abusing moment that forgets some of this, and also now because architects doing geographies may come to the topic of information with different assumptions than, say, interaction designers, installation artists, or cognitive scientists usually do, it is worth unpacking a few more terms. This will perhaps prove useful for reinterpretation throughout other essays in this volume.

017

"Information" should not always be thought of as signals sent; that is, as successfully encoded and transmitted data. Commonly known as the Shannon-Weaver model of communication, that definition has admittedly been more useful than any other, yet it does have its limits. Not all successful data transmittals inform: some are untrue; many arrive in contexts other than the ones they depend on for disambiguation. Context often provides referents, or what dramatists call "mise-en-scène," that put speech or text in place.[08] So as the eminent epistemologist Luciano Floridi has explained, the better definition of information is "true semantic content," at least some of which is "environmental information."[09] Here "environment" includes artifice, and especially building. For instance, sometimes the scale or form of a space matters: a conversation might go differently in a differently sized room. Sometimes the traces of past use can inform, like a well-worn doorway, footprints on the sidewalk, or physical objects themselves, into which digital devices have been embedded.

Context, then, is not all surroundings, but specifically those which unite with a particular action.[10] The circumstances of engagement make the relation between action and context reciprocal. Activity theory, which is a substantial body of studies in interactivity and cognition, explains engagement in terms of a constant ebb and flow of internalization and externalization of contextual knowledge. Habitual actions and circumstances, especially those that occur with intent, as practice, prove much more significant than casual, anytime-anyplace drift in this regard. For as noted in the cases of bike share, the medical clinic, or the warehouse rental space, practices become situated.

Embodiment proves vital to such actions.[11] No similar dynamic occurs through remote, distal media. For as is increasingly normative in cognitive science and applied in design, embodiment perceives much without names, before deliberation, and not as discrete objects. One can know through acquaintance and not declaration. Such knowledge often remains tacit. For example, possibilities for action may be discovered and known without having been designed and placed, thus without apps, so to speak. One usual word for this is "affordance"—a word overused among interaction designers but perhaps underused among architects, who do not always think in terms of users. In a key point for embodied and tangible interaction, not all affordances are declared. They can be discovered in the intrinsic structure of a situation; for example, that a horizontal surface serves as a table. Indeed, much situational awareness is not only inarticulable but lacks names at all. Especially in scale, configuration, and

movement, embodiment often assists cognition without rising to the level of deliberation, without names or identities as objects. In cognition research, this has overturned previous, more computational models of knowing. So for a simple expression by which to remember the importance of unsent natural data, tangible avatars and props, interpersonal distance, and architectural fixity in the use of situated information technologies, take note of "embodied cognition." Action and context unite in embodiment, often instead of devising namable knowledge representations, in the habitual play of situations. Thus, a hyperlocal topography of action (which may or may not individually dispose or socially aggregate into anything large enough to seem geographical) originates and does not merely receive information. Geography is not just the dropping of pins on Cartesian projection, for it also involves spatial mental models, both individual and cultural. Information is not just disembodied signals received from afar. Context may inform even the use of those. But the point here is that engagement creates information. To use the environment as an active resource often means that skills can neither be acquired nor applied nor explained without it.

What If

So where to move ahead on the active usability of architecture and the city? Under the truism that people understand the world by what they can do with it, and that knowing through doing is more vivid than passive grazing on feeds as to constitute an important component of any local information geography, then, as designers, ultimately we must ask, What shall we build?

Predicting is difficult; especially predicting the future. Technofuturism gets stale when larger, nontechnical social challenges seem more pressing. Information technofuturism has been losing its luster anyway. Frankly, the 2010s have become the decade in which the Internet itself has fallen into darkness (even if net neutrality may somehow be saved). No longer able to maintain its mythology of barefoot California counterculture, Silicon Valley today seems only slightly more loved than Big Oil or the Pentagon. And yet, by the standards of any previous era, ubiquitous information does still count as miraculous. This makes people expect more miracles. That makes design magazines want to speculate. So in lighthearted closing here, with all due disclaimer about any use of the future tense, let us just imagine a local information technology—one for the grounded realities, human dispositions, and embedded information practices described in this essay.

Until someone finds a better name, just call it one more kind of "urban markup." Its minor miracle is this:

no remote transmission (although perhaps some touch-driven local data hop), nothing server side, no internet connection. An only-local format of information technology (as, say, printed handbills in the street long have been) but of digital technology, in a moment where that has otherwise seemed too much about perpetual connectivity to anyplace else. This is not to say that much information technology would or should go off grid, only just that at least some could. This small social fiction is deliberate heresy for a moment in which the peak of technological hype (as measured in the famous annual curve by Gartner) has been the Internet of Things.[12]

Then besides total locality, this imagined urban markup also provides new degrees of usability and engagement. Embedded in form; attached to sites; given stewardship by owners, constituents, and curators, it proves easy enough. A child at play knows that when you tap two objects together they connect somehow. A product designer knows how to embed tags and local links into forms known through some active purpose that those local information features serve. A retailer knows how to sell such wares off the pegboard (no online sales either, for these). A citizen, in neither official nor transgressive capacity, knows where to find, read, and sometime annotate these tag objects. Sometimes artists take interest and demonstrate early prospects. (That much is no fiction. Go google Yellow Arrow, LED Throwies, Siftables, Constellactions, or those early MIT Media Lab projects in Triangles and other such Phicons …) Imagine where everyday work takes up these new means of markup (like the yellow stickies on which the arrows were based). Perhaps some new cultural practices arise, perhaps masters of neighborhood lore, or of excluding corporate distractions from social places, or of ambient cultural ornament. And in all these adaptations, the miracle that at least one format of information technology would have no internet somehow keeps a little bit of autonomy and privacy alive and well. Hey, this is speculation. What's for real is the microgeography of making sense through taking form.

01. Lucy Suchman, *Plans and Situated Actions: The Problem of Human-Machine Communication* (New York: Cambridge University Press, 1987).

02. John Walker, "Through the Looking Glass," in *The Art of Human-Computer Interface Design*, ed. Brenda Laurel (Reading, MA: Addison-Wesley, 1990).

03. This expression may have first arisen in my graduate seminars at Carnegie Mellon University, between 1998 and 2000. See also my much later paper, "On the Urbanism of Locative Media," *Places* 18, no. 2 (Summer 2006).

04. Mike Kuniavsky, "Information Is a Material," in his *Smart Things: Ubiquitous Computing User Experience Design* (San Francisco: Morgan Kaufmann, 2010).

05. One core thinker on sensemaking was University of Michigan sociologist Karl Weick. See "Sensemaking," in *International Encyclopedia of Organizational Studies*, ed. Stewart R. Clegg and James R. Bailey (Thousand Oaks, CA: Sage, 2008).

06. Richard H. R. Harper, *Texture: Human Expression in the Age of Communications Overload* (Cambridge, MA: MIT Press, 2010).

07. *New Geographies* 07, call for papers, http://new-geographies.squarespace.com/new-geographies-07.

08. William Mitchell, "In the First Place," in *Placing Words: Symbols, Space, and the City* (Cambridge, MA: MIT Press, 2005).

09. Luciano Floridi, "Semantic Conceptions of Information," in *Stanford Encyclopedia of Philosophy*, ed. Edward N. Zalta (Winter 2007), http://plato.stanford.edu/archives/win2007/entries/information-semantic.

10. For an authoritative guide on context and activity theory, see Victor Kaptelinin and Bonnie Nardi, *Acting with Technology: Activity Theory and Interaction Design* (Cambridge, MA: MIT Press, 2006).

11. For an authoritative guide on embodiment, see Paul Dourish, *Where the Action Is: The Foundations of Embodied Interaction* (Cambridge, MA: MIT Press, 2001).

12. See "2014 Gartner Hope Cycle Special Report," Gartner Inc., http://www.gartner.com/technology/research/hype-cycles.

Malcolm McCullough

From Digital Exceptionalism to Computational Scarcity

Jean-François Blanchette

A common explanation for the extraordinary success of the Internet is digital exceptionalism. In essence, it contends that we have been blessed with the realization of the dream of which our ancestors caught only imperfect glimpses. Parchment, printing, telegraph, radio, television: each of these technologies led in their own times to their own information revolutions. This, however, is it, the genuine artifact, The Information Age—capital T, capital I, capital A.[01]

This particular sublimity of our times hinges on two distinct assumptions: first, in the words of Nicholas Negroponte, we have finally moved "from atoms to bits."[02] Reduced to its purest representation as 0s and 1s, information has finally reached the end of its historical process of emancipation from the material—le degré zéro de l'information. Bits are wholly indifferent to their particular media carrier (whether hard drive, optical disk, or network wires) and to the particular signal that encodes them (whether magnetic polarities, voltages, or pulses of light). As such, bits transcend the economics and logistics of analog media and are immune to the corruption, degradation, and decay that necessarily result from the handling of material carriers of information.

Second, in the words of Lawrence Lessig, Jonathan Zittrain, and Tim Wu, the Internet is uniquely "generative."[03] Through the modular principles that have guided its design, the Internet's highly interoperable architecture enables the next evolutionary step to the vertically integrated firm: a new and highly flexible market structure that provides a democratic "plug-and-play" environment within which innovators may unleash their creativity. The unique ability of modular architectures to render irrelevant the physical basis of computing allows innovation to bypass the drudgery of physical implementation and proceed on the basis of the creative assembly of high-level components.

According to digital exceptionalism, then, immateriality (or at least, freedom from the constraints of the material world) is fundamental to the ability of the digital to upend the analog world. This is why any media that can be digitized or produced digitally will eventually succumb to the logics of digital information and its circulation through electronic networks.

This putative superiority of our digital age is typically credited as the gift of two exceptional individuals, Alan Turing and Claude Shannon, who are celebrated as the founding fathers of the Internet in light of their contributions to the dematerialization of computing and telecommunications, respectively.[04] Both mathematicians proposed models—the Turing machine and the Shannon-Weaver model—that assimilate computation and communication to symbol manipulation; that is, both models formally manipulate a set of symbolic representations that have themselves been reduced to their most fundamental expression as 0s and 1s.[05] In the service of their theoretical arguments, both models eschew considerations of computational resources in the realization of these manipulations. The Turing machine, for example, enjoys the luxury of infinite storage space, and its operation consumes no power whatsoever.[06]

The lesson of the Turing machine is that software is ontologically superior to hardware, while the lesson of the Shannon-Weaver model is that, no matter how much noise affects the communication channel, bits can always be restored to their original purity. In both cases, the networked computer is a technology that has become indifferent to its material instantiation and whose behavior is fundamentally mathematical. This behavior can be and has been implemented using a broad range of material technologies beyond the silicon circuits that dominate today. Indeed, working computers have been built out of tinker toys, and carrier pigeons have been proposed as a possible medium for the realization of the TCP/IP networking protocols.[07]

There are many reasons to be concerned with digital exceptionalism; among other things, it provides a poor foundation for computing pedagogy.[08] However, the dimension I will focus on here is that digital exceptionalism actively obscures an important technical and social reality, that networked computing is about the sharing of scarce resources. Contrast the idealization of the computer embodied by the Turing machine with its infinite storage and power supply and with various visualizations of computational resources (e.g., processing, energy, memory) offered by Apple's Activity Monitor application, resources that are clearly limited in nature and actively contested between applications.

The focus on the logical dimension of bits—their identity as 0s and 1s—negates their material dimension, their identity as physical entities, whether through light, electricity, or radio waves, or magnetized particles. Yet the debates that today dominate the political economy of computing—net neutrality, access to broadband, technological literacy, the politics of platforms

and standardization—cannot be understood without accounting for the intricate relation between the logical and material dimension of bits and, in particular, how the computational resources that ensure the material realization of bits are, of course, always limited.

The key to the relationship between the logical and material dimension of bits lies in the much-too-obvious fact that the computer is itself computerized. That is, the symbolic manipulations performed by computers concern not only representations of the external world but also representations of their own material resources (e.g., a file, or a TCP/IP packet) as well. These representations are located not at the level of software applications, per se, but at the level of the computing infrastructure. It is at that level that computing's complicated relationship to materiality is played out.

The Computing Infrastructure

The evolution of computing technology is typically portrayed in terms of its extraordinary rates of growth in performance. Year after year, processors perform more instructions at ever-increasing speeds, storage devices are able to pack more bits into ever-smaller amounts of space, and network wires transmit more data at ever-faster rates. Indeed, much of our understanding of the extraordinary spread of computing in the past sixty years is based on the idea that the fundamental computing resources of processing power, storage, and bandwidth have and will continue to become simultaneously more powerful and cheaper.[09]

This particular frame of analysis, however, captures only a limited subset of the forces that have driven the evolution of networked computing. Less visible but equally essential dimensions include, on the one hand, modularity, the design technique used to break down complexity and manage the high rate of technological change characteristic of computing technologies, and on the other hand, the sharing and distribution of limited computing resources. Much of these dynamics take place somewhat out of sight, at the level of computing infrastructure, rather than at the level of applications, the more plainly visible space where users extract personal value from computing technologies. Only by examining these three shaping forces—performance increases, modular design, and sharing—together can the evolutionary dynamics of the computing ecosystem, including its current manifestation as the dematerialized Cloud, be analyzed.[10]

In computing, infrastructure can be defined quite simply as the elements of the computing ecosystem that provide services to applications (for example, that perform arithmetic functions, store and retrieve bits, send packets

App Name	Energy Impact	Avg Energy Impact	App Nap	Requires High Perf GPU	User
▶ Google Chrome	48.9	87.84	No	No	blanchette
Spotlight	24.1	1.76	–	–	–
VLC	15.2	5.31	No	No	blanchette
▶ App Store	4.4	–	No	No	blanchette
Activity Monitor	1.3	0.48	No	No	blanchette
▶ Dropbox	0.6	0.27	No	No	blanchette
▶ Mail	0.1	0.05	Yes	No	blanchette
SophosUIServer	0.1	–	No	No	blanchette
Notes	0.1	–	No	No	blanchette
Microsoft Word	0.1	0.06	Yes	No	blanchette
iTunes	0.1	–	No	No	blanchette
Grab	0.1	0.02	No	No	blanchette
Finder	0.1	0.45	Yes	No	blanchette
System Preferences	0.1	–	No	No	blanchette
Microsoft AU Dae...	0.0	0.01	No	No	blanchette
Contacts	0.0	–	No	No	blanchette
▶ Safari	0.0	0.52	Yes	No	blanchette
Time Machine	0.0	0.03	–	–	–

ENERGY IMPACT

Graphics Card: High Perf.
Remaining charge: 11%
Time remaining: 0:20
Time on battery: 1:33

BATTERY (Last 12 hours)

over networks), in contrast to the applications that provide services to users (for example, that process words, or post a status update). The computing infrastructure is composed of both software and hardware: system abstractions such as file systems or packets, storage media such as flash or hard drives, communication protocols such as TCP/IP or ADSL. It provides the various components from which designers can build computing systems as diverse as the Google search engine, Microsoft Word running on a desktop, and the TiVo software. It is what allows computers to be multipurpose, while simultaneously managing the high rate of technical change of computing resources. These two characteristics of computing systems are easily taken for granted today, but they required considerable design innovation to come into being.

The first electromechanical computing machines could only perform a limited range of computational tasks. Herman Hollerith's first tabulator, developed for the 1890 census, was specifically tailored to add up census schedules. Early digital computers such as the ENIAC could be reconfigured to perform different types of computation only through a time-consuming rewiring of the various hardware components. The concept of the stored program, as formulated by John von Neumann in 1943, provided one elegant solution to the issue: the execution of the different components of computers could be directed by way of a sequence of instructions—a program. A single computer could perform distinct computational tasks merely by executing a different program, and while designing such programs proved to be no simple task, once written, programs could be switched in a matter of seconds.

Modularity

This newfound versatility came with some important trade-offs, however. Even as von Neumann and his coinventors gave birth to the software/hardware division, the two remained fused. In the early days of computing, hardly any distance separated program and hardware. The manual of operations for the first commercially produced stored program computer, the IBM 701, included such specific timing considerations as, "to keep the card reader in continuous motion, it is necessary to give the read instruction between 20 and 70 milliseconds after the 12-right copy instruction."[11] Phrased differently, programmers had to take into account specific characteristics of the hardware—in this case, the number of operations the processor would execute before the next card would be available for reading data or instructions from the punched card reader (the dominant input/output technology in the early 1950s). This rapidly became problematic insofar as each succeeding generation of computers offered new, faster hardware, and programs had to be rewritten from scratch to take advantage of their new characteristics, at great expense of time and money.

Above: Computational resources (processing, energy, memory) represented by Apple's Activity Monitor application.

Jean-François Blanchette

By the 1960s the situation had become a sore point for the industry as a whole, prompting market leader IBM to seek a remedy for the issue. The solution consisted in designing a series of processor lines, each compatible with one another (including peripherals): any program written for one line would be able to execute on any other line, albeit with different levels of performance. To achieve such compatibility, IBM relied on modularity as a design strategy, where each component of the system was conceived as a discrete black box with a standardized interface.[12] In the resulting System/360, for example, all processors responded to the same set of instructions, even though their internal architecture might differ widely. For the first time, programmers could design programs with the confidence that, as long as components retained the same interface, programs would continue to run in spite of technical advances.

Compatibility proved much more than just an engineering feature, however, as it profoundly altered the economics of the computing ecosystem: components with standardized interfaces could just as well be produced by competitors, and many IBM engineers left the company to launch their own lines of cheaper compatible processors and peripherals. Modular computing systems rapidly ushered in an era of vertical disintegration of the industry and a new form of market organization.

Indeed, at the core of Lessig, Zittrain, and Wu's "architecture is politics" argument is the acknowledgment that the extraordinary success of the Internet is a direct outcome of its modular architecture, which effectively lowers barriers to entry for prospective market participants and fosters experimentation at the component level.

Sharing and Virtualization

A parallel historical development involved the emergence of operating systems and virtualization. In the early days of computing, computing speed was hampered by two main bottlenecks. On the one hand, programs were loaded and executed sequentially, in a slow and cumbersome process termed "batch processing": at any given time, only one user could access the machine's expensive resources (processor, storage, etc.). On the other hand, increases in processing speed were limited by the extremely slow speed of storage technologies: program execution was often stalled as the processor waited for data to be loaded or written to storage.

A decisive breakthrough came with the invention of time-sharing. Instead of executing sequentially, multiple programs were loaded simultaneously and executed under the authority a new program—the supervisor. In

Above: Server maintenance at Facebook's Prineville Data Center.

similar fashion to real estate time-sharing, the supervisor amortizes an important capital expense (the processor) by distributing it among multiple noncompeting users. By allocating to each program a slice of processing time and by circling rapidly in round-robin fashion between them, each user enjoyed the illusion of having full control of the computer's resources, although in effect they had that control for only a small fraction of the time. Because the supervisor could use the time previously spent waiting for storage devices to service other users, individual performance did not suffer overall. In today's terms, time-sharing virtualized the processor: it created an abstraction of a computing resource (a whole processor, when only a portion was available) so that it could be more efficiently shared among multiple users. User programs no longer directly interacted with the processor but rather with the abstraction provided by the supervisor, which sliced and diced the actual processor among as many users as could be supported.

Just like modularity, time-sharing profoundly changed the economics of computing. By allowing more users to extract more usage out of the most expensive component of a computer (its processor), institutions were able to make the most out of their (increasingly large) capital investments. Through the design of appropriate abstractions, enormous gains in computing efficiency could be had by the efficient sharing of costly and limited computing resources. At the same time, the supervisor ushered in the era of operating systems—software that would serve as a mediating layer, to control applications' access to computing resources, whether processor, storage, or network.

Distributing Computing

Another strand of the history of computing design involves the distribution of computing resources in space. It addresses the question of where computing resources (processing, storage, data) should be located, in relationship to each other and to users. The criteria for choice includes not only computational efficiency but also crucial issues of control, cost, maintenance, reliability, security, and access, among others. During the relatively short history of the field, different architectures have successively dominated the landscape.

Early digital computers took the shape of mainframes: single-user machines in which all computing resources were centrally located, controlled, and maintained, often in the same room. Users accessed the mainframe through computer operators, who controlled available software and data, both of which had to be loaded on input/output devices located in the same physical space.

The advent of time-sharing dramatically transformed this setup: the virtualized processor of the mainframe was partitioned among multiple users, who accessed it through terminals (connected through either local wires or phone lines). The mainframe functioned as a server to these multiple clients, providing access to software and data stored either locally or remotely. At this stage the data transiting over the wires was textual: commands typed by users, and the results of their queries, typically textual and numeric information contained in databanks or the output of programs. Although access had been expanded, control remained local to the machine. Security became a new problem, as multiple users shared access to processors, storage, data, and programs.

Personal computing provided users with unprecedented control over their own processor, storage devices, software, and data. At the same time, personal computing introduced a host of challenges to the workplace: in contrast to the centralized mainframe, every employee's computer needed to be set up, maintained, upgraded, repaired, and provided with individual copies of software. In addition, processing and storage capacity were potentially wasted as individual machines sat idle by night. Personal computers also integrated with mainframes, insofar as they could be used as terminals to connect to institutional mainframes to access software or commercial services (databanks).

By allowing personal computers to connect with one another, the Internet has yet again broadened the scope of architectural possibilities for the distribution of computing resources. By and large, the dominant relationship has been one of client/server: users' devices download content (query results, for example, or streaming data) from the Cloud to local clients (primarily web browsers). Netflix serves as the paradigmatic example. This is, however, only one of many possible configurations for distributed computing. Peer-to-peer computing, in its many flavors, provides a vibrant example of an entirely different model for pooling distributed resources—one whose applications go far beyond mere illegal file sharing. Grid computing, as exemplified by the SETI@home project, leverages the idle cycles of thousands of machines to solve computationally intensive problems such a protein folding or climate modeling.

Today's age of mobile computing has emerged in symbiotic relationship with the Cloud. Given their limited storage, processing, and energy resources, portable devices such as smartphones, tablets, and netbooks rely on cloud services to provide the required software capabilities on which mobile services users have come to rely, such as maps and voice recognition. This movement of

Server maintenance at Facebook's Prineville Data Center.

processing cycles and storage away from users' machines to data centers is, however, entirely dependent upon the availability of broadband. The more data intensive the service, the more bandwidth that is required. For many classes of applications, such as video editing, bandwidth requirements and availability continue to make cloud-based processing an unattractive option.[13] Indeed, data-intensive services such as Second Life or Google Earth must be accessed through client software (or web plug-ins) that can render 3-D virtual environments with the help of the device's local processor. Furthermore, in the cloud model, reliability is entirely a function of service providers, themselves dependent upon network service providers. We might say, "live by the Cloud, die by the network."

Already, the centralization brought on by data centers is being mitigated by content distribution networks (CDNs) such as Akamai, designed to move resources (processing, storage, and data) closer to the edge of the networks—that is, users' machines. Large content providers like Netflix are developing their own proprietary CDNs (for example, OpenConnect) to bypass the costs and network congestion that result from moving large amounts

of data across the Internet. And of course, data centers are themselves being strategically located so as to minimize not only data movement but also energy costs. Even in a cloud-based world, then, there remain multiple models for the distribution of computing resources, whether by reason of computing efficiency or political conviction, and spatial distribution of these resources continues to matter. The Cloud thus emerges at the historical confluence of several longstanding technical traditions within computing: modularity, which has allowed cloud providers to create unprecedented amounts of computing power by merely bringing together massive numbers of low-cost off-the-shelf components; virtualization, which makes it possible to distribute, meter, and charge for these computing resources in highly granular and flexible ways while allowing for continuity with legacy software designs; and distributed architectures, which allow for the partitioning of computing resources between mobile devices and data centers.

The Era of Computational Scarcity

Digital exceptionalism thus holds limited analytical power to illuminate the dynamics that have resulted in today's particular infrastructural configurations. Conversely, a focus on the material dimension of bits provides an explanatory framework that does much for understanding the debates that currently animate the world of computing. Perhaps the most important of these debates (and the one that stands in starkest contrast to the vision of digital exceptionalism) concerns the supply and demand of computational resources. The demand for these resources is virtually inexhaustible because there are, in effect, no particular limits on the amounts of digital information that can be created. Indeed, digital images, films, and sounds are constantly gaining in resolution. Internet traffic increased eightfold between 2006 and 2011 and is expected to continue growing at an annual rate of 30 percent. Mobile traffic now accounts for 45 percent of all IP traffic.[14] There is little end in sight for such demand. The project of computing as it stands today is to provide no less than a computational mirror of the whole world, a global simulation that would augment its physical counterpart so as to make it more predictable and more amenable to manipulation.[15] The resolution of this simulation increases with each new sensor developed, deployed, and plugged into the network, with each new data point integrated into its statistical machinery. The consequence is that the rate of growth of digital data will in all likelihood continue to exceed the available material resources to manipulate, store, and move about this data for the foreseeable future.

A more useful framework, then, for understanding the evolution of computing is one of computational scarcity—that is, of differential access to these limited computing resources by different groups, whether the result of geography, socioeconomic status, legal status, or other causes. These differentials will manifest themselves in familiar ways—individuals will or will not have access to computing devices, bandwidth, or data—but also in new and unfamiliar ways, such as through the design and deployment of largely invisible infrastructural elements that will enable or disable certain kinds of sharing and distribution of computational resources. Indeed, our era's true claim to exceptionalism will likely lay in the subtlety and reach of the information inequalities caused by the computing infrastructure.

01. This article draws in part from Jean-François Blanchette, "Computing's Infrastructural Moment," in *Regulating the Cloud: Policy for Computing Infrastructure*, eds. Christopher S. Yoo and Jean-François Blanchette (Cambridge, MA: MIT Press, 2015).

02. Nicholas Negroponte, *Being Digital* (New York: Random House, 1996).

03. Lawrence Lessig, "The Architecture of Innovation," *Duke Law Journal* 51 (2002): 1783–1801; Jonathan Zittrain, *The Future of the Internet—and How to Stop It* (New Haven, CT: Yale University Press, 2008); Tim Wu, *The Master Switch: The Rise and Fall of Information Empires* (New York: Alfred A. Knopf, 2010).

04. See James Gleick, *The Information: A History, A Theory, A Flood* (New York: Pantheon Books, 2011); and George Dyson, *Turing's Cathedral: The Origins of the Digital Universe* (New York: Pantheon Books, 2012).

05. This is the doctrine of binarism, an ancillary principle to digital exceptionalism. For more on this, see Mathieu Triclot, *Le Moment Cybernétique: La Constitution De La Notion d'Information* (Seyssel: Champ Vallon, 2008).

06. Indeed, Turing himself viewed the physics of computation as wholly subordinate to its mathematics, as he noted in a speech in 1947: "From the point of view of the mathematician the property of [an electronic digital computing machine] being digital should be of greater interest than that of being electronic. That it is electronic is certainly important because these machines owe their high speed to this, and without the speed it is doubtful if financial support for their construction would be forthcoming. But this is virtually all there is to be said on that subject." Alan Turing, "Lecture on the Automatic Computing Engine (1947)," in *The Essential Turing: Seminal Writings in Computing, Logic, Philosophy, Artificial Intelligence, and Artificial Life: Plus the Secrets of Enigma*, ed. B. Jack Copeland (New York: Oxford University Press, 2004), 362.

07. See A. K. Dewdney, "Computer Recreations: A Tinkertoy Computer That Plays Tic-Tac-Toe," *Scientific American* 261, no. 4 (October 1989): 119–23; and D. Waitzman, "A Standard for the Transmission of IP Datagrams on Avian Carriers," *IETF RFC 1149* (April 1, 1990).

08. In Jean-François Blanchette, "Computing as if Infrastructure Mattered," *Communications of the ACM* 55, no. 10 (October 2012): 32–34, I argue in favor of a focus on infrastructural forces and that the material foundation of computing resources provides an appropriate pedagogical framework for teaching the historical evolution of computing over the current emphasis on mathematical abstraction.

09. For example: "The unprecedented evolution of computers since 1980 exhibits an essentially exponential speedup that spans 4 orders of magnitude in performance for the same (or lower) price. No other engineered system in human history has ever achieved that rate of improvement.... Whole fields of human endeavors have been transformed as computer system capability has ascended through various threshold performance values." Lynette I. Millett and Samuel H. Fuller, eds., *The Future of Computing Performance: Game Over or Next Level?* (Washington, DC: National Academies Press, 2011), 25.

10. See Jean-François Blanchette, "A Material History of Bits," *Journal of the American Society for Information Science and Technology* 62, no. 6 (June 2011): 1042–57.

11. *Principles of Operation—Type 701 and Associated Equipment* (New York: International Business Machines Corporation [IBM], 1953).

12. Carliss Young Baldwin and Kim B. Clark, *Design Rules*, vol. 1, *The Power of Modularity* (Cambridge, MA: MIT Press, 2000).

13. Ironically, in many cases, the transfer of datasets to the Cloud can be cost prohibitive leading Armbrust et al. to recommend the "FedEx disk option," that is, ship them using a more traditional infrastructure. See M. Armbrust et al., *Above the Clouds: A Berkeley View of Cloud Computing*, Technical Report UCB/EECS-2009-28 (Berkeley CA: EECS Department, University of California, Berkeley, 2009).

14. See *Cisco Visual Networking Index: Global Mobile Data Traffic Forecast Update, 2012–2017*, http://newsroom.cisco.com/documents/10157/1142732/Cisco_VNI_Mobile_Data_Traffic_Forecast_2012_2017_white_paper.pdf.

15. See, for example, David Hillel Gelernter, *Mirror Worlds, or, the Day Software Puts the Universe in a Shoebox: How It Will Happen and What It Will Mean* (New York: Oxford University Press, 1991).

Image Credits
024, 026: Photos by Shuli Hallak.

Stealth Architectures and the Geographies of Backup

Stephen Graham

In the summer of 2004, a vast, squat, and anonymous building was completed next to US Route 71 on the edge of the unprepossessing Midwestern town of Jane, Missouri. Apart from a complete lack of the usual corporate signage and iconography, this 133,000-square-foot structure is virtually indistinguishable from the countless other suburban distribution centers that colonize the vague margins between urbanity and rurality which encircle the world's towns and cities.[01]

"There is nothing about the building to give even a hint that Wal-Mart owns it," writes Max McCoy for the *Joplin Globe*. "Despite the glimpses through the fence of manicured grass and carefully placed trees, the overall impression is that this is a secure site that could withstand just about anything."[02] The center was deliberately placed on solid bedrock and is designed to withstand powerful local thunderstorms, earthquakes, and terrorist attacks. "Earth is packed against the sides," explains McCoy. "The green roof—meant, perhaps, to blend into the surrounding Ozarks hills—bristles with dish antennas. On one of the heavy steel gates at the guardhouse is a notice that visitors must use the intercom for assistance."[03]

Rather than orchestrating the physical transportation of products, this center operates at the heart of an equally vital but far less visible process: the continuous flow of digital data. The US Route 71 complex is the epicenter of Walmart's global architecture of data traffic—an assemblage developed specifically to ensure that the 100 million or so apparently mundane digital transactions, communications, and surveillance events that sustain the world's largest retailer each day carry on, relentlessly, no matter what extreme events, malfunctions, or acts of political aggression target the firm's operations.

Architectures of Anticipation

The center concentrates, and backs up, all data captured across the firm's stores and online transactions worldwide. This process allows sophisticated data-mining software to predict market trends, thus allowing the global chains of production and distribution to synchronize as nearly as possible with changing market geographies as they play out.

As Hurricane Frances bore down on Florida in the summer of 2004, for example, Walmart's data-mining center quickly analyzed consumption patterns from similar previous events. It predicted that local stores would need large quantities of a range of products beyond the obvious torches and candles. "We didn't know in the past that

029

strawberry Pop-Tarts increase in sales, like seven times their normal sales rate, ahead of a hurricane," Linda M. Dillman, Walmart's CIO, said in a *New York Times* interview conducted at the time. "And the pre-hurricane top-selling item was beer."[04] Thanks to those analyses, large loads of these items were soon speeding down highways toward Walmart stores located in the projected path of the hurricane.

Stealth Data Architecture

Walmart is only the largest and most spectacular of a whole new field of stealth data-center architecture—what London architectural critic Martin Pawley called "terminal architecture" in his 1998 book of the same name. Such buildings are springing up in the most unlikely locations, spreading a whole incipient geography of backup and repair across the world. Near the core of global finance epicenters such as London and New York, for example, bunkerlike business continuity facilities cluster, ready to go into operation to support corporate data flows and archives whenever the main corporate headquarters or electronic trading floor faces a disruption of any kind. Areas adjacent to corporate and financial downtowns, such as London Docklands and New Jersey, are now chock-full of such fortified centers, and the specialized firms that operate them now constitute an important economic sector in their own right.

Meanwhile, in the downtown cores, disused and obsolescent modernist tower-blocks have been converted into so-called telecom hotels. Their windows blacked out, these structures house web servers and major digital switching systems connected directly to the planet's fiber-optic grids. They allow the world's major communications providers to serve the world's major metropolitan markets cheaply, efficiently, and with minimal vulnerability to disruption.

Far away from these metropolitan hubs, data backup and storage centers increasingly occupy the world's nooks and crannies. The accumulated regolith of military architecture, abandoned since the late twentieth century, offers prime real estate for reconstruction as data centers. Abandoned military bunkers, especially, lend themselves to repurposing as ultrasecure data archiving and backup facilities. In northern Washington, DC, for example, a missile control bunker from the early years of the Cold War has been turned into an ultrasecure data center known as "Titan 1." An abandoned intercontinental ballistic missile silo near Albuquerque, New Mexico, has been similarly retrofitted. In Europe parallel refits have been completed using World War II antiaircraft forts off the coast of South East England and civilian antinuclear bunkers deep below the Swiss Alps.

Big Box, Big Data, Big Brother

To the list of corporate data centers we should also add, of course, the burgeoning data collection, surveillance, and "fusion" centers of national security states, emboldened by the rapidly extending "national security" initiatives resulting from the global "war on terror." In such complexes, the commercial innovations of data mining, communication tracking, and profiling are now mutating into new assemblages directed at social and political control. Often such operations blur troublingly with protocols like Walmart's, for the very commercial firms that specialize in such tasks for corporate clients are taking up the mantle of national security data mining as they take advantage of the contracting opportunities created by privatized and neoliberal states.

The daddy of all security data centers is the US National Security Agency's hub in Bluffdale, Utah. The nexus of a vast, global data-intercept cloud that dwarfs even Walmart's, the center seamlessly links together the world's most powerful supercomputers, satellites, and transnational snooping systems with primary transnational telecom and internet service providers. It has been estimated that the NSA intercepts 1.7 billion items of data per day and harvests 2.1 million gigabytes of data per hour. They then pour this data into the largest server banks on Earth.[05]

Imperatives of Backup
and the Always-On Economy

All of the world's major telecommunications outfits now operate their own large-scale bunker complexes. These are designed to allow for the automatic or near-automatic repair of data and communications networks in the event of catastrophic events such as the 9/11 attacks or Hurricane Katrina in New Orleans. With their room-sized digital world maps displaying real-time events, monitored by operators in tiered ranks, these bunkers look more like the nuclear weapons control rooms of Stanley Kubrick's *Dr. Strangelove* (1964) than sites dedicated to managing more mundane threats involving automatic teller machines, mobile phones, supermarket checkouts, gas pumps, and internet "network unavailable" messages.

In a global, digital, twenty-four-hour economy, the absolute imperative is to ensure continuity of service and connectivity. For e-commerce firms, financial services corporations, worldwide logistics and transport providers, call centers, and international information and consumer data companies, continuous data flow and archiving are,

Opposite: Walmart's data "super center" in Jane, Missouri.

Stephen Graham

The NSA's million-square-foot data center in Bluffdale, Utah.

Stephen Graham

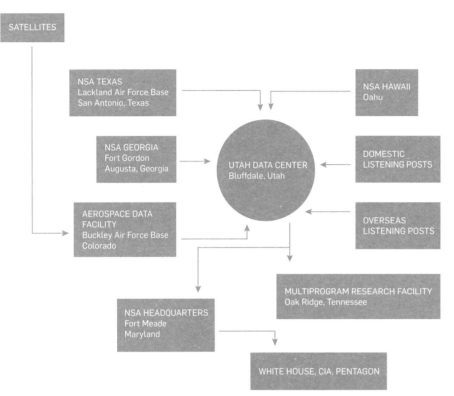

The global data architecture of the NSA with the Utah Data Center as a key hub.

SATELLITES

NSA TEXAS
Lackland Air Force Base
San Antonio, Texas

NSA HAWAII
Oahu

NSA GEORGIA
Fort Gordon
Augusta, Georgia

UTAH DATA CENTER
Bluffdale, Utah

DOMESTIC LISTENING POSTS

AEROSPACE DATA FACILITY
Buckley Air Force Base
Colorado

OVERSEAS LISTENING POSTS

MULTIPROGRAM RESEARCH FACILITY
Oak Ridge, Tennessee

NSA HEADQUARTERS
Fort Meade
Maryland

WHITE HOUSE, CIA, PENTAGON

very literally, the only possible means of operation. The costs incurred when the data flow is disrupted quickly lead to the very erasure of these firms. Neil Stephenson, CEO of the Onyx Group—a major developer of business continuity centers—commented in 2006 that, according to statistics produced by the Office of the Deputy Prime Minister in the United Kingdom, 80 percent of businesses affected by a major incident that disrupts their digital operations or erases their database archives close within eighteen months of the event.[06]

It is not surprising, then, that in the remote and bunkered spaces of the post–Cold War landscape, a new brand of stealth architecture is mushrooming. So anonymous are these buildings, so ubiquitous and generic their urban or suburban presence, they are rendered invisible—undiscoverable except by a handful of hardcore infrastructure enthusiasts and researchers of the urban esoteric, impenetrable by all but a few highly skilled hackers.

Still, these built architectures remain more manifest than their vital, digital shadow. The backup and repair centers perform the powerful job of hiding data infrastructures—the fibers, servers, programs, and code—that link together the interstitial economic geographies

of the world. Most invisible of all is the growing universe of software that automatically detects, diagnoses, and attempts to repair interruptions to flow and connectivity within transnational data systems, routing traffic away from failing nodes within the Internet's famous "packet-switching" architecture and backing up data records on the most secure sites, housed within transnational networks of linked data centers. Together, these spaces and systems constitute what we might call the global assemblage of digital flow. The most crucial infrastructure of globalization, this pervasive digital skein of communications systems works continually to bring the global digital economy, with its mobilities and flows, somehow magically into being.

And yet, like all true infrastructures, the invisibility of global data systems in everyday life means that they are only really noticed (and then, only fleetingly) when they cease to function. At such moments, the constant calculative operations sustaining global digital capitalism momentarily materialize, until reinstatement occurs and the assemblage sinks into the background once again.

Such a perspective has clear analytical implications. It suggests that it is best not to see the so-called network or information society as some extraterrestrial impactor, miraculously transforming cities and societies in its wake. Rather, we would be wise to stress that such transformations are the result of new systems, built spaces, and digital architectures and practices having been brought into being and sunk anonymously, and often invisibly, into the places of the world.

If we were to pay more attention to the mundane infrastructures, landscapes, and assemblages involved, and the ways in which they quite literally surround and sustain our everyday lives, we might be less likely to wrap these transformations in the hype of utopia—or dystopia—with all the unhelpful gloss that doing so invites.

01. An earlier, shorter version of this essay, titled "Automated Repair and Back-up Systems," appears in *Globalization in Practice*, ed. William Rupp, Nigel Thrift, Adam Tickell, and Steve Woolgar (Oxford, UK: Oxford University Press, 2014).

02. Max McCoy, "Wal-Mart's Data Center Remains Mystery," *Joplin Globe*, May 28, 2006, http://www.joplinglobe.com/news/local_news/wal-mart-s-data-center-remains-mystery/article_5f088740-04ea-531d-b526-a2cc9862c8aa.html.

03. Ibid.

04. Linda M. Dillman, quoted in Constance L. Hays, "What Wal-Mart Knows about Customers' Habits," *New York Times*, November 14, 2004, http://www.nytimes.com/2004/11/14/business/yourmoney/14wal.html.

05. Figures are drawn from Kunal Jasty, "The Five NSA Programs You Should Know About," *RadioOpenSource*, July 14, 2014, http://radioopensource.org/the-five-nsa-programs-you-should-know-about.

06. This figure comes from the UK's Federation of Small Businesses, "Three Very Good Reasons Why You Should Have a Plan," http://www.fsb.org.uk/thamesvalley/info/community.

Stephen Graham

Invisible Networks

Shuli
Hallak

The Internet is inherently decentralized; no one entity owns or controls it and it does not exist in one place. Many disparate parts must interconnect at critical junctions in order for information to move seamlessly. In the physical layer, Layer 1 of the Open Systems Interconnection (OSI) model, internet submarine cables must connect to terrestrial cables and networks at interconnection facilities, or "carrier hotels." This is where core networks interconnect as well. Fiber cables are the veins that pulse binary bits of data between the numerous carrier hotels, data centers, nodes, cell towers, and end users around the globe. Each part is equally important because it is critical to the functioning of a whole, efficient network of networks.

Cable tank of subsea cable ship holding internet submarine fiber-optic cable.

Subsea repeater deployment, Caribbean Sea.

Subsea Cables

Fiber-optic cables are built or specially modified for under-water and deep-sea deployment. Laying a cable requires the use of a subsea cable ship and takes several weeks to a month. Usually these cables are financed by a consortium of carriers networks. They are built out by companies such as Alcatel-Lucent and TE SubCom. Subsea cables are deployed with repeaters, part of an optical amplification system that recovers loss of light over transmission distance.

Shuli Hallak

Facebook's Prineville Data Center.

Core Networks

A core network is a central part of the telecommunications network. Typically, this refers to high-capacity communication facilities that connect to primary nodes. Also known as backbone networks, core networks provide paths for the exchange of information between different subnetworks. Facebook is a core network, operating at the physical layer. This massive data center facility houses physical servers. Fiber-optic cables connect to the data center. Data in the form of bits moves through the fiber-optic cables to and from the data center.

041

Facebook's Prineville Data Center.

Shuli Hallak

Meet Me Room, Colo Atl, Atlanta, Georgia.

Carrier Hotels (Interconnection Facilities)

Core networks physically interconnect in network-neutral facilities called carrier hotels. Networks are able to house their equipment (not servers) and connect directly to one another via patch panels. These cross-connects might include, for example, a subsea cable network and a carrier. Within the carrier hotel, peering can happen and that can be at higher layers of the OSI.

Dark Fiber (Terrestrial)

Dark fiber, or unlit fiber, is the equivalent of wholesale fiber: neither owned nor controlled by a traditional carrier, dark fiber is available for lease. Whatever entity leases the fiber becomes responsible for "lighting" it with its own network equipment. In general, Fiber-optic networks are also referred to as broadband. Dark fiber provides certain advantages. By enabling more providers to enter the marketplace, it increases competition, leading to better pricing and higher speeds of data transmission. It also provides an alternative to the net neutrality paradigm, as dark fiber is not regulated by the Federal Communications Commission (FCC). Like any other fiber-optic cable network, dark fiber can be configured for long-haul and short-haul routes and deployed within cities on a municipal level.

Top: Inside a New York City manhole. Bottom: Dark fiber deployment by Stealth Communications, Midtown Manhattan.

Shuli Hallak

Choreographies of Information

The Architectural Internet of the Eighteenth Century's Optical Telegraphy

Dimitris Papanikolaou

Today, with the dominance of digital information and communications technologies (ICTs), information is mostly perceived as digital bits of electric pulses, while the Internet is seen as a gigantic network of cables, routers, and data centers that interconnects cities and continents. But few know that for a brief period in history, before electricity was utilized and information theory formalized, a mechanical version of what we call "Internet" connected cities across rural areas and landscapes in Europe, the United States, and Australia, communicating information by transforming a rather peculiar medium: geometric architectural form.

The Origins of Territorial Intelligence

Telecommunication was not a novelty in the eighteenth century. Early data networks communicated intelligence across land and sea through such media as fire, sound, light, pigeons, mirrors, and flags. In the twelfth century BCE, for example, Agamemnon used a bonfire relay line across six hundred kilometers of ocean and terrain

to communicate the news of Troy's fall to Mycenae. In 150 BCE, Greek historian Polybius described a system of sending pre-encoded messages with torches combinations.[01] And in 1453, Nicolo Barbaro mentioned in his diary how Constantinople's bell-tower network alerted citizens in real time to the tragic progress of the siege by the Ottomans.[02] It wasn't until the mid-eighteenth century, however, that telecommunications developed into vast territorial networks that used visual languages and control protocols to disassemble any message into discrete signs, route them wirelessly through relay stations, reassemble them at the destination, and reformulate the message by mapping them into words and phrases through lookup tables. And all of this was done in unprecedented speeds. Two inventions made it possible: the telescope and the optical telegraph.

The telescope's invention in 1608 improved telecommunications as nothing else before. With a thirtyfold magnifying power, telescopes expanded communication links more than an order of magnitude, while dropping dramatically their infrastructure and operational costs.[03] Optical telegraphs were mechanically transformable structures—partly buildings, partly machines—that could reconfigure their silhouettes to visually manifest signs. Together with telescopes, they created a powerful mechanical internet that could automatically transmit any arbitrary message, independent of its length, through a choreography of mechanical transformations. Through its brief history, the mechanical internet of optical telegraphy introduced fundamental concepts of communication and computing like error detection, data compaction, flow control, encryption, handshaking, clock synchronization, signal restoration, routing, regulation and even fraud that are all present today on the Internet.

The contribution of this essay is twofold: on the one hand, it sheds light to the techno-sociopolitical context of the history of optical telegraphy, a topic that is largely disregarded in architectural and urban history; on the other hand, it makes three thesis statements on the relation of optical telegraphy to the contemporary critical discourse on architecture, media, and urban intelligence.

The Architectural Internet

In March 1791, Claude Chappe, a French cleric and inventor, placed with his brother two synchronized pendulums with ten signs each on their clock faces several hundred meters apart. His goal was to send a message as a combination of signs across the two devices.

To send a sign, the transmitting clock emitted a sound precisely at the moment when the indicators of both clocks passed from the specific sign. By combining signs, predetermined messages could be found in a dictionary.[04] The solution, however, was cumbersome, mechanically complex, and operationally complicated. Two years later, Chappe came up with a new idea, conceptually, mechanically, and operationally simpler: one mechanically transformable structure configured its silhouette to visually represent a sign; then, it waited for the remote structure to replicate the silhouette, thus confirming the sign. By placing the devices on high enough towers, the sky could be used as a bright background to visually enhance the silhouettes. Relay cascades could transmit messages by copying each other's silhouette through a domino effect. Chappe named his invention "telegraphy" from the Greek words *tele* (distant) and *graph* (writing). An architectural form of communication had just been invented.

The Signaling Apparatus: Form Follows Information

The evolution of optical telegraphy was an interplay between communication protocols, engineering ingenuity, operational simplicity, and cost. The concept though remained the same: form follows information. Over the years two designs prevailed: the semaphore and the shutter telegraph.

The semaphore, invented in 1793 by Chappe, consisted of a thirty-foot-high mast with a pivoting arm on top called the regulator. At the two ends of the regulator, which measured fourteen feet long and thirteen inches wide, there were two smaller rotating arms called the indicators, which measured six feet long and one foot wide each. Chappe found through experiments that their thin silhouettes were easily distinguishable from large distances. Both the regulator and the indicators could rotate in forty-five-degree intervals: the regulator could take four positions (horizontal, vertical, and the two diagonals), while each indicator could take eight positions. The apparatus, which was painted black to contrast with the blue sky, could take a total of 256 (eight by eight by two) different positions, or eight bits of information storage. Not all positions were retained, however: Chappe eliminated the positions in which the two indicators were parallel to the regulator and pointed inward because they were hidden. Furthermore, from the four positions of the regulator, he only kept the vertical and horizontal ones. After eliminating a few other positions, the semaphore telegraph eventually encoded a total of ninety-two signs.[05]

The shutter telegraph, first invented in 1794 by the Swedish baron Abraham Niclas Edelcrantz and modified in 1796 by the British lord George Murray, utilized a matrix of flipping shutters, pivoted on horizontal axes, that could open and close individually. Edelcrantz's apparatus had ten shutters organized in a three-by-three matrix, with a tenth shutter mounted on top of the middle column. It could encode 1,024 signs, or ten bits. Murray's apparatus used only six shutters, organized in a two-by-three matrix, with a capacity of sixty-four different alphanumerical characters or six bits. Like Chappe, both Edelcrantz and Murray optimized the design of their devices through experimentations. Edelcrantz found that the gap between shutters needed to equal the width of one shutter, at least, to prevent the human eye from mistakenly blending adjacent shutters when viewing the apparatus from a great distance. He also determined the size and angle of the matrix as a function of the distance the towers had between them, the magnitude of the telescope used, and the minimum visual angle of a human eye.[06] Likewise, Murray standardized the design of his matrix on two supporting posts twenty feet high and twelve feet apart; each shutter was roughly six feet by five feet in size.[07]

Opposite: Chappe semaphore.

Dimitris Papanikolaou

Skala.

The Control Room and the Operators: The Puppeteers

Optical telegraphs were remotely linked to an interface that a human operator could manipulate inside a control room. Chappe's device was mechanically connected through pulleys, disks, gears, belts, and cables to a miniature replica of the device inside that room. Likewise, Edelcrantz's and Murray's signaling devices each linked through strings to a small control box with ten rings, which the operator could pull with his fingers. Like puppeteers, operators could manipulate the miniature devices inside the control room, and the large apparatuses atop the tower would silently replicate the postures. Edelcrantz developed an even more sophisticated mechanism that used foot pedals to control the shutters, leaving the hands of the operator free to turn the pages of the codebook.[08]

Inside the control room, telescopes mounted on the walls pointed to the apparatuses of the nearby telegraph towers. Each relay tower had three to four operators: two watchmen, who monitored nearby towers for incoming or outgoing signals, and a third (and occasionally fourth) worker who operated the apparatus to transmit signals. A terminal station had only two operators, as it only connected to one nearby tower. Occasionally, a single highly skilled worker could both watch and manipulate the

apparatus, if the telescope and control mechanism were located close enough to each other.[09] Operators replicated signs without knowing how to interpret them. Only authorized officers with frequently updated codebooks could interpret signs. This knowledge separation decoupled operations from intelligence, enhancing security throughout the entire communications system.

The Building Typology: The Mechanical Puppet

In dense urban environments, optical telegraphs were often placed on top of high-rise public buildings, like churches, town halls, or bell towers. In rural areas, however, optical telegraphs developed their own typologies in which the signaling apparatuses were architecturally integrated to the building. These typologies evolved based on available materials, human factors, and communication protocols. Towers were built out of timber or masonry and were often fortified, as they constituted military targets. They often contained a kitchen, bedroom, storage for food and fuel supplies, and external water well.[10] Their design typically employed simple geometries such as rectangular or cylindrical prisms; however, more complicated types existed. T. W. Holmes, for example, mentions four building typologies in the British system: a bungalow and three-, four-, and five-story types. Selection was based on the tower's location and the size of the operator's family. Typologies, however, depended also on the landscape and network topology. In his treatise, Edelcrantz explains that on the plains or in flat landscapes telegraphs need to be positioned above

Opposite: Swedish shutter telegraph system. Above, left: The Furusud shutter telegraph in Sweden. Above, right: Inside an operator's room at the Furunsud telegraph.

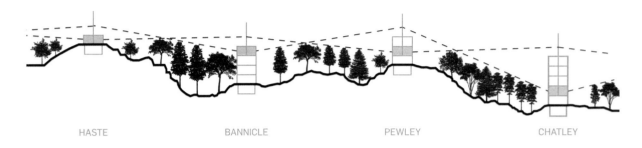

◀ to HOLDER

to COOPERS ▶

the level of fog, mist, or any mirage effects of the hot season, using the sky as much as possible as a background.[11] Furthermore, he determined the distance of towers as a function of the curvature of the earth, mirage effects, and natural geography of the landscape. The height of the control room and the signaling apparatus in the towers varied based on the location and the height of nearby trees or other obstacles, resulting in each tower having a different architectural configuration.

Transmission: Form Follows Form

Relay towers transmitted data by copying each other's form in a domino effect. Hence, form followed form at its most literal sense. Transmission speeds were remarkably high. According to Edelcrantz, Chappe's device could manually change position every twenty seconds, sending approximately two to three signs per minute.[12] Assuming the device utilized 128 of its total 256 signs, this would be equivalent to a transmission speed of 0.5 bits per second. Edelcrantz's ten-bit code could change every eight to ten seconds, while Murray's six-bit code could change every five seconds, both giving a signaling speed of approximately one bit per second.[13] With that speed, a message could traverse the 120 stations of the Paris–Toulon line in less than twelve minutes.

Although signs were transmitted at the aforementioned speeds, their information content depended on how they were utilized to construct messages. Two methods were used: in the first, signs pointed to predefined sentences in lookup codebooks; in the second, signs pointed to alphanumeric characters used for explicitly spelling out messages. While the second method was admittedly slower, it was also logistically simpler and cheaper as it did not rely on voluminous dictionaries that were updated and reprinted often.

Both Chappe and Edelcrantz used codebooks in their systems. In Chappe's system, each transmission consisted of two consecutive signs, the first pointing to a page and the second pointing to an entry in that page. Chappe's codebook had ninety-two pages of ninety-two entries each, for a total of 8,464 predefined messages. Holzmann estimated that Chappe's telegraph was capable of sending up to twenty characters per minute,[14] an astonishing rate compared to the twenty-five characters per minute of the first electromagnetic telegraph in 1837.[15] Edelcrantz's system also used a lookup table with 1,024 entries. To map his device's configurations to index numbers he came up with the following: from top to bottom, he assigned the values 1, 2, and 4 to the shutters of each of the three columns. Then, for each column, he added the values of the closed shutters producing a triplet of octal numbers ranging from zero to seven. The complete code for each signal consisted of the three numbers, prefixed by letter A if the tenth large shutter was closed. For example, code A636 meant a configuration in which the top two shutters of the middle column, the bottom two shutters of the first and third columns, and the tenth shutter were closed. Murray's system was simpler: with a limited range of only sixty-four entries, it was based on explicit spelling.

Optical telegraphs developed sophisticated protocols for communication, addressing, and error detection that are found today in modern telecommunication systems. In the French system, for example, only terminal stations could send or receive messages while all other stations served as relays. In the Swedish network, however, any station could send or receive messages to or from any other station. This addressing detail affected the

Above: Heights of operator room and semaphore apparatus in relation to landscape topography and tree height. A portion of the semaphore line in England.

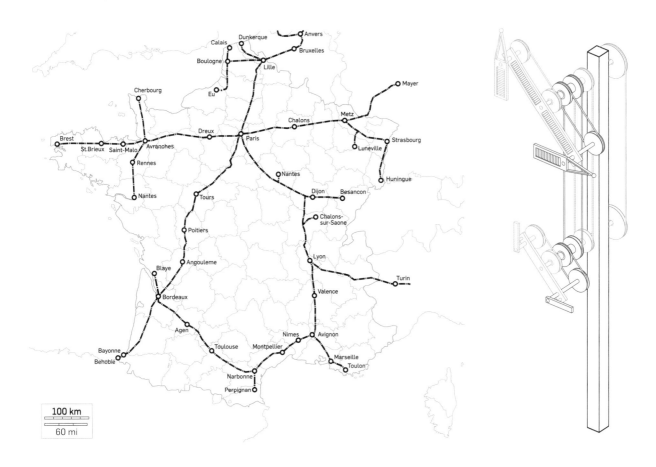

format, size, and eventually transmission speed of the messages as in the former case the messages did not include recipient or sender information while in the latter case they did.[16] Special regulations were invented to deal with message traffic, which was bidirectional and often heavy. When traffic accumulated in a station, for example, rules prioritized which message to switch and which one to hold, especially in hubs. As networks grew, so did their complexity, vulnerability, and ingenuity. Both Chappe and Edelcrantz knew that their system would be as strong as its weakest link: a single error in one relay station could shut down an entire line. Self-reporting mechanisms identified problematic nodes in the network: towers kept logs and reported their peer towers if they were slow in responding. Penalties included fines and imprisonment.[17]

Geographies of Information
Telegraph relay towers were erected at eight- to fifteen-kilometer intervals across the landscape, creating networks of various topologies. The location of each tower was of paramount importance to the reliability of the network: even one misplaced or problematic station

could affect the entire line. As telegraphs had only a front and a back facade, they could be read only from a certain viewing angle, which restricted how towers could be placed. In France, a trial period of one year typically existed for new stations: during this time, stations were often moved around until a good location was found.[18]

By the early nineteenth century, optical telegraphy networks in Europe were vast and busy. More than a thousand telegraphs connected cities from Paris to Perpignan and Toulon in the south, to Amsterdam in the north, to Brest in the west, and to Venice in the east, streaming information at full capacity. In France, for example, traffic averaged several hundred messages per year, serving mostly military, governmental, and stock or commodity market purposes.[19] The Paris–Lille line was completed in 1794, with the first official message sent from Lille to Paris on August 15.

Above, left: The Chappe network in France, showing major cities. Above, right: Axonometric drawing illustrating how the Chappe mechanism worked. Colors indicate the individual pulley systems for manipulating the device. The blue bar controls the regulator while the green and red handles control the left and right indicators.

Dimitris Papanikolaou

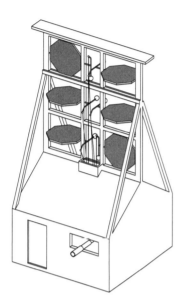 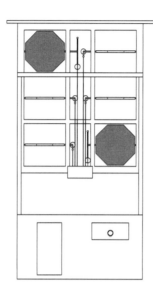 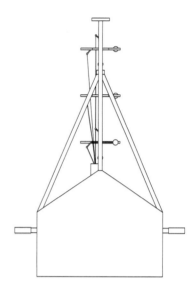

Optical telegraphy operated in France from 1794 to 1855, growing gradually and steadily. In 1816, a line was constructed from Paris to Calais. In 1821, a new line connected Lyons to Toulon. Two years later, Paris connected to Bordeaux, while in 1828 Avignon connected to Perpignan. By 1852, the network reached its peak with 556 stations and more than 4,800 kilometers of relay line serving twenty-nine of France's largest cities. All of these lines were operated and maintained by the French Ministry of War,[20] and employed more than three thousand workers.[21]

Similar networks connected other European countries. In 1801, Sweden had four operating lines connecting Stockholm to Fredriksborg, Grisslehamn, Signilskär, Helsingborg, and Eckerö, while in 1809, its network expanded to fifty stations linking Gävle and Landsort. In the United Kingdom, by 1808, the British Admiralty had a network of sixty-five stations that could send messages form London to Deal, on the English Channel, in about one minute.[22] Soon networks expanded in the rest of Europe, connecting cities in Norway, Finland, Denmark, the Netherlands, Germany, and Russia, as well as on the East Coast of the United States and in Australia.[23] Although optical telegraphy networks covered large areas in Europe, most national networks were incompatible and fragmented. Having different communication protocols and signaling mechanisms, there was often no means for information to smoothly flow from one system to another.

Sociopolitical Context

In the midst of the Napoleonic Wars in Europe (1803–1815), the majority of optical telegraphy networks were developed, operated, and maintained almost exclusively by governmental authorities for diplomatic and military purposes. As war and funding came to an end, telegraphs found new applications where time-sensitive information had to travel faster than material resources. Such applications included trading stocks and commodities in financial markets or operating steam-powered trains in rapidly expanding railway networks.

The new technology was not always embraced by the public. Like most communication media, optical telegraphs and their buildings symbolized instruments of governmental authority, control, surveillance, conspiracy, and oppression. In Chappe's early experiments, some believed he was trying to communicate with the Austrians and Prussians.[24] Later, during the upheaval of the French Revolution, many telegraph towers were burned and torn down with their operators nearly saving their lives from the mobs.

Despite overall skepticism, optical telegraphs constituted also technological achievements of wonder, admiration, and envy. Many inventors claimed ownership of the new invention and the patent war among them was fierce. As Edelcrantz wrote in his treatise,

Above: British admiralty shutter telegraph building.

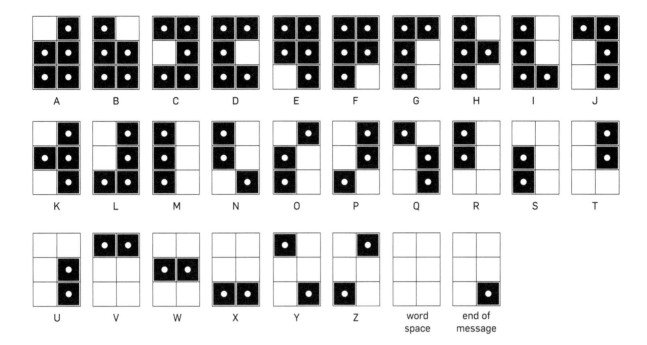

It often happens, with regard to new inventions, that one part of the general public finds them use-less and another part considers them to be impossible. When it becomes clear that the possibility and the usefulness can no longer be denied, most agree that the whole thing was fairly easy to discover and that they knew about it all along.[25]

The extraordinary maintenance costs, the political instability, and the rapid technological advancement of Samuel F. B. Morse's electric telegraph seized optical telegraphy and its nascent architecture permanently in 1844. It lasted fifty years and it was the fastest and most reliable communication system ever conceived until then.

Three Theses on the Architectural Internet of Optical Telegraphy

Little is known about the architecture of optical telegraphs. Within only fifty years from their first implementation until their replacement by the electric telegraph, optical telegraphs remained partly machines, partly buildings never managing to develop a mature architectural typology. Through their short evolution, though, they demonstrated a remarkably novel concept: that abstract architectural language can semantically construct and mediate urban intelligence. After portraying their techno-sociopolitical context from an architectural perspective, I conclude with three theses.

The Eighteenth Century's Smart Cites

First, *optical telegraphy networks constituted cybernetic predecessors of smart cities.* In his book ME++, William Mitchell portrays the urban condition of the twenty-first century as an intelligent, networked landscape that uses electronic nervous systems to serve the needs of its users in more efficient and sustainable ways.[26] It is fair to say that nearly two centuries ago, optical telegraphy created a mechanical nervous system with a similar rhetoric but a more tangible implementation. Optical telegraph networks merged synergistically human operators, mechanical interfaces, and telescopes with decision makers and financial institutions, creating self-regulating cybernetic systems with urban-scale feedback loops.[27] Brokers in Paris could arbitrage from rising trading prices in Amsterdam in a matter of minutes. Train stations could inform awaiting passengers of the imminent delay of an arriving train in nearly real time. Military commanders could organize their army and fleet in response to enemy's tactics. And corporate businessmen could send frequent optical mails, or "omails," to arrange time-sensitive deals.

Form as a Medium of Information

Second, *information was manifested through abstract architectural language, both the control and interpretation of which were critical in closing the feedback loop of intelligence.* While

Above: The British admiralty alphabet code.

Dimitris Papanikolaou

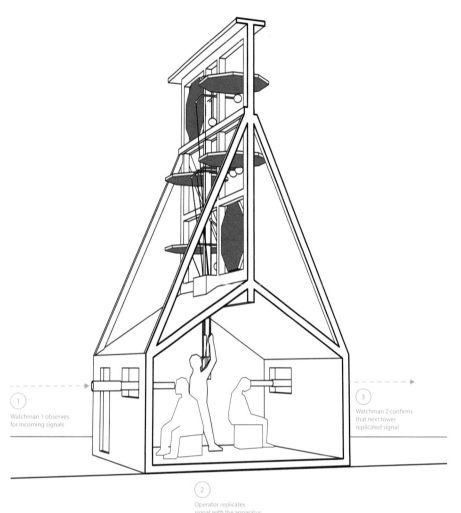

Diagram illustrating how the British shutter telegraph worked.

1
Watchman 1 observes for incoming signals

3
Watchman 2 confirms that next tower replicated signal

2
Operator replicates signal with the apparatus

in Mitchell's rhetoric intelligence is mediated through digital bits, in Chappe's, Edelcrantz's, and Murray's it was mediated through physical space and geometry. This is not to argue that manipulating form is a better medium than flipping digital bits. But in a contemporary discourse on intelligent environments where materiality, information, and human perception seek new models for seamless integration, such rhetoric gives new directions for critical exploration.

Optical telegraphy illustrated both how form can mediate information and how in turn communication requirements can drive architectural, urbanistic, and planning decisions. On the one hand, it produced a self-referring, signifying, and performative (almost postmodern) architecture.[28] On the other hand, its (almost modern) language—abstract and functionalistic—derived through experiments instead of imitation. The form in this case was the medium, not the message.[29]

Form as a Manifestation of Computation

Third, *optical telegraphs were early manifestations of architectural computing automata*. Through their reconfigurable forms, optical telegraphs not only represented information bits but also stored them in their finite formalistic states. Furthermore, by the highly mechanized process by which human operators executed tasks without knowing their meaning, optical telegraphy introduced basic concepts of computation in which routines, when followed methodically, produce logical and consistent outcomes. With their strict procedural protocol of finite states and lookup tables, the constrained inputs and outputs of their control rooms, and the separation of execution from interpretation, optical telegraph towers resemble urban manifestations of architectural Turing machines.[30] No one knows where this technology, idea, and typology would have been taken, had information and computation theory been known then.

Optical telegraphy has often been coined as history's *mechanical Internet*, a term with an emphasis on the mechanisms with which the telegraphic apparatuses worked. Throughout this essay I favor *architectural Internet* as a new term with an emphasis on the medium through which intelligence was implemented. Information etymologically means giving shape to communicate knowledge. Nowhere in the history of communications has this term been more literally implemented than in the eighteenth century's optical telegraphy networks. And nowhere in the history of architecture has knowledge been most closely associated with built form. In an architecturally mediated internet, "form follows information" and "form follows form" would probably be the two most succinct principles of essence.

Acknowledgments: The author would like to acknowledge Tekniska Museet in Stockholm and the Archives and Special Collections at Harvard University for their generous help in accessing their archive materials.

01. See Gerard J. Holzmann and Björn Pehrson, *The Early History of Data Networks* (Los Alamitos, CA: IEEE Computer Society Press, 1995), 26–29.
02. Nicolò Barbaro, *Diary of the Siege of Constantinople, 1453*, trans. J. R. Jones (New York: Exposition Press, 1969).
03. Holzmann and Pehrson, *The Early History of Data Networks*, 31–44.
04. Ibid., 51–53.
05. For a thorough description of Chappe's device see M. Chappe (Ignace Urbain Jean), *Histoire de la télégraphie* (Paris: L'auteur, 1824).
06. See Abraham Niclas Edelcrantz, "A Treatise on Telegraphs" (1796), translated and republished in *The Early History of Data Networks*, 129–78.
07. T. W. Holmes, *The Semaphore: The Story of the Admiralty-to-Portsmouth Shutter Telegraph and Semaphore Lines, 1796 to 1847* (Ilfracombe, UK: Stockwell, 1983).
08. Holzmann and Pehrson, *The Early History of Data Networks*, 105.
09. Holmes, *The Semaphore*.
10. Ibid.
11. Holzmann and Pehrson, *The Early History of Data Networks*.
12. Operators could change the device in one to two seconds, but they held each signal for twenty to thirty seconds to ensure reception from the remote towers.
13. Gerard J. Holzmann, *Design and Validation of Computer Protocols* (Englewood Cliffs, NJ: Prentice Hall, 1991).
14. Considering a rate of twenty characters per minute, about two to three words of ten characters each could be sent per minute.
15. Holzmann and Pehrson, *The Early History of Data Networks*.
16. Ibid.
17. Holmes, *The Semaphore*.
18. Duane Koenig, "Telegraphs and Telegrams in Revolutionary France," *Scientific Monthly* 59, no. 6 (December 1944): 431–37.
19. Holzmann and Pehrson, *The Early History of Data Networks*, 75.
20. Koenig, "Telegraphs and Telegrams in Revolutionary France."
21. Gerard J. Holzmann and Björn Pehrson, "The First Data Networks," *Scientific American* 270, no. 1 (1994): 124–29.
22. Holzmann and Pehrson, *The Early History of Data Networks*.
23. Tom Standage, *The Victorian Internet: The Remarkable Story of the Telegraph and the Nineteenth Century's On-Line Pioneers* (New York: Bloomsbury, 2014).
24. Koenig, "Telegraphs and Telegrams in Revolutionary France."
25. Edelcrantz, "A Treatise on Telegraphs," in *The Early History of Data Networks*, 129–78.
26. See William J. Mitchell, *Me++: The Cyborg Self and the Networked City* (Cambridge, MA: MIT Press, 2003).
27. For an analysis of the synergies between human administration, software, and hardware in applications of optical telegraphy see Alexander J. Field, "French Optical Telegraphy, 1793–1855: Hardware, Software, Administration," *Technology and Culture* 35, no. 2 (April 1994): 315–47.
28. For an analysis on the role of architectural language as a signifying medium, see Charles Jencks, *The Language of Post-modern Architecture* (New York: Rizzoli, 1977).
29. A paraphrase of Marshall McLuhan's quote "the medium is the message"; McLuhan advocated the importance of media over the content it caries in shaping social perception. While optical telegraphs used shape to construct content, their form was decontextualized from meaning. See Marshall McLuhan, *Understanding Media: The Extensions of Man* (New York: McGraw-Hill, 1964).
30. Turing machines, formalized by computer scientist Alan Turing, are hypothetical computing automata that compute by manipulating strings of symbols through finite states and rule tables. For a thorough description see Alan Mathison Turing, *The Essential Turing: Seminal Writings in Computing, Logic, Philosophy, Artificial Intelligence, and Artificial Life; Plus The Secrets of Enigma* (Oxford: Clarendon Press; New York: Oxford University Press, 2004).

Image Credits
047: Chappe (Ignace Urbain Jean), *Histoire de la télégraphie* (Paris: L'auteur, 1824).

048, 049: Tekniska Museet, Stockholm.

050: Illustration reproduced based on Holmes, *The Semaphore*, 89.

051–054: Illustrations by the author.

Preliminary Findings toward an Architectural History of the Network

Kazys Varnelis

As a set of technical protocols determined by the limitations of technologies, the network has received much critical attention since the Internet began to proliferate in the 1990s. By contrast, there has been little research on networks from an architectural perspective. The network as a material fact, as a geographic condition shaped by the constraints of the physical world and punctuated by buildings, remains to be written. Any such investigation would necessarily consider the network's infancy; that is, its historical emergence in typological terms.

But how can we understand the data center as a building type? Can we even speak of a building type when centers encompass at once repurposed buildings, such as One Wilshire in Los Angeles, as well as purpose-built skyscrapers such as 60 Hudson Street or the AT&T Long Lines Building in New York, and warehouse-like, horizontal facilities in exurban areas like Google's data center at The Dalles, Oregon, or the NYSE Euronext Liquidity Center in Mahwah, New Jersey? Data centers, it would seem, have radically different architectural manifestations and appear in remarkably different sorts of geographic conditions.

To study a building type, we must begin with both a definition and a historical genealogy. At its most essential, the data center is a structure dedicated specifically to the transmission of information. The specific nature of the communication media is unimportant to our analysis here; rather, the focus is on the processing of data. One could examine a number of different media that might lay claim to originating the data center. We might start with a very old type—the library. Its rows of shelves have long carried information banks in the form of books. Networks, however, constituted only a minor aspect of libraries, as the circulation between one branch and another, or from main library to branch library, represents only a small part of a library system's total circulation, with formalized interlibrary loans emerging only recently, at the tail end of the nineteenth century. The earliest building type that might confidently be identified as a data center is, instead, the post office, which developed in the United

States in the mid-nineteenth century. Immediately, we are confronted by the link between data center and territory. More than any other country had done previously, the United States placed emphasis on the mail system throughout its political development.

From the onset, the Constitution invested Congress with the expressed power "to establish post offices and post roads." Understanding the service as essential for building a sense of nationhood among the far-flung states and spreading information necessary for the operation of the republic, Congress enacted the Postal Act of 1792. Through the act, Congress took direct responsibility for the control of the mail and encouraged the circulation of information by discounted rates to newspapers. It rapidly expanded the network of postal routes and offices across the country: by 1828 there were 114,536 miles of post roads across the country, up from 1905 in 1791 (a year prior to the Postal Act). The postal system soon became the largest branch of the federal government, with outposts in every town in the country. Historian Richard John writes, "it would hardly be an exaggeration to suggest that for the vast majority of Americans the postal system *was* the central government."[01] By 1831, postal service employees made up just over three-quarters of all federal civilian employees. That same year Alexis de Tocqueville observed that the typical frontiersman, although he might appear rude and ignorant, is actually "a highly civilized being, who consents, for a time, to inhabit the backwoods, and who penetrates into the wilds of the New World with the Bible, an axe, and a file of newspapers." That file of newspapers was not brought from the city; rather, it came by mail. De Tocqueville continued, "It is difficult to imagine the incredible rapidity with which public opinion circulates in the midst of these deserts."[02] Another writer of the time, impressed by the ease of communication made possible by the US postal system, stated, "Time and distance are annihilated."[03]

During the first half-century of mail service, post offices had no specific form. In small towns they could be located within stores or even the home of a postmaster. In cities, post offices rented existing buildings in business centers. Historian David Henkin describes the vicissitudes of the New York office, the busiest in the nation, writing that it "occupied a two-story wooden house in Lower Manhattan in 1825 that was known as the Academy Building. Two years later, the post office moved to the merchants' exchange, then to the rotunda near City Hall, and from there in 1845 to a Dutch Reformed Church, where it remained until after the Civil War."[04] This itinerant condition was intentional: for the network to take visible architectural form would have been risky in an era of widespread anti-Federalist

sentiment. The only exception to this was the General Post Office Building in Washington, DC, constructed in 1836 and housing not only the District of Columbia's post office but also the quarters of the postmaster general and the central administration. One observer called it "perhaps the most beautiful edifice at the capital."[05] But outside the capital, the appearance of the post office as more than an infrastructural element would have risked disrupting the tenuous territorial balance between the federal system and local autonomy.

In 1800 the postal service implemented a hub-and-spoke system for its network, replacing the earlier point-to-point system with the delivery of mail sacks via stagecoach to distributing post offices in key logistical locations. By 1828 there were some forty-eight distributing offices acting as data processing facilities: a letter sent from one location to another would be taken to the nearest distributing office and sorted into the appropriate category for delivery by stagecoach or boat to the distributing office nearest its destination, where it would again be sorted into packets. In a footnote, John observes that the creation of this network was a revolutionary shift in communication since, for the first time, "postal officers routinely distinguished between the *conveyance* of the portmanteau that protected the mail and the *transmission* of the mail itself."[06] Put another way, a level of abstraction between the message being carried and the way it is being carried had entered the system.

The geographical mandate of the federal postal system—to serve more than 1.5 million square miles, encompassing the original colonies, Northwest Territory, and Louisiana Purchase—necessitated the growth of the distributing offices. Thus, while some of the distributing offices doubled as main post offices in major cities (in 1851, fourteen of the fifteen largest cities in the United States had distributing offices), others were located in strategic exurban locations, such as Cumberland Gap, Kentucky; Napoleon, Arkansas; and Vicksburg, Mississippi.[07]

If the distributing office served as a hub in this network, post roads formed the spokes. Proponents of the federal construction of roads understood the Constitution's mandate to "establish … post roads" as authorizing it to construct a nationwide public transportation network; stagecoach routes that operated on it were private, profiting off of postal service contracts.[08] But given continued resistance to the expansion of the federal government, coupled with the government's lack

Opposite: First Assistant Postmaster, Abraham Bradley Jr., *Progress of the Mail on the Main Line*, detail, from *A Map Of The United States Exhibiting Post Roads & Distances*, 1796.

	POST TOWNS	Summer Establishment *from April 15th to October 15th*		Winter Establishment *from October 15th April 15th*	
Miles		Progress Southward.	Progress Northward.	Progress Southward.	Progress Northward.

Miles	Post Towns	
	Brewers M⁰	Leave
40	Machias	
6	Chandler's River	
9	Columbia	
10	Narraguagus	
16	Gouldsboro'	
12	Sullivan	
12	Trenton	
10	Blushill	
	Castine	Arrive / Leave
4	Penobscot	
4	Prospect	
12	Belfast	
12	Duck Trap	
7	Camden	
7	Thomaston	
7	Warren	Arrive / Leave
12	Waldoborough	
10	Newcastle	
10	Wiscasset	Arrive / Leave
13	Bath	
12	Brunswick	
17	North Yarmouth	
14	**PORTLAND**	Arrive / Leave
18	Biddeford	
10	Wells	
20	York	
10	**PORTSMOUTH - N.H.**	Arrive / Leave
22	Newbury Port M⁵	
12	Ipswich	
10	Beverly	
4	Salem	Leave
	Lynn	
14	**BOSTON**	Arrive / Leave
48	Worcester	
31	Brookfield	
28	Springfield	
18	Suffield C.	
10	**HARTFORD**	Arrive / Leave
	Wethersfield	
10	Middletown	
13	Wallingford	
	NEW HAVEN	Arrive / Leave
11	Milford	
3	Stratford	
	Fairfield	
12	Norwalk	
10	Stamford	
29	Kingsbridge N.Y.	
15	**NEW YORK**	Arrive / Leave
9	Newark N.J.	
6	Elizabethtown	
6	Bridgetown	
4	Woodbridge	
10	New Brunswick	
18	Princeton	
12	Trenton	
1	Morrisville P.	
9	Bristol	
20	**PHILADELPHIA**	Arrive / Leave
15	Chester	
13	**WILMINGTON** D.	Arrive
5	Newport	
6	Christiana	
12	**Elkton** M⁴	
10	Charlestown	
6	Havre de Grace	
12	Hartford	
25	**BALTIMORE**	Arrive / Leave
38	Bladensburg	
4	**WASHINGTON** C.	
4	Georgetown	
8	**Alexandria** V.	Arrive / Leave
16	Colchester	
10	Dumfries	
25	Falmouth	
1	**Fredericksburg**	Arrive / Leave
22	Bowling Green	
25	Bowser C.H.	
25	**RICHMOND**	Arrive / Leave
15	Osbornes	
10	**Petersburg**	Arrive / Leave
33	Harris's	
30	Goldans	
54	Warrenton N.C.	
25	Louisburg	
33	**RALEIGH**	Arrive
34	Averysborough	
25	Fayetteville	
32	**Lumberton**	Arrive
54	Cheraw C.H. S.C.	
52	Camden	
55	**COLUMBIA**	Arrive
60	Edgefield C.H.	
25	**AUGUSTA**	Leave
37	Waynesboro'	
25	**LOUISVILLE** G.	Arrive / Leave
100	Savannah	Arrive / Leave
34	Newport	Arrive
25	St. Mary's	Arrive
1799		
	RICHMOND V.	Leave
30	New Kent	
30	Williamsburg	
12	York	
21	Hampton	Arrive
16	Norfolk	Arrive
111		
	Camden S.C.	Arrive
20	Statesbury	
100	Charleston	Arrive
120		

Explanation.

Figures under the days of the week denote the hour { a. afternoon / f. forenoon

The mail leaves Brewers every Monday at 10 o'clock forenoon arrives at Castine the next Sunday 6 o'clock afternoon, and tracing its arrivals and departures along the double line it arrives at Philadelphia on Wednesday 7 a.m. & at St. Mary's in Georgia on Thursday at 10 f. the 46th day from its departure from Brewers.

From New York Southward the Summer Establishment is from May 1st to Nov 1st and the Winter Establishment from Nov 1st to May 1st.

The Winter establishment is the same as the Summer.

of capital, post roads (and later, railroads) were typically funded by private investors, who would derive their profits from the postal contracts or tolls until (at least in the case of the roads) their grant of monopoly status ended and the roads became public.[09]

Throughout the nineteenth century, customs tariffs made up a majority of the federal government's revenue. The employment of architects from the US Treasury's Office of the Supervising Architect (founded in 1852) to construct new customs houses underscores the revenue produced by this branch of government and echoes the earlier status of the customs house in England. To save time and money, the architecture of customs houses and post offices was standardized: identical structures were often constructed in multiple locations. Thus, a building in Cleveland, Ohio, had a near-identical twin in Wheeling, Virginia (now West Virginia). Still, in a country that had not yet been accustomed to architectural production by the government, and had seen virtually no construction at a federal level outside of the US capital, these works were considered so worth recording that the Treasury Department sent out

lithographed copies of the design to depository libraries, the Smithsonian, and other institutions.[10]

Changes in the postal system led to a greater need for a public face for dedicated post offices in cities. In 1845 Congress reformed the pricing of the postal system to radically lower the price of postage required on letters written by individuals. This significantly boosted the volume of personal and business correspondence. As the postal service did not offer home delivery until the 1860s, individuals were forced to visit post offices during the course of the business day to post and retrieve letters. Post office lobbies became clamorous spaces of social mixing and, given that sending large amounts of currency through the mail was the most common means of transmitting money over a distance, often dangerous spaces as well, frequented by pickpockets and con artists looking for an easy mark.

Above: First Assistant Postmaster, Abraham Bradley Jr., *Postal Routes Between New York City and Boston*, detail, from *A Map Of The United States Exhibiting Post Roads & Distances*, 1796.
Opposite: Post Office, New York City, 1910.

The mail service largely fostered intercity communications until 1863, when Congress (following an earlier British innovation) enacted home delivery in the nation's fifty largest cities. Home delivery served a number of social purposes: it responded to concerns about the danger that the heavily male space of the post office posed to women, and made the receipt of letters from Union soldiers during the Civil War a private matter. But for postal reformers, its main purpose was to make intracity mail viable.[11] With the increase in letter writing due to lower postage costs and the advent of urban home delivery, new pressure was placed on the postal network, even as the role of the post office itself changed. Although still necessary for some transactions, post offices became hubs in the system, dedicated to processing, rather than end nodes.[12]

By this point, however, the postal service had encountered its first competitor—the telegraph. Optical telegraphs had been developed in France in the 1790s and were employed in the northeastern United States in the early nineteenth century for ship-to-shore communication. Optical telegraphs had severe limitations: it could only function in daylight and good weather. Still, the potential of telecommunications to bind together territory on a global scale more rapidly and thoroughly than the postal service ever could was clear. In 1800 polymath and architect of the US Capitol building, William Thornton, in calling for the creation of a United North and South Columbia to rule the hemisphere, wrote, "Telegraphs, when perfected, will convey from the remotest bounds of this vast Empire, any communication to the supreme government in twenty-four hours, with ease."[13]

Such links finally became possible when, on May 24, 1844, Samuel F. B. Morse transmitted the words "What hath God wrought?" over an electric telegraph line stretching from Baltimore to Washington, DC. Morse had hoped his invention would be adopted by the government and integrated into the postal service, a reasonable idea given that in 1837 the Secretary of the Treasury had requested proposals for a "system of telegraphs" across the country. But increased opposition to federal spending undid his hopes. After an initial burst of public excitement, private interest waned as well, and the telegraph came to be considered more of a novelty—a feeling inspired in part by the carnival-like atmosphere around demonstrations of it being used to play chess or checkers. Even as more far-sighted investors began building out telegraph networks, the system became plagued by problems. In comparison to the mail, telegraph service was limited to routes connecting major cities: by 1851 the

telegraph had only as many miles as the post office had in 1801. Telegraph carriers generally had little interest in routing a message from a competing network through their own lines. Bad weather interfered with transmission and fallen trees repeatedly knocked out service altogether. Moreover, a telegraph was far more expensive to send: fifty cents for the transmission of a mere ten words from Washington, DC, to New York, and $2.20 from Washington, DC, to New Orleans, as opposed to just three cents for the delivery of a letter.[14]

Telegraphy consolidated in the 1860s. The first transcontinental telegraph line was completed in 1861, eight years ahead of the first transcontinental railroad; a huge influx of messages and government funding boosted telegraphy during the Civil War (1861–1865); and Cyrus Field's development of the first successful transatlantic cable in 1866: all of these events helped both the industry and the network mature. At the same time, one company—Western Union, founded in 1851—had shrewdly overcome or absorbed all of its rivals to dominate the telegraph market. The result was the largest corporation in the country, exceeding any single railroad in size and small only in comparison to the postal service.[15]

The growth of telegraphy was also boosted by its alliance with the media; specifically a consortium of newspapers called the Associated Press (AP). In a country stretched across a continent, newspapers fulfilled an important role: businessmen came to rely on them for the timely news upon which they would gauge important decisions. Founded in 1846, the association of newspapers played a crucial role in strengthening this reliance by effectively consolidating news-gathering agencies and making what were once local or regional stories available to newspapers nationwide. The AP dictated the terms of the association, insisting that only its own wire dispatches could be printed in the newspapers that subscribed to its service.[16] As of 1867, Western Union dedicated the fourth floor of its general office in New York to the AP, offering the first example of a company collocating inside a carrier's facility.[17]

Newspaper editors and publishers frequently voiced their opinion that both the AP and Western Union constituted monopolies, posing threats to the competition as well as to the freedom of the press. In this, telegraphy produced another first: until this time monopolies had only been produced by grants from the state. The concerns raised against Western Union prefigured twentieth-century concerns about AT&T.[18]

Western Union managed to defend itself against its critics (as did the AP) and, after initial tension subsided, it found new allies in the railroads, which used telegraphy

BROADWAY. NEW YORK.
FROM THE WESTERN UNION TELEGRAPH BUILDING LOOKING NORTH.

to coordinate train travel; for example, the telegraph allowed a single track to be used by trains bound in both directions. In 1870, "Commodore" Cornelius Vanderbilt, who had made a fortune in shipping and rail, secretly acquired Western Union. The result was a symbiosis between rail and telegraph industries, as railroads allowed Western Union to outfit train stations with telegraph offices and to use their rights of way to erect telegraph poles.[19] In addition to the AP and the railroads, the major commodities exchanges also relied on the telegraph. Understanding the advantage on the market that even a minute of advance warning in the news could bring, agents sought to get their messages out first by any means possible, including bribing telegraph operators.[20]

More than any other enterprise to date, with the exception of the post office, Western Union faced the problem of administering and coordinated a large number of employees, dispersed among thousands of offices (7,672 in 1878). Compounding this effort was the vast amount of data the firm had to handle. In 1878, 93,127 messages were handled within the headquarters alone.[21] Although

a recent study by historian Joshua Wolff suggests it was a plodding process of trial and error, Western Union eventually developed one of the first modern corporate organizational structures.[22] Reflecting this, the company built a massive headquarters across from the George B. Post–designed New York Post Office, beginning construction in 1872 and finishing in 1875. Not only was this a symbolic challenge to the rival postal service, the site also abutted Printing House Square, (now Park Row), home to a number of the city's newspapers.[23] Like the Post Office across the way, inside the building was a blend of spaces, including an imposing public lobby and facilities for staff from telegraphy operators to managers, as well as batteries and dynamos for the telegraph equipment.

The new Western Union Building—which, at ten stories, held the title of tallest building in the city for four months—was organized vertically; circulation was provided by elevators, a new invention of the time. The

Above: Currier & Ives, *Broadway, New York. From The Western Union Telegraph Building Looking North*, 1875.

"receiving room," where the public would come to send messages, was located on the ground floor, together with various support facilities such as cashiers' offices. In another one of the earliest instances of collocation, related industries were allowed to rent rooms on the second and third floors, those floors serving as a buffer into which Western Union could expand.

The sixth floor of the Western Union building housed some six thousand batteries weighing about two hundred tons, which were used in transmitting messages. Telegraph wires were carried into the structure via wooden conduits on the facade, entering through a balcony at the seventh floor. Messages were inserted into pneumatic tubes in the receiving room on the ground floor and conveyed upward to the seventh floor "operating room." From there they were transmitted to (as well as received from) other offices, in code. Spanned by a roof truss, the 150-foot-long, sixty-foot-wide room had an open plan with no internal obstructions. It contained eighty-seven tables, each of which accommodated four operators. Above the operating room was a story occupied by the AP, and above that, a final story housing a kitchen and lunchroom.[24] Horizontal expansion across territory and verticality within the city were now firmly linked.

The topology of the Western Union network differed from that of the postal service. Here, major post roads were replaced by trunk lines from which sprang branch lines. Whereas letters were abstracted from their means of transmission through the process of sorting, telegraph messages had to travel over a single connection as much as possible. Information identifying the destination of a message would preface the message itself sent over a line. All offices on a line would receive all messages, and it was up to the destination office to respond with a notice that it had received a message. If possible, switchboards connected branch offices to the line; if this was not possible, messages had to be repeated by hand and sent on their way. Initially, only one telegraph message could be transmitted on a given line, but eventually technologies were developed to transmit messages in both directions and then to transmit two messages simultaneously in both directions.[25]

With the Western Union building adding the skyscraper to the previous two models—the rented post office and the horizontal postal sorting center—the third and final manifestation of the data center was put in place together with two network topologies, based on decentralized models. In contrast, the telephone system would initially take a step back, focusing on

Above, left: C. K. Bill, Western Union Telegraph Building, New York, General Operating Department, half of stereoscopic slide, 1875. Above, right: Irving Underhill, view of Western Union Telegraph Building showing carts and wagons on street, 1912.

short distance, intracity communication, dominated by exchanges serving neighborhoods, with central offices located downtown only slowly becoming integrated in a long-distance network.

Even as they annihilated time and space, communication networks have been dependent upon them from their inception. Our own networks and data centers, located according to a complex calculus of the availability of power grids, security, latency, legal rights-of-way and even topography, are little different. These constructions are both architectural and territorial, tied to both urban and planetary scales. Designing the networks of our time demands that we consider such scalar qualities as well.

01. Richard R. John, *Spreading the News: The American Postal System from Franklin to Morse* (Cambridge, MA: Harvard University Press, 1995), 3–4.
02. Alexis de Tocqueville, *Democracy in America*, trans. Henry Reeve (New York: Colonial Press, 1899), 322–23.
03. John, *Spreading the News*, 10. The original words, "Ye Gods! annihilate but space and time, And make two lovers happy," so often bent to apply to communications and capital are Alexander Pope's.
04. David M. Henkin, *The Postal Age: The Emergence of Modern Communications in Nineteenth-Century America* (Chicago: University of Chicago Press, 2006), 65.
05. Eli Bowen, *The United States Post-Office Guide* (New York: D. Appleton, 1851), 15. No matter what service, the federal government would typically rent existing buildings for its own purposes when outside of the District. Antoinette J. Lee, *Architects to the Nation: The Rise and Decline of the Supervising Architect's Office* (New York: Oxford University Press, 2000).
06. John, *Spreading the News*, 304.
07. Bowen, *The United States Post-Office Guide*, 34.
08. Daniel P. Carpenter, *The Forging of Bureaucratic Autonomy: Reputations, Networks, and Policy Innovation in Executive Agencies, 1862–1928* (Princeton, NJ: Princeton University Press, 2001), 69; and Theodore Sky, *The National Road and the Difficult Path to Sustainable National Investment* (Newark: University of Delaware Press, 2011).
09. John B. Miller, *Case Studies in Infrastructure Delivery* (Boston: Kluwer Academic Publishers, 2000), 120.
10. Lee, *Architects to the Nation*, 60–61.
11. Ibid., 82–83.
12. Ibid., 84.
13. William Thornton, "Thornton's Outlines of a Constitution for United North and South Columbia," *Hispanic American Historical Review* 12, no. 2 (May 1932).
14. Joshua D. Wolff, *Western Union and the Creation of the American Corporate Order, 1845–1893* (Cambridge: Cambridge University Press, 2013), 16–24. On Morse's attempts to secure congressional sponsorship of the telegraph network, see Richard R. John, *Network Nation: Inventing American Telecommunications* (Cambridge, MA: Belknap Press, 2010). The statistic about post road mileage appears in Dow, "The Progress and Present Condition of the General Post Office," 203.
15. John, *Network Nation*.
16. Wolff, *Western Union*, 122.
17. "The General Telegraph Office of Western Union in New York City," *Telegrapher* 3, no. 56 (July 15, 1867): 1.
18. Wolff, *Western Union*, 2, 53, and 116.
19. Ibid., 133–34, 204.
20. Ibid., 204.
21. Joseph J. Korom, *The American Skyscraper, 1850–1940: A Celebration of Height* (New York: Brenden Books, 2008), 72–73.
22. Wolff, *Western Union*, 264.
23. Robert A. M. Stern, Thomas Mellins, and David Fishman, *New York 1880: Architecture and Urbanism in the Gilded Age* (New York: Monacelli Press, 1999).
24. Korom, *American Skyscraper*, 72–77; "The New Telegraphic Heart of America," *New-York Daily Tribune*, February 1, 1875, 12; and "The Western Union Telegraph Building," *Manufacturer and Builder* (December 1873): 280.
25. For a detailed explanation of the operation of telegraph networks, see International Correspondence Schools, *Elements of Telegraph Operating Systems* (Scranton, PA: International Textbook Company, 1912). For their history, see Ken Beauchamp, *History of Telegraphy* (London: Institution of Electrical Engineers, 2001).

Image Credits

All images are courtesy of the Library of Congress.

Farm/Cloud

Mason White

It could be argued that the data center—the product of cloud computing, virtual communication, and the Information Age—is the first distinct new building type to emerge in this young twenty-first century. The data center is also, possibly, the first building type dedicated almost exclusively to the machine as its user. It could also be argued that architecture, frequently entangled in biological associations throughout the past several decades, has a correlation with "speciation."[01]

In some instances, building types are ushered into being by the abrupt need to address highly specific programs. These building types emerge from demands within economics and development trends, though sometimes they advance and proliferate rapidly before architects are able to place their imprints on them. Speciation of a building type was evident, for example, in the early 1900s when the modern factory appeared as pioneered by the Detroit-based architect Albert Kahn. Speciation surfaced again in the 1950s when the shopping mall was given form by the Austrian-born architect Victor Gruen. The data center is a significant new type within a series of types that have been added to the architectural species. In contrast to other architectural speciations, however, this type has no identifiable architect associated with it to date. The overlaps with both the shopping mall, determined as much by shopping environments as economic markets, and the factory, designed with assembly line and manufacturing systems in mind, are undeniable.

Harvesting Information

Various physical manifestations of the Internet have appeared since the 1990s, conceived as efficient spaces for storing digitized information and carrying out various processes. What initially began as a computer closet later became a server room, before emerging as a stand-alone building housing servers and the infrastructure that powers them. Similarly, what began as a process (information technology) able to be managed in-house later became one requiring specialists and peripheral equipment. Throughout this transformation, the logistical requirements for this technologically intensive program governed all significant space and design decisions. This program demands cooling and power, as well as access for maintenance and oversight. There is very little human demand on the spaces of the type: it is an architecture (or infrastructure) that privileges the (utilitarian) needs of the machine.

It is not surprising, then, that this machinic space is described as fieldlike—as a place for the cultivation of information, such as a "farm," and also as an atmospheric nonspace, like a "cloud." These two common characterizations—specifically, the "server farm" and "cloud computing"—are ideally suited to describe something as abstract as the physical spaces dedicated to the operations of the Internet. Nor is it unrelated that the term "farm" connotes a productive field located at the periphery of modern urban life, yielding sustenance for the masses while remaining largely out of sight, and that the term "cloud" invokes a visible yet shape-shifting mass of liquid droplets. The associations of both terms, when used in regard to the structures dedicated to the Internet, refute the presence or physicality of the Internet in the minds of those who are unable to see its infrastructure firsthand.

There are two predominant spatial conditions for the physical internet: the dedicated data center and the colocation center. Dedicated data centers are used exclusively by a single company, such as Microsoft, Facebook, and Google, who are among the largest operators of the physical spaces of the Internet. Colocation centers (or "colos") are rented and may be partitioned to allow for multiple tenants. Typically, the renting company provides its own equipment, whereas the host company provides the space, power, and cooling. Centers of both types may vary in size and can be located in preexisting buildings, making them ideal as adaptive reuse projects.

Following the proliferation of distinct computing rooms within company offices in the 1990s, the stand-alone data center grew in popularity in the early 2000s. Companies embraced the opportunity offered by operators to store data off-site and to outsource the complex requirements of data management to specialists in cloud computing services. Emboldened by its own success, the data center proliferated, further increasing its viability as an emerging building type. Like other rapidly surfacing architecture speciations, however, this nascent building type exhibited a contradictory relationship both to its site and to its context.

From Nonplaces to "Superplaces"

In *Non-Places*, Marc Augé, the French anthropologist, observes that a number of spatial types exhibiting an ambivalence toward site specificity surfaced in the late twentieth century to disturb conventional understandings of place. He identifies these types as spaces of circulation, consumption and communication, such as highways, airports, and supermarkets, among others.[02] Rather than owned and occupied, these "non-places" are intended to be consumed and traversed. Additionally, they "cannot be defined as relational, or historical, or concerned with identity."[03] Although information technology had not yet advanced to the point where it exerted a physical presence in 1992, the year Augé published his book, the data center (and other internet-initiated building types) could now be considered among his nonplaces.

Is the data center a nonplace? Although initial consideration might suggest it is, further reflection offers a counterpoint. Like Augé's nonplaces, the data center is a space of passage and transmission, albeit digital ones. It cannot be defined as historical or concerned with identity in any way. This comparison is misleading, however, as the data center is not a public building, as is the case with the majority of Augé's nonplaces. The data center is private, and equipped with considerable security. Although it eludes conventional understandings of place and site specificity involving cultural signs, it is certainly not unspecific. Rather, the structures associated with the physical internet engage hyperspecific site conditions: climate, economics, energy, and parallel infrastructure, to name only a few. These factors of place occur at a regional, infrastructural, jurisdictional, and even geological scale, resulting in a "scaling-up" of place: this tests the elasticity of architecture to acknowledge site beyond the immediate or legible proximate. The data center type therefore suggests an alternate understanding of site and place, one that is hyperspecific, yet megaregional.

Augé suggests that the expansion of nonplaces is a logical extension of what he calls "supermodernity," a situation characterized by one essential quality: excess. The oversaturation of the built environment "is the price we pay for the overabundance of events" characteristic of supermodernity.[04] The excess of supermodernity depends upon its participating spaces acting as an extension of each other, stitching together a continuous experience that is simultaneously fluid and familiar.

The data center offers a larger conception of place, outside the reductive binary of place versus nonplace. Today, conceptions of place include geoeconomics. The idea of supermodernity is useful here as it was further developed by Hans Ibelings in his 1998 book *Supermodernism: Architecture in the Age of Globalization*. Ibelings identifies the neutral, abstract work of contemporary architects as a latent extension of the International Style. To make this case, he bundles together several 1990s architecture preoccupations—lightness, transparency, minimalism—under a shared ambition of neutrality and boundlessness. He observes that it seemed as though the "ideal of boundless and undefined space is set to become the main Leitbild for architects."[05] Redirecting Augé's notion, Ibelings cites supermodernism as an apt descriptor of such architectures. Although the stand-alone data center was in its embryonic state in the 1990s, "boundless," "undefined," and "neutral" certainly characterize the emerging type. Building upon both Augé and Ibelings, we might posit the data center as both a by-product and example of "superplace," a playful portmanteau of supermodernity and nonplace.

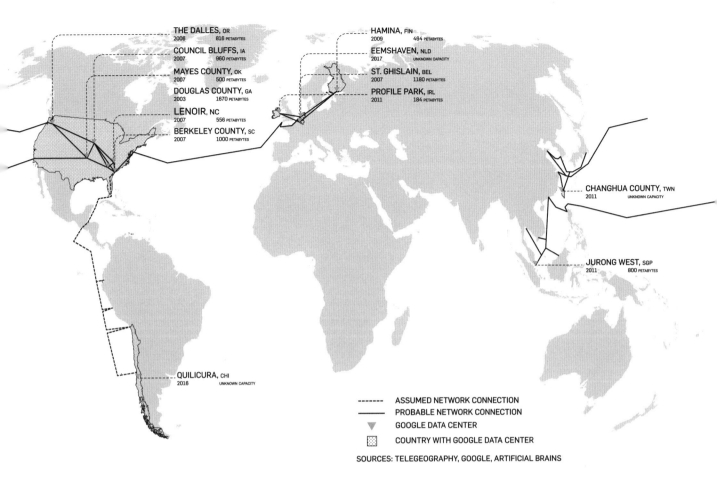

THE DALLES, OR
2006   816 PETABYTES

COUNCIL BLUFFS, IA
2007   960 PETABYTES

MAYES COUNTY, OK
2007   500 PETABYTES

DOUGLAS COUNTY, GA
2003   1670 PETABYTES

LENOIR, NC
2007   556 PETABYTES

BERKELEY COUNTY, SC
2007   1000 PETABYTES

HAMINA, FIN
2009   464 PETABYTES

EEMSHAVEN, NLD
2017   UNKNOWN CAPACITY

ST. GHISLAIN, BEL
2007   1180 PETABYTES

PROFILE PARK, IRL
2011   184 PETABYTES

CHANGHUA COUNTY, TWN
2011   UNKNOWN CAPACITY

JURONG WEST, SGP
2011   800 PETABYTES

QUILICURA, CHI
2016   UNKNOWN CAPACITY

------- ASSUMED NETWORK CONNECTION
———— PROBABLE NETWORK CONNECTION
▼ GOOGLE DATA CENTER
▦ COUNTRY WITH GOOGLE DATA CENTER

SOURCES: TELEGEOGRAPHY, GOOGLE, ARTIFICIAL BRAINS

The Strategy of Superplace

It is now irrefutable that the Internet produces physical spaces and exerts its presence in considerable ways in specific territories. The architectures of the Internet are comprised of the following: a series of massive buildings conspiring to bridge significant distances, a network of undersea cables linking landmasses in an abstract reversal of continental drift, and a land-based, high-capacity fiber-optic network backbone. Although it is distinctly physical, the built form of the Internet is not Manuel Castells's "Informational City," nor is it Silicon Valley.[06] Instead, these spatial manifestations seek to allay claims of insidiousness on the part of the Internet's chief controllers, which recently released images of Heatherwick Studio and BIG's Google campus perpetuate. By contrast, the architectures of the Internet are not actually recognizable as a form of urbanism: they are a mutant hybrid of infrastructure and architecture. The Cloud and the farm are equal parts atmospheric mass and productive surface. Google advocates for cloud computing as a sustainable solution for businesses since it allows them to outsource server storage to a concentrated off-site venue. Its products also suggest Google's investment in making the Cloud appealing. However, the Internet only becomes spatial when its conduit roots within a plot meticulously selected for particular geographic and economic attributes.

How is a site selected? And what kind of place does it become? The data center is primarily invested in site qualities related to available infrastructure. When Google began looking to site a data center in 2004, it cryptically codenamed its search "Project 02," so as to keep it anonymous and covert for as long as possible. But why did they choose a thirty-acre plot in The Dalles, Oregon, a town of barely 14,000 residents, located eighty miles from Portland along the Columbia River—a town that one resident described as "a dusty town on the edge of oblivion"?[07] A 2006 *New York Times* article on the opening

Above: Global network of Google data centers.

Mason White

NG07—Geographies of Information

of Google's $600 million center observes, "odd as it may seem, the barren desert land surrounding the Columbia [River] along the Oregon-Washington border—at the intersection of cheap electricity and readily accessible data networking—is the backdrop for a multibillion-dollar face-off among Google, Microsoft and Yahoo that will determine dominance in the online world in the years ahead."[08] The site was ideal because of its inexpensive hydroelectric power and its proximity to the Internet's backbone of fiber-optic cable dating from the dot-com era. Journalist Andrew Blum, in his 2012 book *Tubes*, suggests that the debate on siting strategy is central to data center design. Blum writes that "siting a data center is like the acupuncture of the physical internet, with places carefully chosen with pinpoint precision to exploit one characteristic or another."[09] The imminent arrival of Google at the time even sparked a small-scale real estate boom in The Dalles, with property values rising 60 percent in the early half of 2005. The complex received a fifteen-year property tax exemption and massive discounts on electricity usage rates. The savings is estimated at about $8.5 billion annually, as compared to typical rates from the local Northern Wasco County People's Utility District.

Some believe that "the physical network is Google's 'secret sauce,' its premier competitive advantage."[10] This secret—not only project sites but also the data center architecture itself—had to be closely guarded. A 2008 article in *Harper's Magazine* published the blueprint of Google's Dalles data center with very little information other than a measured site plan, devoid of interiors but with more than adequate parking. The article by Ginger Gail Strand, a writer on hydroinfrastructures, cites "Google's addiction to cheap electricity" as an immense bias in the strategic placement of energy-intensive data centers.[11] Echoing the complicated reading of the data center as a type, it has alternately been described as a prison, a shopping mall, and an "information-age factory."[12] Andrew Blum's 2011 tour of The Dalles Google project led to his observation that its architectural presence and siting was reminiscent of "the back of a shopping mall, with broad parking lots, loading docks, and a tiny polite nod toward landscaping."[13] This is unsurprising given that the data center harbors little ambition to be "Architecture"; rather, it simply wants to be a machine-building, efficiently consuming and producing in information space.

While Oregon offered a strategic point at a geographic edge, Google's data center in Iowa, completed in 2009, offered a calibrated midspine location along the fiber-optic network. A border town of 62,000 residents across the Missouri River from the larger city of Omaha, Google's thousand-acre Council Bluffs site transformed a derelict farm into a server farm. The conversion of agricultural land to server farm boosted wind farm development in the region in response to the demand for convenient energy. In April 2014 Google announced it would be partnering with MidAmerican Energy, the local utility company in Iowa, to supply up to 407 megawatts of wind energy. Based in Des Moines, MidAmerican Energy currently operates more than 1,200 wind turbines.

Data center experts expect that server farms will continue to have high energy demands. Therefore, to be in the data center business is to also be in the energy business. The bias toward sites that supply abundant, affordable energy is therefore understandable. The strategy of data center site selection implies place as defined by the forecasted availability of certain inputs and outputs—from energy to water to tax incentives to employment base. With an estimated $2 billion per quarter invested into its global data center construction program, and thirteen data centers in existence worldwide, Google is helping solidify the type into a quasi-architecture-infrastructure vernacular.

A Data-Space Vernacular

Architect and theorist Keller Easterling identifies what she calls "broadband urbanism" as compound dispositions of terrestrial fiber-optic cables and airborne mobile telephony. She suggests that each aspect of this system "has the power to territorialize, alter settlement patterns, and redistribute resources."[14] Although Easterling refers specifically to telephony within telecommunications, her observation could be extended to data centers, especially in light of her subsequent claim that "social structures and physical organizations of urban space in turn influence the development of the technology."[15]

This leads us to consider two remaining provocations: Is the data center architecture? And does this building type extend or contribute to notions of architecture's relationship to place and site? In spite of certain shared attributes with nonplace, the data center posits a new, contemporary understanding of place operating at a scale difficult to quantify. It establishes a new scale for architecture, much larger than itself and larger than architecture's immediate registration of site. Factors of economy, energy, and geology extend from, and feedback to, globalization and Easterling's notion of broadband urbanism. The data center can be distinguished as the hybrid

Opposite, from top: Deer at the Council Bluffs, Iowa, Google data center. Plumes of steam rise above The Dalles, Oregon, Google data center.

Google data center in
Douglas County, Georgia.

Google | google.com/datacenters

Mason White

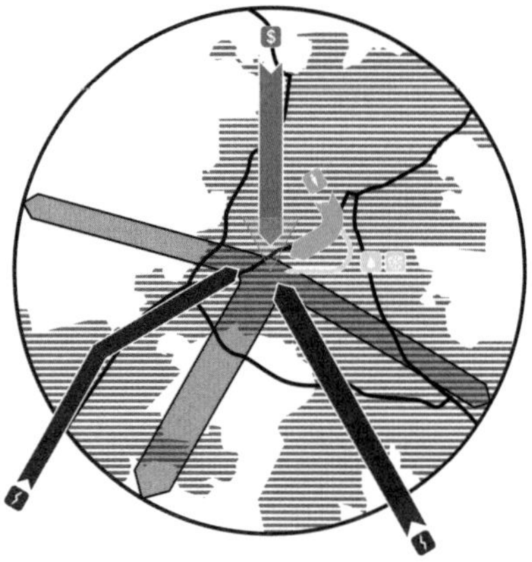

LENOIR
NORTH CAROLINA

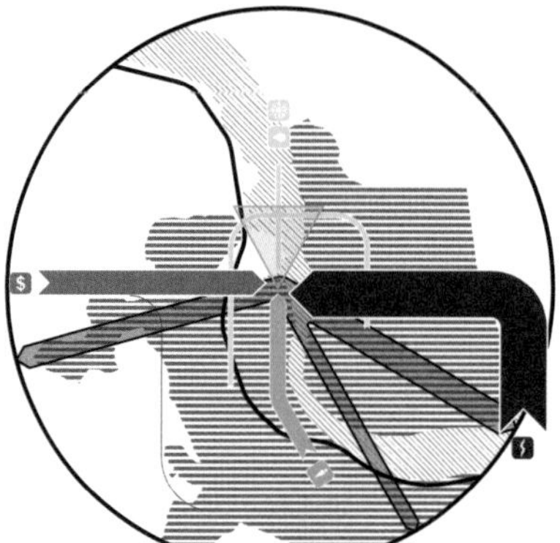

THE DALLES
OREGON

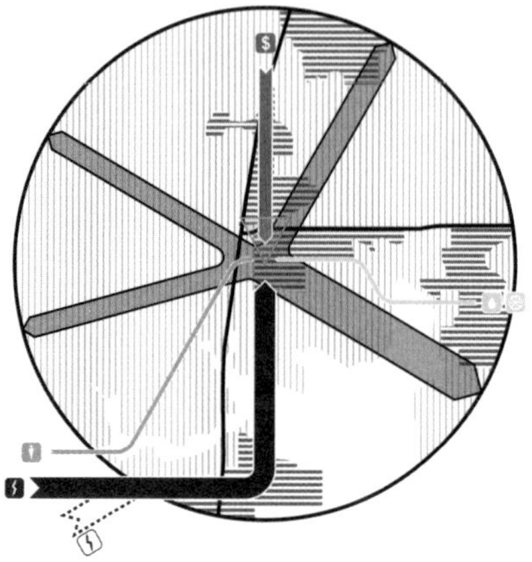

MAYES COUNTY
OKLAHOMA

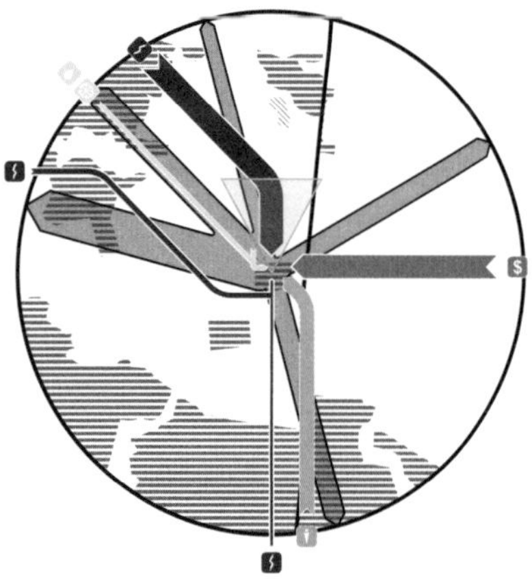

BERKELEY COUNTY
SOUTH CAROLINA

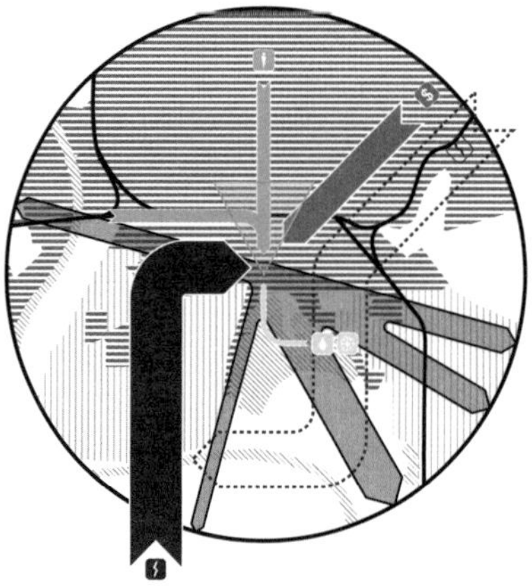

COUNCIL BLUFFS
IOWA

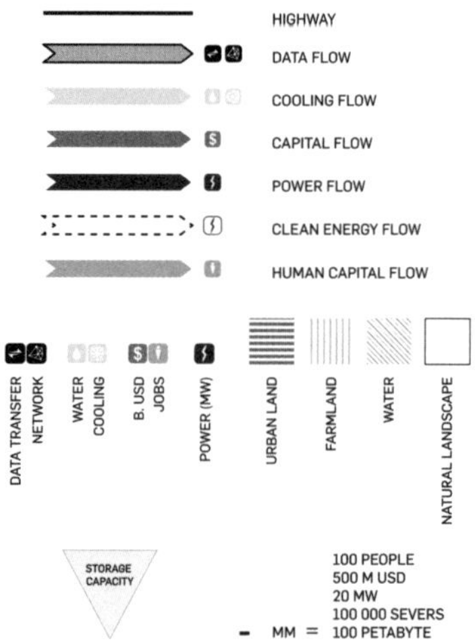

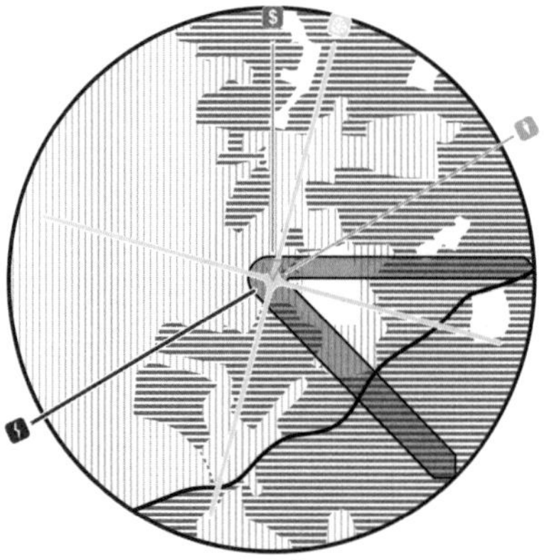

PROFILE PARK
DUBLIN

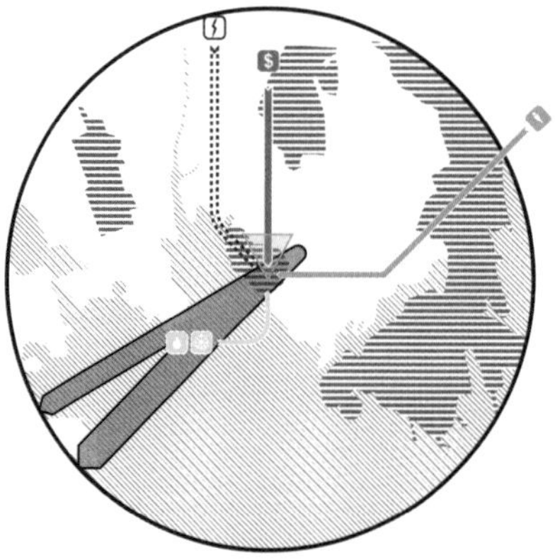

HAMINA
FINLAND

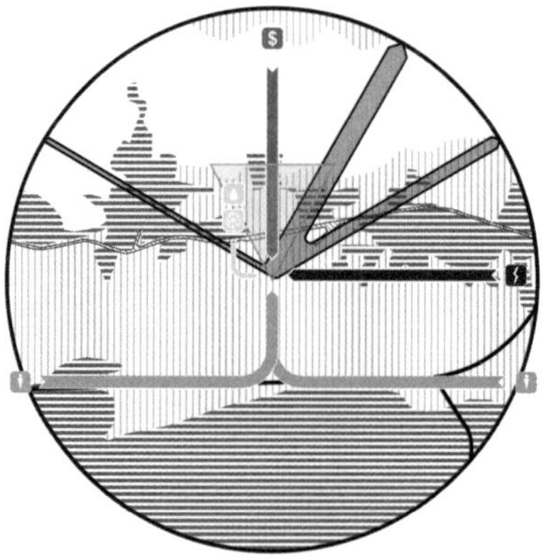

ST. GHISLAIN
BELGIUM

HIGHWAY

DATA FLOW

COOLING FLOW

CAPITAL FLOW

POWER FLOW

CLEAN ENERGY FLOW

HUMAN CAPITAL FLOW

DATA TRANSFER NETWORK

WATER COOLING

B. USD JOBS

POWER (MW)

URBAN LAND

FARMLAND

WATER

NATURAL LANDSCAPE

STORAGE CAPACITY

100 PEOPLE
500 M USD
20 MW
100 000 SEVERS
— MM = 100 PETABYTE

architecture-infrastructure recalling public utilities. Equally, the type offers an abstract, deceptively neutral superplace. This is data at its most vernacular—server corridors, chillers, parking lots, hydroinfrastructures, and all.

A preliminary study of quantified factors supports the notion of the data center as a superplace. The study focuses on Google's data centers as a way to isolate a leader in the development of the building type. It could be argued that Google is the architect of the data vernacular, like Kahn and Gruen before it. The collision of information architecture and spatial, physical architecture is manifest in the physical internet within its superplace.

Acknowledgments: The author would like to acknowledge the following for contributions and insight: Karan Manchanda (University of Waterloo) in the development of the graphics supporting this text; Andrew Blum in early conversations about the space of data; and Jon Hjembo and Markus Krisetya at TeleGeography on recent history of data centers.

01. Speciation is a term coined by American botanist Orator F. Cook Jr. He used the term to refer to the process by which new species emerge from existing ones. The term is borrowed to suggest that building type is analogous to species, and emerges from circumstances within a wider environment.
02. Marc Augé, *Non-Places: Introduction to an Anthropology of Supermodernity*, trans. John Howe (London: Verso, 1995).
03. Ibid., 77.
04. Ibid., 29.
05. Hans Ibelings, *Supermodernism: Architecture in the Age of Globalization* (Rotterdam: NAi, 1998), 62.
06. Google owns or leases about 7.3 million square feet of office space in Mountain View, California. That includes most of the property around its headquarters on the north side of the city near Highway 101, which cuts the length of the valley, according to Transwestern, a commercial real estate brokerage. Mountain View, about 40 miles south of San Francisco, has close to 80,000 people; with its strip-mall thoroughfares and streets of single-family homes, it looks like a sleepy suburb. Conor Dougherty, "Google Plans New Headquarters, and a City Fears Being Overrun," *New York Times*, February 25, 2015, http://nyti.ms/18kF13C. Byron Beck, "Welcome to Googleville," *Willamette Week*, June 4, 2008, http://www.wweek.com/portland/article-9089-welcome_to_googleville.html.
07. John Markoff and Saul Hansell, "Hiding in Plain Sight, Google Seeks More Power," *New York Times*, June 14, 2006, http:// www.nytimes.com/2006/06/14/technology/14search.html.
08. Andrew Blum, *Tubes: A Journey to the Center of the Internet* (New York: Ecco, 2012), 232.
09. G. Pascal Zachary, "The Unsung Heroes Who Move Products Forward," *New York Times*, September 30, 2007, http://www.nytimes.com/2007/09/30/technology/30ping.html.
10. Ginger Gail Strand, "Keyword: Evil: Google's Addiction to Cheap Electricity," *Harper's Magazine*, March 2008, 64.
11. Markoff and Hansell, "Hiding in Plain Sight."
12. Blum, *Tubes*, 244.
13. Keller Easterling, *Extrastatecraft: The Power of Infrastructure Space* (Brooklyn, NY: Verso, 2014), 124.
14. Ibid., 125

Image Credits
069, 074: Illustration by Mason White and Karan Manchanda.

070, 072–073: Photos courtesy of Google/Connie Zhou.

Opposite: Comparative study of select Google data centers flow of energy, information, and capital.

Mason White

The Limits of Intelligence
On the Challenges Faced by Smart Cities

Antoine
Picon

During the past decade we have witnessed the rise of the smart city both as a new urban ideal and as a concrete process of transformation in cities around the world. Although the term may spark thoughts of London, New York, or Singapore—metropolises positioned on the cutting edge of technology—the smart city movement encompasses many cities, in developing countries as well as in wealthy, technologically advanced ones. An estimated total of nearly $39.5 billion is due to be invested in the field of smart cities in 2016, as compared to just $8.1 billion in 2010.[01]

The notion of the smart city is grounded in the intensive use of information and communications technology (ICT). It works through the development of electronic content and the increased hybridization of that content with the physical world, a mingling that is often referred to as augmented reality. Its construction engages a number of key issues, such as reconciling sustainable development with quality of life issues through the close management of technological resources and infrastructure. Smart grids and other networks optimize the urban metabolism of the smart city. In addition to these highly reactive systems, however, new interactive opportunities emerge. Both for individuals equipped with mobile devices and for new collectives, formed along the lines of organizations such as Wikipedia and OpenStreetMap, the smart city enables collaboration on a massive scale.

Beyond its technological basis and its mobilization of inhabitants, a number of additional features may be said to characterize this new understanding of the urban.[02] The "smart city" perspective is progressively replacing the "networked city" ideal, which emerged at the time of the industrial revolution and developed throughout the nineteenth and twentieth centuries as the dominant model to conceptualize the city in both technological and sociopolitical terms.[03] Contrary to the networked city, organized almost exclusively around the mastery of flows, from water supply to transportation systems, the smart city gives greater importance to the control of events, of what happens at all scales, within the urban infrastructure and on the streets. These events range from the millions of ordinary occurrences recorded by the sensors and meters of the smart city to the various festivals that play a more and more essential role in the affirmation of the city's identity. This accent on events has generated two competing interpretations of the smart city: a top-down one, permeated with managerial concerns, that possesses a clear neocybernetic and technocratic tone; and a bottom-up one that relies instead on the capacity of individuals to collaborate in productive ways.[04] One must imagine, I think, the mature smart city as a complex combination of top-down, neocybernetic control systems and bottom-up initiatives led by digitally empowered individuals.

Equally important is the spatial dimension that characterizes the ongoing process of transformation that constitutes the other side of smart city dynamics. With the increasing hybridization of atoms and bits, of the physical and electronic worlds, fostered by technological developments such as augmented reality and geolocalization, smart cities are inseparable from a "spatial turn" of the digital. Urban geographer Edward Soja coined this phrase to refer to the recent evolution of the social sciences, a turn that will eventually impact the urban morphology, even if its effects remain, as for now, limited.[05]

Finally, one additional characteristic of the smart city may be worth noting, or rather, reconsidering: the expression "smart city" should be taken much more literally than is usually the case. Rather than conceiving of a city whose circuits of information and communications are simply sprawled out and whose intelligence continues to reside exclusively within the men and women who communicate through them, why not imagine the progressive development of nonhuman forms of reasoning and even of consciousness? At the final stage of such development—the seeds of which have already been sown in current research on algorithms, artificial intelligence, robotization, and cyborg-type assemblies between biological organisms and machines—the entire city could be considered intelligent in a new way, founded on and composed of the interaction of the perceptions and deliberations of multiple entities: human, nonhuman, and often a mixture of the two.

Now, both as an ideal and as a process, the smart city faces a number of challenges that are simultaneously technological, social, and cultural. It is not that any one of them represents an insurmountable obstacle or an asymptotic limit that cannot be crossed; rather, each might be considered an incitement to enrich current approaches. In particular, we need to leave in the past what is still the overly simplified quality of representations of the smart city proposed by its various stakeholders. While I am certainly not "against the smart city"

like the American urbanist Adam Greenfield, I cannot satisfy myself with one or two simple models of what it should be.[06] The head-on conflict between neocybernetic-inspired management and participatory logic should not lead to limit the range of possibilities we might envision. Instead, by extending this range one may reveal the existence of alternatives, taking local situations into account, such as the targets that leaders and the general public themselves set.

The Shortcomings of All-Digital Solutions

As is the case with all positive interpretations, that of the smart city leaves aside a whole set of troubling realities, starting with the emerging tensions between the intensive use of ICT and the need for sustainable development. Is digital technology really as "green" as its stalwart supporters claim? It is worth reminding ourselves that the smart city is not merely an ethereal presence but exists materially. The smart city's servers, cables, and aerials—not to mention its millions of chips and sensors—exert a heavy impact on the environment.[07] The annual volume of electronic waste produced across the planet was estimated at 41.5 million tons in 2011, and may well reach 93.5 million in 2016.[08] Discarded cables, circuit boards, and screens bring up sensitive issues regarding recycling, which is often subcontracted to developing countries with barely a thought for the health of the people taking it on. ICT already consumes almost 10 percent of the global electricity supply: that is, 50 percent more energy than the entire air transport industry.[09] Servers give off heat, raising issues of climate change and global warming.

These statistics do not call the ideal of the smart city into question, but they do point toward a need for greater discernment in harnessing the technologies on which it depends. Digital technology has both a financial and an environmental cost. Consequently, its use needs to be modulated in relation to the characteristics of the urban areas that it is set to serve. To put it in the simplest terms, the greater the density of capital and population (as typically exists in the heart of major cities) the greater the investment in information and communications technology that can be justified, even if this risks exacerbating the imbalance between centers and suburbs—a subject to which I will return. A specific economy for the smart city is crucially needed.

This economy needs to be coupled with moral standards that are both collective and individual. Reviving a sort of behavioral restraint, they should go against the inducements to consume ever-greater quantities of digital resources and equipment, which that sector's main

stakeholders constantly direct at the public. It is worth remembering that even carrying out a Google search on a mobile phone at a street corner consumes energy. Aside from broader questions such as those concerning the relationship between humans and machines that are invested with some sort of intelligence, the morality of the smart city should probably begin with more judicious use of smartphones.

In addition to environmental challenges, there are other pitfalls that threaten the viability of the smart city. Despite the growing presence of surveillance cameras scrutinizing the whereabouts and activities of its residents and visitors, the smart city is particularly vulnerable to vandalism and terrorism, which can quite easily disrupt the workings of its essential infrastructure. Added to threats in physical space is the prospect of cyber-attack. Cities made of atoms and data bits sometimes seem more fragile than their predecessors built of brick, stone, and concrete.

But, at the same time, it is worth remembering that every new type of technology has its own specific forms of vulnerability. Electricity remains the city's principle source of weakness: it is no accident that so many futuristic novels depict its disappearance as a precursor to the apocalypse or to a return to barbarity. Living in a city means accepting its weaknesses, while constantly thinking of ways to mitigate its most disastrous effects. For example, where digital technology is concerned, it is advisable to establish ways of getting around the automated management of vital infrastructure in case of a major malfunction, whether accidental or criminal in origin. Think, for example, of the electric cars whose windows cannot be opened if their electrical system fails, or elevators that get stuck and hold their users prisoner during a power outage. With the onslaught of ICT, this type of problem needs to be limited as much as possible. This is the price that has to be paid for city intelligence.

Above: Ghanaians working in Agbogbloshie, Ghana, 2011.

Antoine Picon

The Necessary Diversification of Scenarios

Other challenges to the smart city stem from the emphasis that most stakeholders place on the knowledge economy, to the detriment of more traditional manufacturing activities. Smart cities are often interpreted as places primarily geared toward scientific and business elites. This explains the emblematic role played by urban areas such as Silicon Valley and the region around Boston, where universities and high-tech businesses requiring very highly educated individuals predominate. It sometimes seems as though industrial towns are not called to become intelligent, especially when situated in developing countries where the rights of individuals are still not widely respected. It bears asking whether the techniques of urban management that form the basis of the smart city can be productively applied to situations of postindustrial decline. It is noteworthy that Detroit rarely features among the examples cited in relation to the hypothesis of the smart city.

I referred above to the need to introduce sorts of gradients, for example, between the center and the suburbs, when equipping cities with ICT. Does this mean that the outskirts are called to become less intelligent than city centers? And what of the countryside? Is the establishment of the smart city leading to a reinvention of the split between town and country, which had been gradually questioned under the influence of factors such as modern media (chiefly radio and television)?

On a more general level, questions might be asked about the political and social ideals to which most advocates of the smart city subscribe, whether implicitly or explicitly. In *Splintering Urbanism*, Stephen Graham and Simon Marvin hold digital technology responsible for an increasing series of ruptures: between hyperconnected neighborhoods, in touch with the global economy and linked together by high-speed communications tunnels, and neglected urban areas; or between stakeholders in the global economy and residents relegated to menial tasks.[10] Graham and Marvin claim that the age of urban networks that served to integrate society has given way to an era in which technology shows itself to be incapable of curbing the most glaring differences. Worse, it has even exacerbated them.

Above: B+H Architects, SmartCity Kochi, Kerala, India, 2015.

In fact, these authors fail to recall that there was nothing egalitarian about the political project that underpinned the emergence of the networked city of the industrial era. Far from seeking to eradicate social differences, Paris in the age of Napoleon III and Baron Haussmann simply set out to make these differences tolerable by inserting middle-class districts and working-class suburbs within a single mesh that combined water and sanitation systems, a road network, pleasure gardens, and parks such as the Buttes-Chaumont.[11] The Internet has merely appropriated this ideal of cohabitation without reducing its inherent inequality. By the same token, narratives on the smart city are neither more nor less generous than the ones that presided over the establishment of the major urban networks of the industrial era.

Again, the problem has more to do with the failure to take the diversity of city functions into account and with the impossibility of reducing this to a simple question of intelligence. Writers from Richard Florida to Edward Glaeser have arguably placed too much emphasis on the brain of the smart city—its "creative class"—and not enough on the role of its muscles—traditional services and industry.[12] Above all, there cannot be only one or two scenarios that lead to this city. Diversification is clearly necessary at this point, even if only because situations differ greatly from one country to another.

India's decision to develop intelligent cities can only be applauded. It is still reasonable, however, to question the country's strategy of imitating Western, Middle Eastern, Chinese, and Korean models without seeking to capitalize on the inventiveness of its own urban population, accustomed to using smartphones even in the slums of megalopolises such as New Delhi and Mumbai.[13] As expressions of "impatient capital," to borrow the term coined by Rahul Mehrotra, which is causing a proliferation of glass office buildings and conference centers all over the planet, the Indian projects would certainly benefit from being linked up to the rich range of digital practices that are already present in the country's cities.[14]

The paths leading to the smart city in Europe—where cities possess a rich heritage of traditional infrastructure, from sanitation to public transport—cannot be the same

Above: Las Vegas Strip, Las Vegas, Nevada, 2010.

Antoine Picon

as in the metropolises of developing countries, where this infrastructure is often lacking. In the latter, the inadequacy of facilities is often offset by residents' resourcefulness: their ability to make do and mend through inventively blending technologies and devices, wheelbarrows and multimedia sound systems, broken robots and interactive screens.[15] Without questioning the need for large cities in developing countries to be gradually provided with facilities, it is possible to imagine other ways to approach the smart city than through a proliferation of sensors intended to better control the functioning of heavy infrastructure. Once more, the scenarios need to be diversified, and well beyond what companies such as IBM and Cisco Systems are proposing, just as the networked city of the industrial era took very different forms in Europe, the United States, and Japan in the nineteenth and twentieth centuries.

Public/Private

"All that happens must be known," "Secrets are lies," "Privacy is theft": in *The Circle*, the American novelist Dave Eggers imagines a business based on Google and Facebook where these sorts of slogans make the rounds.[16] There could be no better way of summarizing the main ambiguities of the political and social discourse put forward by the advocates of a digital brave new world in which nothing would escape the notice of either the decision makers or the public: a modern version of Bentham's Panopticon and Foucault's panopticism, in which the major part of the surveillance was carried out by inmates themselves.[17] The smart city is not immune to this ambiguity, given that it seems to rely partially on individuals' acceptance of repeated intrusions into their private lives. Even if these intrusions are accepted by large swaths of "digital natives" (members of the generations that have grown up with the Internet), not all aspects of this evolution are beneficial.[18]

The increasing privatization of entire areas of cities, which generally goes hand in hand with a reinforcement of surveillance, is a move in the same direction, blurring and even questioning the dividing line between public and private. Does this mean that we should accept everything for the sake of security, control, and the need to share information? Here again, the solution may well lie in the emergence of new codes of ethics, undoubtedly quite different to the ones that governed the relationship between public and private in the past, but sufficiently prescriptive to preserve the essential aspect of the right to a private life and personal secrets (as long as they are neither "lies" nor "theft").

From Event to History

Despite the challenges described here, the rise of the smart city constitutes a genuine revolution, comparable in significance to the birth of the major industrial cities in the nineteenth century and the emergence of the networked city as both an urban ideal and a physical process of city transformation. While this revolution's impact on urban form is still shrouded in uncertainty, its influence on the temporal structures of urban experience can already be observed. We live in cities that move to the rhythm of increasingly numerous events that can be followed in real time.

But with this proliferation of happenings comes a glaring absence of historical perspective, as if the possibility of history had been suspended indefinitely in favor of an eternal present, or of a future so close to what we already know that it seems to be a mere intensification of current conditions. The environmental apocalypse still remains the only notable prospect of change.

Of course, digital technology plays a key role in generating this impression. Indeed, the Internet is the most obvious embodiment of this world of events without clear historical pointers, into which we often find ourselves thrust. In this respect it remains faithful to the original metaphor of cyberspace, like the sort of giant Las Vegas Strip proposed by authors such as William Gibson in *Neuromancer*.[19] In Las Vegas, there is always something going on. Spectacular and saturated with clashing signs, atmospheres, and colors, the giant hotels—from Caesars Palace to the Venetian, from the New York–New York to the Paris—appear as events in themselves. But nothing ever seems to change, and the feverish activity of tourists and personnel alike generates nothing other than its own repetition. Facebook and Twitter give a fairly similar impression of hyperactivity and repetition. This, in turn, is communicated to cities, which we willingly see as set in a state of eternal youth, with electronic exchanges playing the role of regenerating fluid. The era when the city appeared as a palimpsest of interventions recalling the role of history seems to be over. And yet the world still marches on. Social and political change looms on the horizon of an enlightened dream, sometimes reminiscent of the "spectacle" that Situationist leader Guy Debord so tirelessly denounced.[20] How can we escape from this both enchanted and vicious circle? How can smart cities be made to age? This last challenge is closely linked to the need for a diversification of the models that guide these cities' development. It is a challenge that urgently needs to be met. That is the price to be paid for the future: a different future, rich in promise.

01. "$39.5 Billion Will Be Spent on Smart City Technologies in 2016," ABI Research, September 8, 2011, https://www.abiresearch.com/press/395-billion-will-be-spent-on-smart-city-technologi.

02. These characteristics are outlined in Antoine Picon, *Smart Cities: A Spatialised Intelligence* (Chichester: Wiley, forthcoming).

03. On the networked city as a technological as well as political and social ideal and process, see Gabriel Dupuy and Joel A. Tarr, eds., *Technology and the Rise of the Networked City in Europe and America* (Philadelphia: Temple University Press, 1988); Olivier Coutard, Richard Hanley, and Rae Zimmerman, eds., *Sustaining Urban Networks: The Social Diffusion of Large Technical Systems* (London: Routledge, 2004); and Antoine Picon, *La ville des réseaux: Un imaginaire politique* (Paris: Editions Manucius, 2014).

04. A similar distinction between top-down and bottom-up interpretations can be found in Anthony Townsend, *Smart Cities: Big Data, Civic Hackers, and the Quest for a New Utopia* (New York: W.W. Norton & Company, 2013).

05. Edward W. Soja, *Postmodern Geographies: The Reassertion of Space in Critical Social Theory* (London: Verso, 1989).

06. Adam Greenfield, *Against the Smart City* (New York: Do projects, 2013).

07. See Andrew Blum, *Tubes: A Journey to the Center of the Internet* (New York: HarperCollins, 2012).

08. "E-Waste to Exceed 93.5 Million Tons Annually," *Environmental Leader*, February 24, 2014, http://www.environmentalleader.com/2014/02/24/e-waste-to-exceed-93-5-million-tons-annually/.

09. Mark P. Mills, "The Cloud Begins with Coal: Big Data, Big Networks, Big Infrastructure, and Big Power; An Overview of the Electricity Used by the Global Digital Ecosystem" (research report for the National Mining Association and the American Coalition for Clean Coal Electricity, August 2013), http://www.tech-pundit.com/wp-content/uploads/2013/07/Cloud_Begins_With_Coal.pdf?c761ac.

10. Stephen Graham and Simon Marvin, *Splintering Urbanism: Networked Infrastructures, Technological Mobilities and the Urban Condition* (London and New York: Routledge, 2001).

11. Picon, *La ville des réseaux*.

12. Richard Florida, *The Rise of the Creative Class: And How It's Transforming Work, Leisure, Community, and Everyday Life* (New York: Basic Books, 2002); Edward Glaeser, *Triumph of the City: How Our Greatest Invention Makes Us Richer, Smarter, Greener, Healthier, and Happier* (New York: Penguin Press, 2011).

13. Uma Vishnu, "34% in Slums Have No Toilet, but 63% Own Mobile Phone in India," *Indian Express*, March 22, 2013, http://archive.indianexpress.com/news/34-in-slums-have-no-toilet-but-63-own-mobile-phone/1091573.

14. Rahul Mehrotra, *Architecture in India since 1990* (Mumbai: Pictor Publishing, 2011).

15. See Nicolas Nova, *Futurs?: La panne des imaginaires technologiques* (Montélimar: Moutons Electriques, 2014), 72; and Adam Greenfield, "The Smartest Cities Rely on Citizen Cunning and Unglamorous Technology," *The Guardian*, December 22, 2014, http://www.theguardian.com/cities/2014/dec/22/the-smartest-cities-rely-on-citizen-cunning-and-unglamorous-technology.

16. Dave Eggers, *The Circle* (San Francisco: McSweeney's Books, 2013).

17. See Michel Foucault, *Discipline and Punish: The Birth of the Prison (Surveiller et punir: Naissance de la prison* [1975]), trans. Alan Sheridan (New York: Vintage Books, 1995).

18. John Palfrey and Urs Gasser, *Born Digital: Understanding the First Generation of Digital Natives* (New York: Basic Books, 2008).

19. William Gibson, *Neuromancer* (New York: Ace Books, 1984).

20. Guy Debord, *The Society of the Spectacle (La Société du spectacle* [1967]), trans. Donald Nicholson-Smith (New York: Zone Books, 1994).

Image Credits

079: Marlenenapoli/ Wikimedia Commons.

080: Courtesy of B+H Architects.

081: Lasvegaslover / Wikimedia Commons.

Antoine Picon

Profit Uber Alles
Networked Mobility as the Successful Socialization of Risk

Adam
Greenfield

We can think of the propositions the so-called smart city is built on as belonging to three orders of visibility. The first is populated by exotica like adaptive sunshades, fully automated supply and removal chains, and personal rapid transit ("podcar") systems. These systems feature prominently in the smart city's advertising, promotional renderings, and sales presentations. They may or may not ever come into being—complex and expensive, they very often wind up value-engineered out of the final execution, or at least notionally deferred to some later phase of development—but by announcing that the urban plan in question is decidedly oriented toward futurity, they serve a valuable marketing and public relations function. Whether or not they ever amount to anything other than what the technology industry calls "vaporware," they are certainly highly visible and can therefore readily be held up for consideration.

A second order consists of the behind-the-scenes working of algorithmic systems, the black box churn of "big data" analytics that, at least in principle, affords metropolitan administrators with the predictive policing, anticipatory traffic control and other services on which the smart city value proposition is premised. These systems are hard to see because their operations are inherently opaque. While the events concerned are inarguably physical and material, they are far removed from the phenomenological scale of human reckoning. They unfold in the transduction of electrical potential across the circuitry of databases and servers, racked in farms that may be hundreds or even thousands of miles from the city whose activities they regulate. Such systems are, therefore, generally discernible only in their outputs: in the differential posture or disposition of resources, or the perturbations that result when these patterns are folded back against the plane of experience. At best, the dynamics involved may show up in data visualizations bundled into a "city dashboard"—access to which itself may or may not be offered to the populace at large—but they otherwise tend to abscond from immediate awareness.

The third order, however, may be the hardest of all to consider analytically, and this is because it is predominantly comprised of artifacts and services that are already well-assimilated elements of everyday urban life. Being so well woven into the fabric of urban experience, the things that belong to this category, like other elements of the quotidian, fade beneath the threshold of ordinary perception; we only rarely disinter them and subject them to critical evaluation. In this category we can certainly place the smartphone itself: a communication device, intimate sensor platform, and aperture onto the global network of barely half a decade's vintage, that has nonetheless utterly reshaped the tenor and character of metropolitan experience for those who wield one. Here as well we can situate big-city bike-sharing schemes—each of which is, despite a certain optical dowdiness, a triumphant assemblage of RFID, GPS, wireless connectivity, and other networked information-processing technologies. And here we find the network-mediated mobility-on-demand services that have already done so much to transform what it feels like to move through urban space, at least for a privileged few.

Inordinately prominent among this set of mobility brokers, of course, is the San Francisco–based Uber. So hegemonic is the company that its name has already entered the language as a shorthand for startups and apps dedicated to the smartphone-mediated, on-demand provision of services: we hear the Instacart offering referred to as "an Uber for groceries," EvoLux as "an Uber for helicopters," Tinder as "an Uber for dating," and so on. If we are to understand personal mobility in the networked city—how it works, who has access to it, which standing patterns it reinforces and which it actually does disrupt—it might be worth hauling Uber up into the light and considering its culture and operations with particular care.

It may seem perverse to describe something as "difficult to see" when it is so insistently, inescapably visible. To be sure, though, Uber's sudden prominence is not merely due to the esteem in which its users hold it; the company has a propensity for becoming embroiled in controversy unrivaled by its peers, or indeed by just about any commercial enterprise, regardless of scale or sector.[01] That any given mobility technology should become a flashpoint for so many controversies so widely dispersed is remarkable; that all of them should involve a sole mobility provider may well be unprecedented. The truth is that we certainly do see Uber … but not for what it is. Its very prominence helps to mask what's so salient about it.

What is Uber? Founded in 2009 by Travis Kalanick—a UCLA dropout whose only previous business experience involved the peer-to-peer file-exchange applications Scour Exchange and Red Swoosh—Uber is a company valued as of the end of 2014 at some $40 billion, currently operating in more than two hundred cities worldwide.[02] Like others of its ilk, it allows customers to arrange point-to-point journeys as and when desired via an application previously loaded on their Apple or Android smartphones; all billing is handled through the application itself, meaning that the rider needn't worry about the psychological discomfort of negotiating fares at origin or tips at their destination. Its various offerings, which range from the "low-cost" uberX to the superpremium UberLUX, are positioned as being more convenient, and certainly more comfortable, than existing municipal taxi and livery ("black") car services. Regardless of service level, the vehicles involved are owned and operated by drivers the company has gone to great lengths to characterize not as employees (with all that would imply for liability insurance, wages, and the provision of employee benefits) but as independent contractors.

Uber is classified under California law as a "network transportation company," and while the dry legal taxonomy is technically accurate, it masks what is truly radical about the enterprise. Seen clearly, Uber is little more than a brand coupled to a spatialized resource-allocation algorithm, with a rudimentary reputation mechanic running on top. The company owns no fleet, employs relatively few staff directly, and—as we shall see—may not even maintain public offices in the commonly understood sense of that term.

What distinguishes it from would-be competitors like Hailo and Lyft isn't so much any particular aspect of its organization or technical functionality but rather its stance. Uber comes with an overt ideology.[03] Despite a tagline positioning itself as "Everyone's Private Driver," Uber has never for a moment pretended to universality. Just the opposite: every aspect of the marketing and user experience announces that this a service consciously designed for the needs, tastes, preferences, and status anxieties of a very specific market segment—the aspirant global elite.

Uber makes no apologies about its policy of adaptive surge pricing, in which fare multipliers of up to 8x are applied during periods of particularly heavy demand.[04] But at an average fare of around $20, a single Uber ride can still be justified by most members of its target audience as an "affordable luxury"—all the more so when enjoyed as an occasional rather than a daily habit. Availing oneself of this luxury, and being seen to do so, is self-evidently appealing to a wide swath of people living in densely built-up places around the world, necessarily including among their number a great many who would likely be appalled by the company's politics, were they ever unambiguously forced to consider them.

With Uber, Kalanick has made it clear that a service founded on a relatively high technological base of ubiquitous smartphones, sophisticated digital cartography, and civilian GPS can be wildly successful when it is wrapped in the language not of technology itself but of comfort and convenience. So enticing, indeed, is this combination that hundreds of thousands of users are willing to swallow not merely the technologically complex but the politically unsavory when sugarcoated in this way. While this will likely strike most observers as rather obvious, it is an insight that has thus far eluded other actors with a rhetorical or material stake in the development of a heavily technologized urbanity.

This state of affairs, however, is unlikely to last forever. Other interested parties will surely note Uber's success, draw their own conclusions from it, and attempt to apply whatever lessons they derive to the marketing of their own products and services. If Uber is a confession that the "smart city" is a place we already live in, then, it is also a cautionary case study in the kinds of values we can expect such a city to uphold in its everyday operations—some merely strongly implicit, others right out there in the open. Just what are they?

Those who can afford to pay more deserve to be treated better.

Uber's proposition to its users collapses any distinction between *having* and *deserving*; quite simply, its message is that if you can afford to be treated better than others, you're entitled to be treated better than others.

This is certainly one of the logics of resource allocation available in the late-capitalist marketplace. As Harvard's Michael Sandel observes in his 2012 *What Money Can't Buy*, this particular logic is increasingly filtering into questions traditionally decided by different principles, such as the (at least superficially egalitarian) rule of first come, first served.[05] And it is not, after all, very different from the extant market segmentation dividing public transit from taxi or livery service: money to spend has always bought the city dweller in motion a certain degree of privacy and flexibility in routing and schedule. What specifically distinguishes Uber from previous quasiprivate mobility offerings, though, and takes it into a kind of libertarian hyperdrive, is its refusal to submit to regulation, carry appropriate insurance, provide for the workers on whom it depends, or in any way allow the broader public to share in a set of benefits distributed all but exclusively between the rider and the company. (Driver comments make it clear that it is possible to make decent money as an Uber driver, but only with the most exceptional hustle; the vigorish assessed is significant, and monthly payments on the luxury vehicles the company requires its drivers to own saddle them with an onerous, persistent burden.)

Uber's "disruptive" business model forthrightly treats the costs of on-demand, point-to-point mobility as externalities to be borne by anonymous, deprecated others, and this is a strong part of what makes it so corrosive of the public trust. This becomes most acutely evident when Uber drivers are involved in fatal accidents during periods when they do not happen to be carrying passengers, as was the case when driver Syed Muzaffar struck and killed six-year-old Sofia Liu in San Francisco, on the last day of 2013.[06]

That "better" amounts to a bland generic luxury.

Uber's conception of user comfort pivots largely on predictability and familiarity. Rather than asking riders to contend with the particularities and idiosyncrasies of local mobility culture, or any of the various factors that distinguish a New York City taxi cab from one in London or Delhi or Beijing, the Uber fleet offers its users a mobile extension of international hospitality nonplace: a single distributed site where globalized norms of blandly aspirational luxury are reinforced.

The suggestions Uber drivers leave for one another on online discussion sites are revealing in this regard. Those who wish to receive high ratings from their passengers are advised to ensure that their vehicles are well-equipped with amenities (mints, bottled water, WiFi connectivity) and remain silent unless spoken to. The all-but-explicit aim is to render the back of an Uber S-Class or 7 Series experientially continuous with the airport lounges, high-end hotels, and showplace restaurants of the business-centric generic city hypostatized by Rem Koolhaas in his 1994 article of the same name.[07]

Interpersonal exchanges are more appropriately mediated by algorithms than by one's own competence.

This conception of good experience is not the only thing suggesting that Uber, its ridership, or both are somewhat afraid of actual, unfiltered urbanity. Among the most vexing challenges residents and other users of any large urban place ever confront is that of *trust*: absent familiarity, or the prospect of developing it over a pattern of repeated interactions, how are people placed (however temporarily) in a position of vulnerability expected to determine who is reliable?

Like other contemporary services, Uber outsources judgments of this type to a trust mechanic: at the conclusion of every trip, passengers are asked to explicitly rate their driver. These ratings are averaged into a score that is made visible to users in the application interface: "John (4.9 stars) will pick you up in 2 minutes." The implicit belief is that reputation can be quantified and distilled to a single salient metric, and that this metric can be acted upon objectively.

Drivers are, essentially, graded on a curve: their rolling tally, aggregated over the previous five hundred passenger engagements, must remain above average not in absolute terms, but against the competitive set. Drivers whose scores drop beneath this threshold may not receive ride requests, and it therefore functions as an effective disciplinary mechanism. Furthermore, judging from conversations among drivers, the criteria on which this all-important performance metric is assessed are

087

subjective and highly variable, meaning that the driver has no choice but to model what they believe riders are looking for in the proverbial "good driver," internalize that model, and adjust their behavior accordingly.

What riders are not told by Uber—though, in this age of ubiquitous peer-to-peer media, it is becoming evident to many that this has in fact been the case for some time—is that they, too, are rated by drivers, on a similar five-point scale. This rating, too, is not without consequence. Drivers have a certain degree of discretion in choosing to accept or deny ride requests, and to judge from publicly accessible online conversations, many simply refuse to pick up riders with scores below a certain threshold, typically in the high 3s.

This is strongly reminiscent of the process that I have elsewhere called "differential permissioning," in which physical access to everyday spaces and functions becomes evermore widely apportioned on the basis of such computational scores, by direct analogy with the access control paradigm prevalent in the information security community.[08] Such determinations are opaque to those affected, while those denied access are offered few or no effective means of recourse. For prospective Uber patrons, differential permissioning means that they can be blackballed and never know why.

Uber shares this feature in common with algorithmic reputation-scoring services like Klout. But all such measures stumble in their bizarre insistence that trust can be distilled to a unitary value. This belies the commonsense understanding that reputation is a contingent and relational thing—that actions a given audience may regard as markers of reliability are unlikely to read that way to all potential audiences. More broadly, it also means that Uber constructs the development of trust between driver and passenger as a circumstance in which algorithmic determinations should supplant rather than rely upon (let alone strengthen) our existing competences for situational awareness, negotiation, and the detection of verbal and nonverbal social cues.

Interestingly, despite its deployment of mechanisms intended to assess driver and passenger reliability, the company goes to unusual lengths to prevent *itself* from being brought to accountability. Following a December 2014 rape in Delhi, police investigators were stunned to realize that while Uber had been operating in India for some time, neither the .in website nor any other document they had access to listed a local office. They were forced to register for the app themselves (as well as download a third-party payment application) simply so they could hire an Uber car and have the driver bring them to the place where he believed his employers worked. Here

we see William Gibson's science-fictional characterization of twenty-first century enterprise ("small, fast, ruthless. An atavism … all Edge") brought to pungent life.[09]

Private enterprise should be valorized over public service provision on principle, even when public alternatives would afford comparable levels of service.
Our dissection of Uber makes it clear that, in schematic, the company offers nothing that a transit authority like Transport for London (TfL) could not in principle furnish its riders. Consider that TfL already has everything it would need to offer not merely a comparable, but a better and more equitable, service: direct operational control over London's fleet of black cabs, a legendarily skilled and knowledgeable driver pool, the regulatory ability to determine fares, and a set of existing application programming interfaces giving it the necessary access to data. Indeed, coupling an on-demand service directly to its standing public transit capacity (at route termini, for example, or in neighborhoods of poor network coverage) would extend its reach considerably and multiply the value of its existing assets. Even after accounting for operating costs Uber is unwilling to bear, the return to the public coffers could be substantial.

Like other transit authorities of its scale, TfL possesses the sophistication needed to perform such an analysis. But the neoliberal values on which Uber thrives, and the concomitant assumption that public transport is best provisioned on a privatized, for-profit basis, have become so deeply embedded into the discourse of urban governance just about everywhere that no such initiative is ever proposed or considered. The implication is that the smart city is a place where callow, "disruptive" services with poor long-term prospects for collective benefit are allowed to displace the public accommodations previous generations of city dwellers would have demanded as a matter of course and of right.

Conclusion
Quite simply, the city is smaller for people who have access to Uber. The advent of near-effortless, on-demand, point-to-point personal mobility has given them a tesseract with which the occasionally unwieldy envelope of urban space-time can be folded down to something more readily manageable. It's trivially easy to understand the appeal of this—especially when the night is dark, the bus shelter is cold, the neighborhood is remote, and one is alone.

But as should be clear by now, this power to fold space and time comes at a terrible cost. The four values enumerated above make Uber a prime generator of the patterns of spatialized injustice Stephen Graham has called "software-sorted geographies," although it does so in a way unencompassed by Graham's original account.[10] Its ordinary operation injects the urban terrain with a mobile and distributed layer of invidious privilege, a hypersite where practices and values deeply inimical to any meaningful conception of the common wealth are continuously reproduced.

More insidiously yet, these become laminated into journey planning and other services when they position Uber alongside other options available to the commuter, as simply another tab or item in a pull-down menu. Ethical questions are legislated at the level of interface design, at the hands of engineers and designers so immersed in the privileges of youth and relative wealth, and so inculcated with the values prevalent in their own industry, that they may well not perceive anything about Uber to be objectionable in the slightest. (Notable in this regard are Google Maps and Citymapper, both of which now integrate Uber as a modal option alongside public transit and taxis, and Apple's App Store, which lists the Uber app as an "Essential.") Consciously or not, though, every such integration acts to normalize the Randian solipsism, the frat boy misogyny, and the sneering disdain for the very notion of a public good that saturate Uber's presentation of its identity.

Where innovations in personal mobility could just as easily be designed to extend the right to the city, and to conceive of on-demand access to all points in the urbanized field as a public utility, Uber acts to reinscribe and to actually strengthen existing inequities of access. It is an engine consciously, delicately, and expertly tuned to socialize risk and privatize gain. In furtherance of the convenience of a few, it sheds risk on its drivers, its passengers, and the communities within which it operates.

And this is only to consider what is operating in the proposition offered by a single provider of networked mobility services. If there is a distinct set of values bound up in Uber, it is unmistakably enmeshed within the broader ideological commitments all but universally upheld in the conception of the smart city, wherever on Earth the deployment of this particular ensemble of technologies has been proposed. Chief among these are the reduction or elimination of taxes, tariffs, and duties; the concomitant recourse to corporate sponsorship (or outright privatization) of essential municipal services; the deregulation of activity between private actors; and the prioritization of other policies primarily oriented to the needs of classes and sectors within society that benefit from frictionless global trade. A judicious onlooker might of course wonder what anything on this laundry list has to do with the attributes or capabilities of networked digital systems, but that is precisely the point. As articulated on terrain from Dholera to Rio de Janeiro to New York, we can understand the ostensibly utopian smart city as nothing more than the information-technological aspect of a globally triumphant but still-ravenous neoliberalism—a mask this ideology wears when it wishes to dissemble its true nature and appeal to audiences beyond its existing core of convinced adherents.[11]

Dissecting Uber may help clarify the implications of this turn for those whose life chances are and will continue to be affected by it, but it is the merest start. There remain arrayed before the public for its consideration a very great number of other propositions that belong to the latter two of the smart city's three orders of visibility, from security systems equipped with facial-recognition capability to networked thermostats to wearable devices aimed at nothing less than quantification of the self. It is these systems in which even the clearest ideological commitments are most likely to be screened or obscured, whether by the seemingly ordinary nature of the product or service or by the very complexity of the distributed technical architecture that underwrites it. Given what is at stake, it's therefore essential that we subject all such propositions to the most sustained, detailed, and knowledgeable scrutiny before embracing them.

01. Just some of the most widely reported incidents Uber has been involved in during the past year:
    June 2014—European taxi drivers call a one-day strike over the non-regulation of Uber's drivers: Mark Tran, "Taxi Drivers in European Capitals Strike Over Uber—As It Happened," *The Guardian*, June 11, 2014, http://www.theguardian.com/politics/2014/jun/11/taxi-drivers-strike-uber-london-live-updates.
    Summer 2014—insurance providers broadly began to refuse coverage for (and, in some case, claims against) Uber drivers: Carolyn Said, "Leaked Transcript Shows Geico's Stance against Uber, Lyft," *Sfgate*, November 23, 2014, http://www.sfgate.com/business/article/Leaked-transcript-shows-Geico-s-stance-against-5910113.php; and Ellen Huet, "Rideshare Drivers Still Cornered into Insurance Secrecy," *Forbes*, December 18, 2014, http://www.forbes.com/sites/ellenhuet/2014/12/18/uber-lyft-driver-insurance/.
    August 2014—A second wave of complaints emerged alleging that Uber had sabotaged mobility-on-demand competitors Lyft and Gett in certain strategic markets: Erica Fink, "Uber's Dirty Tricks Quantified: Rival Counts 5,560 Canceled Rides," *CNNMoney*, August 12, 2014, http://money.cnn.com/2014/08/11/technology/uber-fake-ride-requests-lyft/index.html.
    September 2014—It is reported that Uber had used ostensibly secure and private user data to

populate a real-time visualization of ridership projected onto the wall at a party: Sam Biddle, "Uber Used Private Location Data for Party Amusement," *Valleywag*, September 30, 2014, http://valleywag.gawker.com/uber-used-private-location-data-for-party-amusement-1640820384.

A persistent drumbeat of allegations of rape and assault lodged against Uber drivers worldwide culminated in decisions by German national (September 2014) and Delhi regional authorities (December 2014) to ban the service entirely. See Kevin Rawlinson, "Uber Service 'Banned' in Germany by Frankfurt Court," *BBC News*, September 2, 2014, http://www.bbc.com/news/technology-29027803; and Aman Sharma, "Delhi Government Bans Uber, Says It Is Misleading Customers," *Times of India*, December 8, 2014, http://articles.economictimes.indiatimes.com/2014-12-08/news/56839680_1_taxi-services-radio-taxi-scheme-customers.

A flurry of dismay predictably greeted the company's active

(i.e., deliberate, conscious, and human, not algorithmic) decision to institute surge pricing during the December 2014 Sydney hostage incident. See Claire Reilly, "Uber Reaches 4x Surge Pricing as Sydney Faces Hostage Lockdown," *CNet*, December 15, 2014, http://www.cnet.com/uk/news/uber-reaches-4x-surge-pricing-as-sydney-faces-hostage-lockdown.

02. Tim Bradshaw, "Uber Valued at $40bn in Latest Funding Round," *Financial Times*, December 4, 2014, http://www.ft.com/cms/s/0/66a76576-7bdc-11e4-a7b8-00144feabdc0.html.

03. Paul Carr, "Travis Shrugged: The Creepy, Dangerous Ideology Behind Silicon Valley's Cult of Disruption," *Pando Daily*, October 24, 2012, http://pando.com/2012/10/24/travis-shrugged.

04. Jessi Hempel, "Why the Surge-Pricing Fiasco Is Great for Uber," *Fortune*, December 30, 2013, http://fortune.com/2013/12/30/why-the-surge-pricing-fiasco-is-great-for-uber/.

05. Michael J. Sandel, *What Money Can't Buy: The Moral Limits of Markets* (London; New York: Allen Lane, 2012).

06. Muzaffar's Uber app was open and running at the time he hit Liu and her family, indicating that he was cruising for fares, but the company refuses to accept any liability for the accident. See Josh Constine, "Uber's Denial of Liability in Girl's Death Raises Accident Accountability Questions," *TechCrunch*, January 2, 2014, http://techcrunch.com/2014/01/02/should-car-services-provide-insurance-whenever-their-driver-app-is-open.

07. Rem Koolhaas, "The Generic City," in *S,M,L,XL* (New York: Monacelli Press, 1994), 1248–64.

08. Adam Greenfield, *Everyware: The Dawning Age of Ubiquitous Computing* (Berkeley, CA: New Riders Press, 2006).

09. William Gibson, "New Rose Hotel," in *Burning Chrome* (New York: Ace Books, 1986).

10. Stephen Graham, "Software-Sorted Geographies," *Progress in Human Geography* 29, no. 5 (October 2005): 562–80.

11. Adam Greenfield, *Against the Smart City* (New York: Do projects, 2013).

Information Infrastructure in Urban Planning

Yannis Orfanos,
Eleonora Marinou,
Vicky Sagia
& Spiro Pollalis

Information as infrastructure constitutes the integrated framework, which allows for the collection, flow, and processing of information. It consists of potentially infinite subsystems, public or private, created and used by individuals and organizations. Although intangible, information strongly impacts physical space, determining how cities are planned and managed, and how they operate. It has the potential to affect the performance of all other infrastructure systems and their ability to respond to continually evolving demands and challenges.

Information as Infrastructure

The concentration of people and economic processes that defines the urban condition requires continuous and reliable flows of resources. Infrastructure is the backbone of these flows. Urban planning and infrastructure development are therefore intertwined.[01]
The planning guidelines for sustainable cities, developed by the Zofnass Program at Harvard Graduate School of Design, attempt to address the integration of infrastructure systems in contemporary city planning for new or expanding, as well as existing, urban developments. The main objective is to provide an analytical framework for achieving urban sustainability through integrated planning by focusing on the services and the performances of a number of infrastructure systems, including energy, water, transportation, solid waste, landscape, information, and food. An "infrastructure system" consists not only of physical structures but also of operation procedures, administration, bylaws, natural processes, and, equally important, the end user. Within this context, information as infrastructure was examined both in itself and as a supportive subsystem of all other infrastructure systems, interconnecting and assisting their high performance. Information as infrastructure per se supports the flow and processing of information. It facilitates communication between communities and enables their interaction and collaboration. In doing so, it transforms the concepts of physical distance and time. Information can extend everywhere and, at any time, affect economic and cultural dynamics. According to Terry Bennett and Lynda Sharkley,

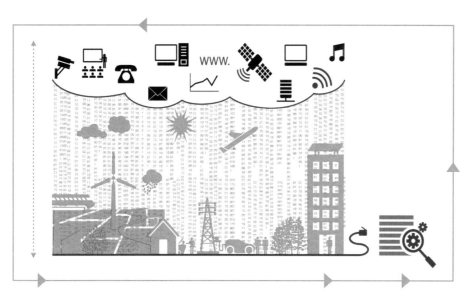

Ubiquitous city diagram: infrastructure with intelligence.

systems driven by information are more adaptive and can reconfigure themselves in response to demands and supply or in the case of an emergency. Over time this performance information allows for more predictive capability and optimization for more efficiency since models of the systems can be created and used in their operations. This integrated system allows supply, consumption and control at many stages or locations helping with redundancy and resiliency.[02]

Specifically, through the main functions of monitoring, controlling, and managing information, urban infrastructure systems can improve their service delivery capacity by securing supply (energy or water, for instance) or adapting their functions to different user demands (for example, trip generation rates). A thorough understanding of the demand for information services by other infrastructure makes it possible to mitigate systems' negative impacts (such as air pollutant emissions), secure service during demand peaks or periods of extreme natural phenomena, and provide balance through the necessary bidirectional communication of supply and demand. All in all it creates the potential for smarter systems. Infrastructure systems are becoming digitized, networked, and thus enhanced in order to better address the complexity of present and future urban challenges.

Examples of Synergies

Within the transportation infrastructure, the performance of transport systems can be optimized with the collection and processing of real-time information on demand regarding trip generation and traffic conditions. In addition, the information infrastructure can provide and promote remote access and e-services so that the need for unnecessary trips is reduced. The Berlin Traffic Control Center (VKRZ) represents one of the most mature implementations of information infrastructure in transportation. Started in 2002 and continuously updated since then, this comprehensive traffic management system monitors and controls traffic in a 1,600-kilometer network of main roads in Berlin while providing online traffic information to the public. Real-time traffic data is collected by a detection network of more than 300 infrared sensors and transmitted via General Packet Radio Service (GPRS) to the traffic control center. The data concerns quantity and velocity of traffic flow and the types of vehicles involved.[03] Additionally, real-time photographs of traffic conditions are regularly transmitted by 300 street cameras. The system also receives reports on construction sites and large-scale events such as the 2006 FIFA World Cup or state visits.[04] The data is continuously transmitted via the information networks and nodes such as traffic computers and substations, then is processed by traffic management software so that traffic models are simulated and short- or midterm forecasts are generated. The system responds accordingly, and when needed the connected 2,000 volume-controlled traffic lights automatically adjust the signal coordination pattern. In parallel, the system responds to traffic updates provided by ten traffic control systems distributed across urban motorways and tunnels. "The traffic control systems inform motorists about congestions on the motorway sections ahead, display speed limits, allocate or close lanes and provide warnings notices concerning possible hazards," as explained on the Verkehrsinformationszentrale Berlin website.[05]

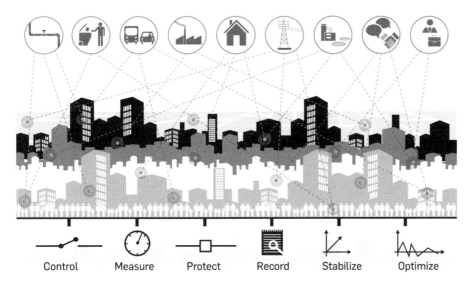

Information needs.

Control Measure Protect Record Stabilize Optimize

While the Berlin Traffic Control Center manages a critical part of Berlin's transportation infrastructure in real time, it serves another role as well: to influence the trip generation. Free online services provide the public with almost real-time access (data is updated with a five-minute delay) to the traffic map, where they obtain information on traffic delays, road work, and closed roads.[06] The intermodal routing planner it offers also includes trip routing recommendations based on different transport modes: public transportation, biking, and walking, alone and in combination. The goal of the Berlin Traffic Control Center is to secure sustainable traffic management and influence user demand. As a system it incorporates all of the main organizational qualities of both transportation and information infrastructure.

Similarly in energy systems—and particularly in electricity networks—information technologies can provide accurate data, analysis, and visualization, as well as faster communications. The integration of these technologies in transmission systems provides a key example, applicable not only to cities but also systemwide. Information infrastructure can contribute toward core transmission objectives, such as the stability of electricity grids and the penetration of renewable energy into the supply mix. Preventing system failures and blackouts requires constant monitoring. Technological advances make it possible to implement such monitoring through measurement devices, communications networks, and visualization software.

Phasor Measurement Unit (PMU) technology serves as one very promising example. PMU hardware measures critical indicators of voltages and currents at load centers, such as urban areas, and at other key locations of the electricity grid. The advantage of this particular technology is

that it allows for very frequent measurements that provide accurate and high-resolution data. PMUs can record data thirty to 120 times per second, more than a hundred times faster than other current technology.[07] However, developing automatic control actions based on raw PMU data still requires significant research and the collaborative efforts of the involved stakeholders. In early 2010, approximately 250 PMUs were installed across North America, with more than 850 additional PMUs scheduled for installation between 2010 and 2013.[08] By October 2014 there were almost 1,700 PMUs installed in the United States and Canada.[09] The "Smart Grid Strategy for Assuring Reliability of the Western Grid" in the United States includes the modernization of the existing grid through the installation of more than 300 PMUs. The objective is to increase reliability and system performance, and to facilitate the exploitation of renewable energy resources available in the region.[10]

The increase in distributed energy production installations, especially when these depend on renewable energy sources, makes grid monitoring and regulating more challenging. Solar and wind, in particular, are considered "variable energy resources," as operators have only limited control over them. The system must therefore have enough response capacity to maintain its stability under unpredictable conditions. Another key shift, however, is found at the heart of this process: grid locations (for example, buildings) that once played only the role of the consumer have now also become electricity-generating entities, requiring additional communication capabilities. "Smart" systems allow distributed energy production to be funneled into the grid. "These systems are made possible by two-way communication technology and computer processing that has been used for

095

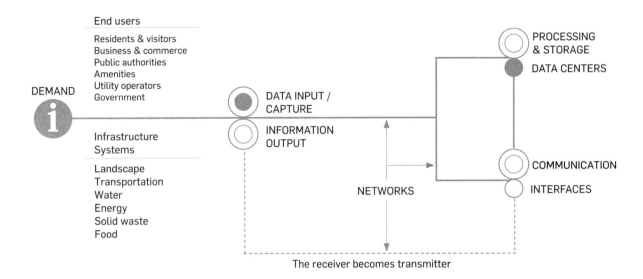

The receiver becomes transmitter

decades in other industries."[11] The widespread use of advanced data-generating hardware and the expansion of two-way communication bring the synergy between information infrastructure and electricity to the center of the discourse on electricity grids. A 2007 National Energy Technology Laboratory report created for the US Department of Energy recognized that "the communications systems utilized in the power industry today are too slow and too localized to support the integrated communications needed to enable the modern power grid."[12] Eight years later the efforts for increased data storage, processing, flexibility, and response capacity are ongoing as evidenced through the US government–sponsored smart grid projects. Managing diverse networked components with multiple roles and variable performance is the coming challenge for engineers and regulators alike.[13]

In water infrastructure, the information system is a strategic enabler for smart water management policies. Information infrastructure as a subsystem offers monitoring of daily and seasonal water consumption, reduction of water losses, leak detection in both water and wastewater networks, reduction of energy costs, storm water management, and urban flooding solutions. It provides real-time monitoring of the reservoir water quality and the volume of discharged effluents to the city's water bodies. Similar to the smart grid developments in the energy sector, integrated information components such as data collection devices and data control software, information communication modes and network optimization fixtures offer real-time tracking and reporting of conditions. As a result, quick response mechanisms can be developed and potential problems can even be predicted. Water utility companies have started incorporating information technologies

to map water resources and predict weather, to develop asset management for water networks or to set up warning systems, and finally, to meet water demand in both urban and agriculture areas.

A smart water grid begins at the source and finishes at the consumption location. Smart meters, pumps, and valves are primarily installed in water resource locations. Later on, flooding, leak, and contaminant sensors are incorporated along the urban water networks. The same logic is followed in the wastewater system and applied in its sewage network, water treatment facilities, and discharge lines. Water consumption locations (buildings, green areas, etc.) are equipped with end-use sensing devices, smart irrigation systems, contaminant sensors, and smart meters.

In Florida advanced information systems are used by the Jacksonville Electric Authority, the water, sewer, and electric provider for Jacksonville. As *WaterWorld* magazine points out: "JEA's new system, Optimized System Controls of Aquifer Resources, or OSCAR, controls the water system in real time, creating what JEA refers to as Operations Optimization."[14] The system regulates the pumping of water from the aquifer, minimizing energy consumption while maximizing water generation during peak periods of consumption. Operations staff that use the software can now develop optimal operation plans through accurate data, reliable forecasting, and real-time alerts.

Today, advanced metering infrastructure (AMI) is the most common type of smart metering. Data flows in both directions, between metering devices and utilities information systems. In Malta, the national water utility Water

Above: Indicative information system diagram.

Services Corporation and IBM began a nationwide AMI and smart grid implementation program in 2009. Today, thousands of smart meters identify water leaks, and IT applications enable remote monitoring and management. The whole system provides insight into water usage patterns and the efficient management of water demand.[15]

As a way of moving forward, IBM points out, "Current systems are generally standalone and limited in scalability, which inhibits effective decision making across departments and organizations. Smarter water management systems need to provide an integrated operating picture with robust real-time analytics, modeling and decision support capabilities."[16]

Hybrid Reading between Physical and Virtual

Although integrating information infrastructure can improve the efficiency of a city's infrastructure systems and increase its sustainability, this integration carries with it implications in the way we address the urban environment. Information infrastructure connects in almost real time the actual conditions of the urban environment with the performance of infrastructure systems. In the case of the Berlin Traffic Control Center, we have seen how the city's urban fabric (street network and trip destinations), physical transportation infrastructure (streets, cars, and public transport), end-user behavior (trip generation realized physically but expressed also digitally), virtual information infrastructure (software and information systems), and physical information infrastructure (sensors and control centers) can be all interconnected through information flow in a dynamic feedback loop. Simultaneously, we can read that continuous information flow as interconnecting the physical space (a city's urban fabric, physical transportation infrastructure, physical information infrastructure, and end-user behavior) with the virtual space (virtual information infrastructure, end-user behavior, and information flow). Similar patterns can be identified in the case of energy, water, and other infrastructure systems.

In practice, the boundaries between physical and virtual spaces are becoming erased. This hybrid reading is the de facto outcome of the synergistic integration of information infrastructure with other urban infrastructure systems. These applied synergies mainly focus on increasing the technical and financial efficiency of an urban infrastructure system through information, while mitigating any negative impact on the environment. Beyond that, however, the question arises, can this rethinking of the city as synergistic hybridization of physical and virtual space lead us to new ways of planning the cities of the twenty-first century?

In transportation, one of the most recent characteristic examples is Uber, a mobile-app transportation network of crowd-sourced taxi drivers that responds to trip requests from customers and operates through dynamic pricing. More advanced examples include the ongoing projects involving driverless cars—autonomous vehicles that are capable of sensing their environment and navigating without human input based on advanced information systems. In energy, the Nest thermostat is a self-learning and programmable Wi-Fi-enabled thermostat that reduces the energy demand of buildings by optimizing heating and cooling.[17] In solid waste, the Bigbelly smart waste management system provides a network of interconnected trash cans across cities that use real-time data and analytics to drive operational planning and resource allocation.[18] In food, research on optimizing urban farming through information infrastructure is growing. For example, the City Farm project in the MIT Media Lab works on rethinking urban food production by combining hydroponic methods with networked sensing and automated feedback.[19] At the intersection of water and landscape, parks are becoming self-watering in Barcelona, where a network of sensors monitors the local conditions to provide the water that is strictly needed for irrigation, preventing any waste.[20]

These developments exemplify current and near future solutions that will introduce new forms of urban infrastructure by integrating information infrastructure with more traditional varieties. Nevertheless, they have been developed with existing cities in mind, and they do not question the predominant spatial arrangements and forms of the urban environment. What kind of urban environments might instead be designed from scratch to accommodate such hybrid, synergistic, and evolving infrastructure systems? How would we design the street network for a city of driverless cars, or address land uses for smart urban farming?

The first steps in this direction have already been taken. Songdo, in South Korea, is considered the most typical example of a new city that has been planned with integrated information infrastructure. Built from scratch on 1,500 acres, construction of the last part of the city will be completed in 2015. Eighty-two thousand people already reside there. A recent review by MIT on smart cities reveals that Songdo "has been touted as a model future city by developers and technology suppliers. The city is home to futuristic technologies that promote sustainability, such as water recycling systems and pneumatic waste disposal systems that eliminate the need for garbage trucks."[21] At the same time, critics have noted that Songdo's urban form is not different from that of other satellite cities of Seoul. They have also

Yannis Orfanos, Eleonora Marinou, Vicky Sagia & Spiro Pollalis observed that some of the city's embedded technologies have already been superseded.[22] This is a general issue for emerging smart cities around the world. While cities like Songdo signify an important start in urban automation, the question of hybrid reading-based urban planning remains open.

Anthony Townsend advocates for a future city where dynamic, adaptive systems respond in real time to changing conditions at the very small and very large scale simultaneously, in ways that both optimize urban infrastructure systems and create a more delightful human experience.[23] The central issue is what kind of new urban environment will support such a development. That can be answered only in practice, through future urban prototypes, although we have to shape the urban planning approaches that will generate such prototypes.

In future cities, urban infrastructure systems will need to address increasingly complex urban challenges. With emerging advances in information and communication networks, the technological capacity to manage such complex synergic ecosystems will increase over the coming years. According to Stephen Goldsmith and Susan Crawford, "machine-organized and -curated responses will dramatically reduce the transaction costs of gathering data and organizing feedback almost to zero."[24] The urban environment can be a physical and virtual interface that derives from new ways of planning and experiencing future cities. Put simply by Townsend, "The real magic of a fully networked and automated city won't be seen until designers start writing code to program truly novel behaviors for entire buildings and neighborhoods."[25]

A hybrid reading of urban space as inherently both physical and virtual, based on a synergic integrated planning between urban infrastructure systems and information infrastructure, would no doubt contribute to devising new ways forward.

Acknowledgments: This research has been supported by the Zofnass Program for Sustainable Infrastructure at the Graduate School of Design. The authors would like to thank the entire research team and the members of the Sustainability Industry Advisory Board of the Zofnass Program for their input and comments.

01. Spiro Pollalis et al., "Information," in *Planning Sustainable Cities: An Infrastructure Based Approach* (forthcoming).
02. Terry Benett and Lynda Sharkley, quoted ibid.
03. Ralf Kohlen, "Berlin Traffic Management Centre (VMZ)—Mobility Management in Conurbation" (paper presented at the Danish Society of Engineers, Copenhagen, January 18, 2010).
04. "Berlin Traffic Control Centre: Traffic Management Ensures Urban Mobility," Verkehrsinformationszentrale Berlin, accessed March 18, 2015, http://www.viz-info.de/documents/10122/0/VKRZ-Flyer-Englisch/c2bfb4a4-d777-42ef-a208-18a24a83f04c.
05. Ibid.
06. Ibid.
07. "A Smart Grid Strategy for Assuring Reliability of the Western Grid," US Department of Energy, 2011, accessed March 17, 2015, https://www.smartgrid.gov/files/WECC_Profile_casestudy.pdf.
08. "The Future of the Electric Grid: An Interdisciplinary MIT Study," Massachusetts Institute of Technology, December 5, 2011, http://web.mit.edu/mitei/research/studies/the-electric-grid-2011.shtml.
09. "Synchrophasor Technology Fact Sheet," North American Synchro-Phasor Initiative, October 2014, https://www.naspi.org/File.aspx?fileID=1326.
10. See "A Smart Grid Strategy for Assuring Reliability of the Western Grid."
11. "Smart Grid," US Department of Energy, accessed January 30, 2015, http://energy.gov/oe/services/technology-development/smart-grid.
12. "Integrated Communications," National Energy Technology Laboratory of the US Department of Energy Office of Electricity Delivery and Energy Reliability, B1-4, February 2007, http://www.netl.doe.gov/File%20Library/research/energy%20efficiency/smart%20grid/whitepapers/Integrated-Communications_Final_v2_0.pdf.
13. See "Smart Grid."
14. "Artificial Intelligence Helps JEA Optimize Water Resources," *WaterWorld*, accessed March 16, 2015, http://www.waterworld.com/articles/print/volume-22/issue-6/automation-technology/artificial-intelligence-helps-jea-optimize-water-resources.html.
15. "ICT as an Enabler for Smart Water Management, " ITU-T Technology Watch Report, October 2010, http://www.itu.int/dms_pub/itu-t/oth/23/01/T23010000100003PDFE.pdf; "The First Nationwide Smart Energy and Water Grid," IBM, accessed March 17, 2015, http://www-03.ibm.com/ibm/history/ibm100/us/en/icons/gridnation.
16. "Smarter Water Management," IBM, accessed March 17, 2015, http://www.ibm.com/smarterplanet/us/en/water_management/nextsteps/solution/J103636F12674V34.html.
17. "Energy Savings from the Nest Learning Thermostat: Energy Bill Analysis Results," Nest, February 2015, https://nest.com/downloads/press/documents/energy-savings-white-paper.pdf.
18. "Cities & Towns," BigBelly, accessed March 18, 2015, http://bigbelly.com/places/cities.
19. "CityFARM Research," MIT Media Lab, accessed March 18, 2015, http://mitcityfarm.media.mit.edu.
20. "Telemanaging Irrigation," BCN Smart City, accessed March 18, 2015, http://smartcity.bcn.cat/en/telemanaging-irrigation.html.
21. "A Closer Look at Smart Cities," *MIT Technology Review*, January/February 2014, 15.
22. Anthony Townsend, *Smart Cities: Big Data, Civic Hackers, and the Quest for a New Utopia* (New York: W. W. Norton & Company, 2013), 28.
23. Ibid.
24. Stephen Goldsmith and Susan Crawford, *The Responsive City: Engaging Communities through Data-Smart Governance* (San Francisco: Jossey-Bass, 2014), 70.
25. Townsend, *Smart Cities*, 28.

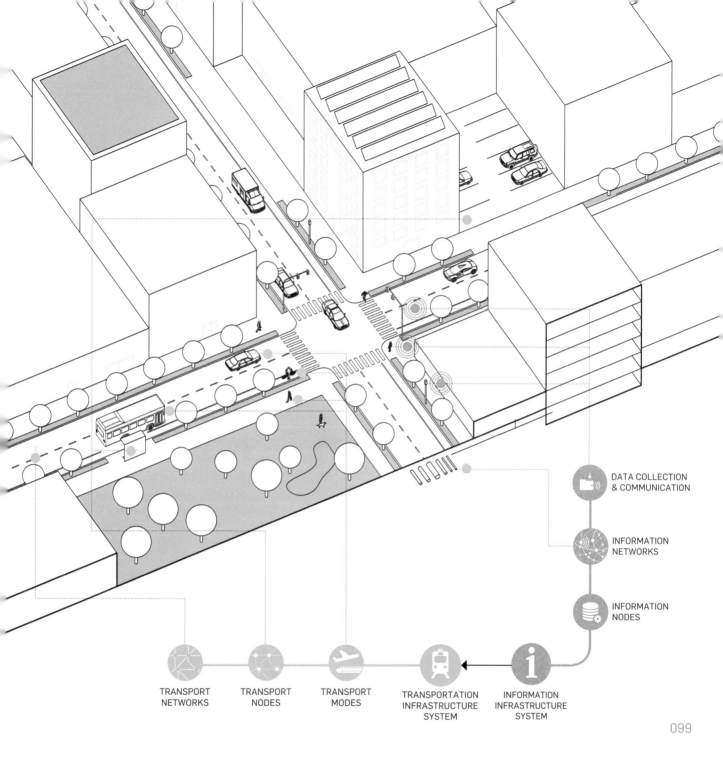

DATA COLLECTION
& COMMUNICATION

INFORMATION
NETWORKS

INFORMATION
NODES

TRANSPORT
NETWORKS

TRANSPORT
NODES

TRANSPORT
MODES

TRANSPORTATION
INFRASTRUCTURE
SYSTEM

INFORMATION
INFRASTRUCTURE
SYSTEM

Synergies of transportation
infrastructure with
information.

Yannis Orfanos, Eleonora Marinou, Vicky Sagia & Spiro Pollalis

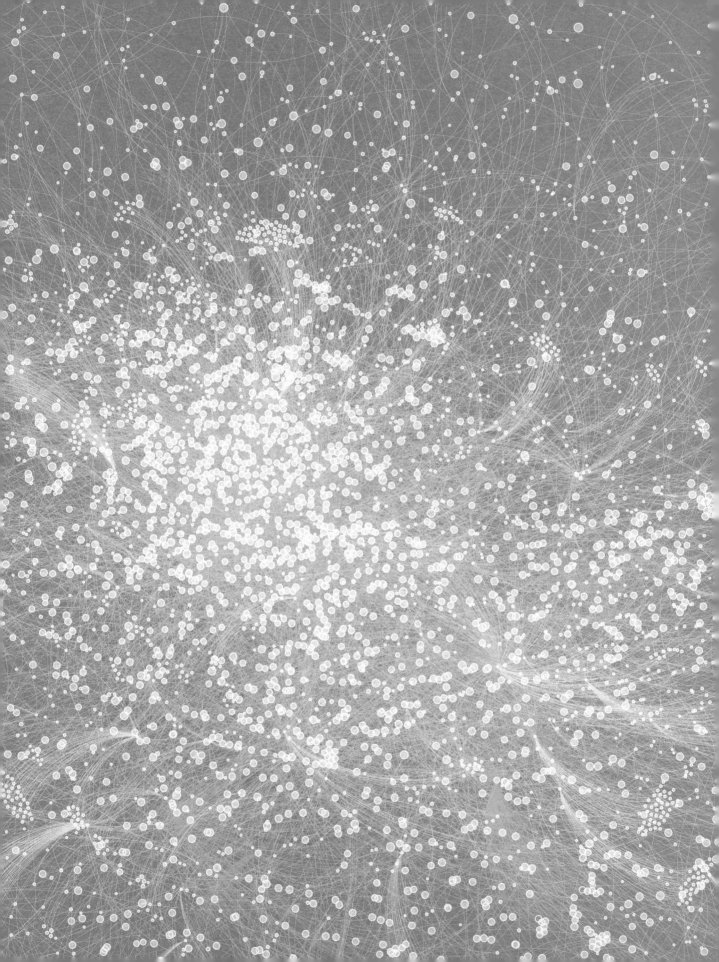

Architecture Machines and the Internet of Things

or, The Costs of Convergence

Molly Wright
Steenson

Does the Internet of Things have a history? If so, it sure doesn't show it.

Coined in 1999, at a presentation to Procter & Gamble given by Kevin Ashton, the term "Internet of Things" (IoT) picked up valence in the early twenty-first century.[01] It connoted a universe full of objects, or "things," that sense, actuate, and respond to us. The idea of networked, sentient objects predates the naming of the Internet of Things, originating with researchers working on networked sensors in the 1980s and gaining momentum with the proliferation of wireless networks in the late 1990s. And since 2008, this idea has largely taken form: as of that year, there were more things on the Internet than there were people on the planet. Gartner, an information technology research firm, estimates that by 2020 there will be twenty-six billion things on the Internet: that is, not devices with screens but everyday objects of all kinds capable of sensing, communicating, and responding to each other and to their users.[02] From environmental monitoring to home automation, from manufacturing to healthcare, from large-scale infrastructure to nanotechnology, the Internet of Things, say its proponents, will alter all aspects of our world.

Even older than IoT, the term "smart city" has been part of our lexicon for more than twenty years, for as long as the commercial World Wide Web has been in existence.[03] Smart cities promise "new generation services and infrastructure with the help of information and communication technologies (ICT)," according to one industry report, and are "differentiated in terms of their governance, technological advances, economic benefits, and social and environmental standards."[04] There are immense possibilities for technology to govern everything, from the minuscule to the monolithic. This is a different situation than what German media theorist Friedrich Kittler described in a 1999 lecture as a world influenced by the "universal discrete machine known as the computer" and "the only medium that combines … storage, transmission, and processing … fully automatically."[05] In this new universe characterized by the IoT, any *thing—anything—*can become a transmitter, a receiver, a processor. Everything is a computer, and everyone resides inside the computer.

The IoT often forgets it has users. It has no idea whatsoever about architecture. Yet the scale of IoT is

101

the same as that of architecture, of the built environment that we navigate. It merges the architecture of the computer with the architecture of the built environment. The history of the IoT needs to be claimed in light of its mythologizing and as part of its cautionary tales. The groundwork for that history is presented here. It is a story of convergence: of architecture and computation, or of the architectures of the built environment and the architecture of the computer.

Half a century ago, architects and computer engineers began a mutual mining of each other's fields in order to express the growing complexity of their own practices. In the earliest days, architects applied cybernetics, artificial intelligence, and computer-aided design to architectural problems. At the same time, technologists used architectural metaphors to explain the increasingly complex functioning of computer systems. Engineers and programmers turned to architecture to describe the complex task of designing computers. What started out as the "organization" and "instructions" of computer design became known as its "architecture" by the late 1950s and early 1960s.

In a paper from 1945, John von Neumann characterized the design of the EDVAC computer (one of the earliest digital computers) and the instruction sets it needed to follow to carry out its operations as the "organization of logical elements." When IBM attempted to build the world's fastest supercomputer, the IBM 7030, its engineers referred to the design as "architecture." "Computer architecture, like other architecture," writes Frederick P. Brooks in "Architectural Philosophy," part of his 1962 *Planning a Computer System*, "is the art of determining the needs of the user of a structure and then designing to meet those needs as effectively as possible within economic and technological constraints." Brooks likens this process of defining the "functional characteristics" of the IBM 7030 to that of an architect designing a building, in which the architect determines the needs of the user and designs accordingly.[06] The architecture needed to reflect how it would be engineered and built, in order to assure a cost-effective and buildable system. Brooks explains, "the emphasis in architecture is upon the needs of the user, whereas in engineering the emphasis is upon the needs of the fabricator."[07] In this definition of architecture, the focus is on the organization of a system's elements with regard to the person who would be using it—a translation between the requirements of the computer's physical design and the experience of the person using it. In other publications in the early 1960s, IBM used "architecture" similarly, to refer to "conceptual structure and functional behavior."[08]

Architects turned to computing to model the complexity they found in architectural practice. As Royston Landau noted in 1968, practitioners found themselves interfacing with more systems, tackling more complicated design problems, and needing to conceptualize their work within a bigger systemic framework than they had had to manage previously.[09] They turned to computers and information processing in search of logical approaches to process the different, more complex stores of information that now fell under the umbrella of architecture. If anything, many architects found this increasing computation inevitable, a fact they approached with both trepidation and excitement. At the 1964 "Architecture and the Computer" conference, attended by a who's who of architecture, planning, engineering, and computation research luminaries, the biggest question was not whether the computer would change architectural practice but rather how it would do so. The conference served to "alert the profession to an irresistible force which will radically alter the practice of architecture whether we plan for it or not," writes conference organizer Sanford Greenfield in his preface to the proceedings.[10]

This convergence of architecture and the computer had profound implications. Working within architecture allowed both technologists and architects to ponder computation at a scale larger than punch cards and terminals. It meant that they could situate architecture as a cybernetic problem, or as an artificial intelligence question. It made architecture the locus of a new form of human-computer interaction, which took place at the scale of architecture itself. In so doing, both architects and technologists discovered the implications of building intelligence at a scale bigger than the screen, along with the problems that come when one expands a model developed for a small scale to a large system. A key example of this sort of experiment took place at the Massachusetts Institute of Technology (MIT) Architecture Machine Group between 1967 and 1984.

Founded by Nicholas Negroponte and Leon Groisser in 1967, the Architecture Machine Group (Arch Mac) was a hybrid laboratory for architecture and engineering research. There, students and researchers split between architecture and engineering built intelligent, computerized environments in collaboration with the Artificial Intelligence (AI) Laboratory and the Departments of Electrical and Mechanical Engineering. While located in an architecture school, Arch Mac's projects followed the same logic and research strategies as did these technical labs. The group was funded by the same Department of Defense (DoD) agencies, such as the Defense Advanced Research Projects Agency (ARPA/DARPA) and the Office of Naval Research, and supported by some of the most powerful people at MIT in artificial intelligence and computer science. These included AI Lab cofounder Marvin Minsky, still on faculty at MIT, and computer science luminary J. C. R. Licklider, who put in place the framework for what would later become networked computing and the Internet.

These financial and personal relationships are an important part of Arch Mac's story. Since Arch Mac relied on DoD funding, it echoed the same dynamics as other defense-funded AI and engineering research groups. In order to understand the scope of Arch Mac's work, it is necessary to understand how DoD funding functioned and the impact it had on research imperatives.

Defense agencies operated in what historian Paul Edwards calls a "closed world."[11] They preferred to channel money within a closed, personal network. This cadre of individuals moved between DoD agencies, universities and technological institutes, and organizations such as RAND Corporation or private contractor Bolt, Beranek and Newman (now Raytheon BBN Technologies). (For example, Licklider worked at MIT, DARPA, and Bolt, Beranek and Newman between 1957 and 1968) The tight network was a way of keeping the braintrust and technological know-how developed during World War II intact during the Cold War. Until the late 1960s, general technical research could be funded by the military—it did not require explicitly military applications. But in 1970, the US Senate passed the Mansfield Amendment, which restricted military funding of academic research to direct, tactical military applications.

In the same period, the big goals that AI pursued in the 1950s to early 1970s did not prove successful, causing the field to suffer major cuts. Originally, much AI research took place in the "microworlds." Such projects often involved the manipulation of stacks of blocks with natural language commands and robotic arms, and accordingly were called "blocks worlds." Microworlds were useful because they focused in on a miniature domain, abstracted from real world constraints. They were also problematic for that very reason. When microworlds fell out of favor, Patrick Winston, director of the MIT AI Lab from 1972 to 1997, encouraged researchers to develop projects with tactical military applications. In particular, this meant projects that met priorities in military command and control. Arch Mac followed suit, and we will see the ways in which the group echoed the imperatives of defense funding.

The term "architecture machine" referred to Negroponte's theories of the impact of AI and computers on the built environment. He coined the term "architecture

machine" to refer to any number of intelligent, adaptive computational environments. In his 1975 book *Soft Architecture Machines*, he imagines what he calls "the distant future of architecture machines: they won't help us design; instead, we will live in them."[12] Beyond teaching architects to tinker and program, or engineers to think about applications for their work, Arch Mac investigated big questions about how computer architectures would permeate the built environment. Negroponte's statements about architecture machines were both bombastic and uncanny, a point that he himself acknowledged. "I strongly believe that it is very important to play with these ideas scientifically and explore applications of machine intelligence that totter between being unimaginably oppressive and unbelievably exciting," he writes.[13] And indeed, Arch Mac's writings, projects, and proposals would skirt the line between "oppressive" and "exciting" throughout its existence.

In the group's early days in the 1960s and early 1970s, Arch Mac worked within microworlds. Users of Arch Mac's URBAN 2 and URBAN 5 computer-aided design (CAD) systems (programs running on an IBM 360 computer) manipulated ten-by-ten-foot cubes by assigning attributes to them and engaging in a question-and-answer dialogue with the computer. URBAN 5 was supposed to be able to demonstrate its intelligence through this dialogue, which would change according to the user's context, but delivering meaningful dialogue was nearly impossible. URBAN 5 did not "admit the necessary ambiguity and the subtle intermingling of contexts that are required in order to respond to a real-world medley of events," Negroponte concedes, in 1970.[14] He deemed the project a failure.

Paradoxically, however, failures justified more funding for blocks worlds. Minsky and MIT Professor Seymour Papert wrote in a 1970 ARPA proposal, "we feel they are so important that we are assigning a large portion of our effort toward developing a collection of these microworlds and finding how to use the suggestive and predictive powers of the models without being overcome by their incompatibility with literal truth."[15] In fact, they were useful precisely because they operated without regard to "literal truth," or reality. Minsky and Papert write that each microworld "is very schematic; it talks about a fairyland in which things are so simplified that almost every statement about them would be literally false if asserted about the real world."[16] This is less of a concern when the blocks world is housed in a laboratory, or on a screen: but blocks worlds did not scale, as was apparent in Arch Mac's SEEK project, exhibited in the "Software" show at New York's Jewish Museum in 1970.

SEEK manipulated and organized blocks to "show how

a machine handled a mismatch between its model of the world and the real world."[17] The project consisted of a pen containing a bevy of two-inch mirrored blocks, which the steel and Lucite robotic hand of SEEK, guided by colored wires and a coiled cord, attempted to stack. The pen also contained a colony of gerbils. SEEK, however, was not apprised of these rodent residents. The exhibition catalog reads, "Unbeknownst to SEEK, the little animals are bumping into blocks, disrupting constructions, and toppling towers. The result is a substantial mismatch between the three-dimensional reality and the computer remembrances which reside in the memory of SEEK's computer. SEEK's role is to deal with these inconsistencies."[18] Unfortunately, the system suffered from the same problems that plagued URBAN 5. "Today machines are poor at handling sudden changes in context in environment. This lack of adaptability is the problem SEEK confronts in diminutive," writes Negroponte.[19] Indeed, in diminutive the model failed for many reasons, and not just because it was a blocks world. SEEK also tended to kill the gerbils.[20]

SEEK serves as a pointed example for criticizing microworlds in their abstractions and reductions. While microworlds provide manageable frameworks for exploration, applying the lessons they offer to larger-scale environments becomes a thornier issue. Rodney Brooks, MIT AI Lab director from 1997 to 2007, argues that the microworld construct is "a dangerous weapon" because it does not scale: "There is no clean division between perception (abstraction) and reasoning in the real world," he writes.[21] "Eventually criticism surfaced that the blocks world was a 'toy world' and that within it there were simple special purpose solutions to what should be considered more general problems."[22]

Arch Mac built an all-encompassing media environment, the Media Room, in the mid-1970s. Rather than sitting at a computer terminal keyboard or operating upon a world composed of blocks, the Media Room put the user inside the computer. Negroponte calls this "being in the interface."[23] The soundproofed, living room–sized apace had dark pile carpet on the floor and walls. Spanning the wall in front of the user was a large light-valve screen. At the center of the room, an Eames lounge chair was equipped with joypads (like joysticks only in the form of touchpads). Two smaller touch screens were positioned within reach of the user, along with a ten-inch-square data tablet.[24] The Media Room provided ways to experience simulations more real than real, claimed the group. Using the joypads on the lounge chair, denizen could drive down the streets of Aspen with the Aspen Movie Map, a sort of Google Street View at the scale of the room.

They could move through the interfaces of the Spatial Data Management System, a forerunner to the graphical user interface. Or, they might move a fleet of ships by voice and gesture with Put That There, or navigate the first digital layered maps in Mapping By Yourself, an augmented reality and handheld mapping system.

In the Media Room, computer architecture and spatial architecture converged. In line with the notion of "integration," the Media Room was a space to explore "supreme usability," a conflation of the human, the interface, and the built environment. It combined comfort and ease, on the one hand—"that one can be oneself in the company of machines," as Negroponte writes in one proposal—with technological integration, on the other.[25] Where usability relates to the ergonomics and affordances of user interfaces, supreme usability is ergonomics on a larger scale, architecture and the machine aligning the human amid dynamic streams of information, military logistics, and the simulation. "We look upon this objective [supreme usability] as one which requires intimacy, redundancy, and parallelism of immersive modes and media of interaction," Negroponte and Richard Bolt write. "The image of a user perched in front of a monochromatic display with a keyboard, is obscured by the vision of a Toscaniniesque, self-made surround with the effervescence of *Star Wars*."[26] A limitless *Star Wars*, it would seem: in a report on the Media Room, Negroponte writes, "As soon as each wall is a floor to ceiling display, or in the limiting case the place is a hemisphere, the room has no presentational extent. Instead, spatiality is only limited by the movements of input, itself confined to the real space of the human network."[27]

This description calls to mind the camera obscura that art historian Jonathan Crary situates in "its relation of the observer to the undemarcated, undifferentiated expanse of the world outside."[28] Arch Mac and Media Lab researcher Andy Lippman uses this notion of limitlessness in his corollaries for effective interaction: the "impression of an infinite database."[29] The user has to have the idea that there are not just one or two possibilities but rather many potential ways to navigate, myriad choices to make: otherwise, it is not interactive. In an infinite database, the simulation knows no bounds. In the warm and exciting integration provided by supreme usability, the Media Room simplifies complex information, while masking the dynamics—perceptual and power both—that lie beneath.

Arch Mac was rolled into the MIT Media Lab, which opened in 1985 with $40 million in mostly corporate, private funding, under a new moniker: media. Inherent in Negroponte's term "media" is political scientist Ithiel de Sola Pool's concept of "convergence." A technological condition in which computing devices become more compatible, convergence referred to the alignment and unification of content, media, delivery, and governance. In his 1983 book *Technologies of Freedom*, Pool characterizes it as follows: "A process called the 'convergence of modes' is blurring the lines between media, even between point-to-point communications." He writes,

> A single physical means—be it wires, cables, or airwaves—may carry services that in the past were provided in separate ways. Conversely, a service that was provided in the past by any one medium—be it broadcasting, the press, or telephony—can now be provided in several different physical ways. So the one-to-one relationship that used to exist between a medium and its use is eroding.[30]

Pool's particular interest in convergence was in the implications of electronic communications on politics and the economics of media ownership, but Arch Mac sheds light on another form of convergence, not just of humans and machines, nor of military and consumer applications, but also of the architectures of computing and lived space. The one-to-one relationship with the built environment, with the infrastructures we don't see, and the everyday interfaces that we do, becomes more complicated as the computational powers within them increase. Arch Mac's research provides early proof of the promise and problems of these forms of convergence.

It may be easy to scoff at Arch Mac's grand pronouncements regarding the future of architecture machines and how they would change the world in which we live, but the fact is that in the more than forty years since they were made we have not come much further. Consider the statements of Google CEO Eric Schmidt at the World Economic Forum in Davos, Switzerland, in January 2015. Schmidt talked about the "disappearing Internet"—so pervasive, it is no longer visible. Schmidt tells his audience, "Imagine you walk into a room, and the room is dynamic. And with your permission and all of that, you are interacting with the things going on in the room. ... A highly personalized, highly interactive and very, very interesting world emerges."[31] This statement represents a gross abstraction: it glosses over issues of privacy, responsiveness, and generativity. Looking back to an even earlier moment, in 1991 Xerox PARC Chief Scientist Mark Weiser introduces the term "ubiquitous computing" in a *Scientific American* article. "The most profound technologies are those that disappear," he writes. "They weave themselves into the fabric of everyday life until they are indistinguishable from it."[32] Weiser's concept of nearly twenty-five years ago is far more nuanced than Schmidt's more recent description of the disappearing Internet.

What Google, Cisco, IBM, or even a feisty startup have to gain from the success of the IoT is clear: there are billions of dollars at stake. The current total market value of smart cities—with their investment in smart buildings, homes, energy, healthcare, industrial automation, transportation, education, and security—is expected to grow from $411 billion in 2014 to more than $1 trillion in just five years. That projected total rises to nearly $40 trillion over the course of the next twenty years.[33] But the stakes revealed by the convergent history of architecture and the IoT are equally evident. As in Negroponte's blocks worlds, the effects of a bad model will become magnified at the scale of the city, with its billions of networked objects, and its users will be humans, not gerbils. How smart is the smart city?

Perhaps it is not so smart after all. Our fine-grained details become coarse when they meet big data, when decision technologies that respond to this data become embedded in the world around us. To return to John von Neumann's characterization, computer architectures organize the logical elements of the machine—the architecture machine. We find that uniting the user with the machine creates sticky problems and that users still do not fare well. From inside the architecture machine—as designed by the architects of the smart city or the Internet of Things—there is no exit.

01. Kevin Ashton, "That 'Internet of Things' Thing," *RFID Journal*, June 22, 2009, http://www.rfidjournal.com/articles/view?4986.
02. "Gartner Says the Internet of Things Installed Base Will Grow to 26 Billion Units by 2020," Gartner, press release, December 12, 2013, http://www.gartner.com/newsroom/id/2636073.
03. Andrew Tokmakoff and Jonathan Billington, "Consumer Services in Smart City Adelaide" (paper presented at Home-Oriented Informatics, Telematics and Automation Conference, Oikos, Copenhagen, June 27–July 1, 1994).
04. "Smart Cities Market by Smart Home, Intelligent Building Automation, Energy Management, Smart Healthcare, Smart Education, Smart Water, Smart Transportation, Smart Security, & by Services—Worldwide Market Forecasts and Analysis (2014–2019)," Markets and Markets, http://www.marketsandmarkets.com/Market-Reports/smart-cities-market-542.html.
05. Friedrich A. Kittler, *Optical Media: Berlin Lectures 1999* (Cambridge, UK: Polity, 2010), 26.
06. F. P. Brooks Jr., "Architectural Philosophy," in *Planning a Computer System: Project Stretch*, ed. Werner Buchholz (New York: McGraw Hill, 1962), 5.
07. Ibid.
08. The *Oxford English Dictionary* cites IBM's use in its listing "architecture."

OED Online, http://www.oed.com/view/Entry/10408.

09. Royston Landau, *New Directions in British Architecture* (New York: G Braziller, 1968), 115.

10. Boston Architectural Center, *Architecture and the Computer* (proceedings, first Boston Architectural Center conference, Boston, MA, December 5, 1964), 8.

11. Paul Edwards, *The Closed World* (Cambridge, MA: MIT Press, 1996).

12. Nicholas Negroponte, *Soft Architecture Machines* (Cambridge, MA: MIT Press, 1975), 5.

13. Ibid.

14. Nicholas Negroponte, *The Architecture Machine: Toward a More Human Environment* (Cambridge, MA: MIT Press, 1970), 95–96.

15. Marvin Minsky and Seymour Papert, "Proposal to ARPA for Research on Artificial Intelligence at MIT, 1970–1971" (Cambridge, MA: MIT Artificial Intelligence Lab, 1970), 34.

16. Ibid.

17. Nicholas Negroponte, "The Return of the Sunday Painter, or the Computer in the Visual Arts" (manuscript, 1976), 9. Nicholas Negroponte Personal Papers, Cambridge, MA.

18. Architecture Machine Group, "SEEK, 1969–70," in *Software: Information Technology; Its New Meaning for Art*, ed. Jack Burnham (New York: The Jewish Museum, 1970), 23.

19. Ibid.

20. Paul Pangaro, telephone interview with Molly Steenson, November 27, 2006. See also Edward Shanken, "The House that Jack Built: Jack Burnham's Concept of 'Software' as a Metaphor for Art," *Leonardo Electronic Almanac* 6, no. 10 (November 1998), http://www.artexetra.com/House.html.

21. Rodney Brooks, "Achieving Artificial Intelligence through Building Robots," 1986, MIT Artificial Intelligence Laboratory, AI Memos (1959–2004), http://dspace.mit.edu/handle/1721.1/6451.

22. Ibid.

23. Nicholas Negroponte, "Books without Pages" (1979), 8. Nicholas Negroponte Personal Papers. Stewart Brand called the Media Room "a personal computer with the person inside." In a reference to the gestural and voice command project he referred to a space as the "Put That There" room, but he is actually describing the Media Room. Stewart Brand, *The Media Lab: Inventing the Future at MIT* (New York: Viking, 1987), 152.

24. William C. Donelson, "Spatial Management of Information," *ACM SIGGRAPH Computer Graphics* 12, no. 3 (August 1978): 205.

25. Nicholas Negroponte and Richard Bolt, "Data Space Proposal to the Cybernetics Technology Office, Defense Advanced Research Projects Agency" (1978), 11. Nicholas Negroponte Personal Papers.

26. Ibid.

27. Nicholas Negroponte, "Media Room," *Proceedings of the Society for Information Display* 21, no. 1 (1980).

28. Jonathan Crary, *Techniques of the Observer: On Vision and Modernity in the Nineteenth Century* (Cambridge, MA: October Books and MIT Press, 1992), 34.

29. Andy Lippman, quoted in Brand, *The Media Lab*, 46–48.

30. Ithiel de Sola Pool, *Technologies of Freedom* (Cambridge, MA: Harvard University Press, 1983), 23.

31. Eric Schmidt, quoted in Stephanie Mlot, "Eric Schmidt: 'The Internet Will Disappear,'" *PCMag*, January 23, 2015, http://www.pcmag.com/article2/0,2817,2475701,00.asp.

32. Mark Weiser, "The Computer for the 21st Century," *Scientific American* 265, no. 3 (September 1991): 94.

33. These statistic originated with Markets and Markets analysis and were provided by http://www.marketsandmarkets.com/Market-Reports/smart-cities-market-542.html.

Grounding Urban Data
Interview with Rob Kitchin

New Geographies: We can say that as a society we are generating, processing, transmitting, and storing massive amounts of information. However, focusing solely on the technical capabilities of new information technologies paints a limited picture of the highly charged and quite complex relationship between information and communications technologies (ICTs) and society as a whole. Perhaps another way of entering this conversation is to read the influence of this information revolution (revolutionary, both in terms of quantity and technology) on our perception of another aspect of the contemporary societal condition: urbanity. Perhaps we can start by discussing the reciprocal relationship between "big data" and urban environments. If past experiments in data-driven urban planning and design have shown us anything, it is that techno-scientific approaches to design can be problematic. They were not able to fully capture the intricacies of the urban environment. But do we have a new potential with big (urban) data for this kind of approach to observing, analyzing, conceptualizing, and constructing our built environment? Beyond theoretical discourse, what practicalities does big data afford our understanding of, and our agency in, the built environment?

Rob Kitchin: There's no doubt that big urban data does offer us a new real-time evidence base from which to understand cities. And new data analytics based on machine learning offer us new opportunities to analyze, map, and model urban environments and processes. We are now generating a phenomenal amount of structured and unstructured data about cities from satellites, aerial surveys, surveillance cameras, sensors and scanners, digital devices such as smartphones, and the interactions and transactions that take place over networked systems relating to consumption, production, travel, social engagement, and so on. Advances in computational power and analytical techniques mean it is evermore possible to store, link, and extract information from these data. And we're only really at the beginning of this era of big urban data. Over time, the flows of data will increase further, and the techniques for making sense of them will advance. That said, cities are incredibly complex, open systems made up of a multitude of diverse, interconnected systems that stretch out across the globe in terms of flows of goods and services. They are embedded in urban hierarchies. They are affected by structural forces and political and business decisions made in a multitude of places.

They are full of millions of people who act in all kinds of ways and are thoroughly infused with culture, history, and politics. Even with more data, new analytics, and enhanced computation, it is therefore very difficult to create robust models of city development, and even more difficult to translate these contextually into policy.

I thus worry when people make pronouncements about how big data and associated models offer a better way forward for knowing and managing cities. Built within these claims is an assumption that big data and the models built on them will ultimately let us divine the truth of cities. Moreover, as the data will speak for themselves and the models will be built through machine learning, how to understand and run cities will manifest itself largely without the need for any deep domain knowledge about cities—their history, their politics and culture, their political economy, their inequalities and tensions and battles, their modes of governance, their environment. This condition promotes particular forms of knowledge about cities, that is, epistemic (scientific knowledge) and technical (practical instrumental knowledge), which work to marginalize and replace phronesis (knowledge derived from practice and deliberation) and metis (knowledge based on experience). Hard facts and models trump other kinds of knowing, and undermine and displace other scientific forms of urban knowledge that are less systematic and continuous, such as policy analysis, interviews, focus groups, surveys, etc. So as a new form of knowledge is developed, other forms are potentially sidelined. That, I think, will be to our detriment, because for all the hoopla about big urban data and urban science, it has numerous limitations, including methodological and technical shortcomings and data quality issues. I would prefer to think about big urban data as complementing—not replacing—other urban knowledges. It's not necessarily better: it offers another perspective.

NG: So much has been said about smart cities recently. How do you define the concept of a "smart" city? What opportunities does this emerging concept present for our current urban condition?

RK: What is interesting to me about the term "smart city" is that it is open to multiple interpretations. For some, a smart city is one that is instrumented; that is, computation is built into the very fabric of the city, so that its data flows can be monitored in real time and it can be programmed to respond in real time. So, for example, in an intelligent transport system, data about traffic is fed back from cameras, sensors, and transponders located across the system and used to alter traffic light sequencing or dynamically change speed signs. For others, a smart city is one that uses information and communication technologies to foster creativity, innovation, productivity, competitiveness, and governance, enhancing human capital and quality of life in order to grow the indigenous economy and attract inward investment.

In both cases, the use of ICTs is central, so a shorthand way of defining a smart city is that it is one that uses ICTs to augment, enhance, and reconfigure its social, economic, and governance systems. The opportunities that the smart city presents are gains in efficiency, effectiveness, productivity, safety, security, creativity, participation, transparency, and accountability in governance. Of course, the smart city also comes with a number of concerns, including technocratic governance, increased surveillance, erosion of privacy, social sorting, anticipatory governance, control creep, buggy and hackable city systems, and widening social inequalities. The challenge facing networked urbanism is to get the balance right between the positives and the negatives.

NG: We have arguably entered an age of real-time information. But are we getting closer to a conception of real-time cities? Can you elaborate on the role of real-time analytics in the monitoring and management of cities? How do you see these practices evolving as the gap between monitoring and action is increasingly shortened through big data urban applications?

RK: In many cases we are already in the age of real-time cities. Big urban data is flowing into control rooms related to transportation infrastructures (road system, public transit), utilities (energy, water), and the environment (sensors monitoring pollution, water levels, noise levels, land movement, etc.). Public service delivery data is increasingly being captured through management systems in use in city departments, public administration databases, social media, and crowdsourcing apps that enable citizens to report issues to city officials. These are complemented by a range of data outputted on a short temporal scale (weekly, monthly, and quarterly) that provides a set of urban indicators for measuring city performance. Together, these data provide a wealth of information about the city that is increasingly used in city management.

In general terms, this use of real-time data happens in two ways. Some municipalities use it to underpin forms of new managerialism—to explicitly guide operational practices and policy formulation. In these cases, the data is reviewed in weekly meetings to assess performance of city service units and managers, reward those meeting and exceeding targets, discipline those underachieving, and guide new strategies, policy, and budgeting. In other cases, such data is used in a more descriptive way, to complement a variety of information derived from other sources. Here, governance is seen as complex and multilevel in nature and not easily captured or steered through data levers.

The way I see big data urban governance developing, if the present trajectory continues, is first, through an attempt to integrate various data silos into centralized facilities. This will enable data to be conjoined. Second, I see it developing through city operating systems that manage and control city services through a single, coordinated platform (much like the ERP systems used by companies to coordinate activities across multiple domains). Third, I think more and more city services will be layered into these city operating systems, which will increasingly become the means by which city workers' performance will be evaluated (and city workers disciplined): it will thus deepen the extent of the emerging audit society. Fourth, these systems will act as a means of disciplining citizens through forms of automated management—autonomous, automatic, and automated means of regulating and socially sorting citizens based on their actions having been surveilled and then evaluated by software. The relationship between ICTs and governance has prefigured this trajectory in countries such as the United Kingdom and the United States during the past twenty years, driven by discourses of safety, security, productivity, efficiency, and transparency, and there is a strong path dependency that I think will be difficult to redirect. However, the extent to which systems actually improve in efficiency and effectiveness, I believe, will be highly variable. The history of IT management systems to date reveals a patchy rate of success in anticipated gains, as well as many unanticipated outcomes.

NG: Smart urbanism, enabled by big data, is increasingly portrayed as a new urban future inherently devoid of the political ideologies that have influenced cities in the past. What challenges can you identify in such a conception? Are smart city projects inherently apolitical, efficient, sustainable, and transparent? Can smart cities create more direct participation and collaboration between citizens and local government?

RK: I do find it odd, the way in which smart city developments are often positioned as pragmatic, commonsensical, and nonideological. Many academics (especially those working on technical developments) frame their work in purely scientific, technical, and pragmatic terms. Businesses aim at presenting their initiatives as inclusive and neutral, as if they did not have a vested interested in, or are not involved in lobbying around, issues such as deregulation, privatization, or other urban policies. The politics of smart cities, and the potentially negative consequences, are either ignored or summarily dismissed as halting progress. Yet, as I've already elaborated, the smart city is far from apolitical and nonideological: it is infused with politics, and with a certain vision of how cities will be managed and run in the future.

There has been some pushback against this apolitical positioning by critical academics, city managers, and citizens, who would like to make explicit and even reimagine the politics of smart cities. The result has been a move within the discourse to highlight ideas of citizen empowerment and participation. On one level this is positive, encouraging more citizen engagement around smart city developments. On another level, the rhetoric is being absorbed into the discourse without altering the underlying structural processes at work. So, for example, there are moves to open data, run hackathons, and conduct citizen consultation, yet the thrust of neoliberal reforms and technocratic governance are not being deflected. In other words, you can now get open data that shows you how the health system is being privatized, you can now create your own apps that tell citizens about the city, but you are still being surveilled and the data is still being used to discipline and socially sort you. You can take part in roundtables about city developments, but the dominant drivers of urban development are still capitalist interests. In other words, the danger is that citizens are given the perception that they are recasting the smart city, whereas in reality they are operating at one scale when the key decisions and processes are operating at another. That's not to dismiss attempts to reimagine smart cities or to create more direct participation and collaboration between citizens and local governments, but only to acknowledge that there are many powerful interests at play in this space.

NG: Given the current wave of privatization of urban command and control systems by multinational IT companies (such as IBM), how do we begin to read the emerging confluence of power and knowledge? Can we say we are entering a new age of neoliberal power/knowledge nexus?

RK: I think the first thing to say here is that urban command and control centers are not yet being fully privatized, though they might be in the future. At present, what I think is happening is that cities are entering into public-private partnerships where companies sell or license urban operating systems, which are then staffed and run by city officials (although they might be serviced and maintained by the company). If cities want such operating systems, they have no alternative but to enter into this partnership: cities do not possess the staff or the skill sets to develop such systems for themselves. This means, however, that private companies are becoming more involved in running and maintaining critical city infrastructure. Over time I imagine there will be pressure to start to outsource the staffing and running of the systems, as has happened with other city services. For example, in countries such as the United Kingdom, much transport and utilities provisions have been privatized, as have large chunks of services such as education, health, security, prisons, etc. This is very clearly part of a neoliberal drive to hollow out the state, turning it into an agency that manages contracts on behalf of cities and citizens rather than delivers services. To my mind, this raises all kinds of questions around the shifting power/knowledge of cities, especially given that whoever controls big urban data gains an enormous bank of information that enables them to intervene in city governance in a variety of ways that might ultimately benefit themselves. It also means that critical infrastructure is being run for profit, not for the public good, the danger there being that the quality and distribution of such infrastructure might become uneven and unequal, in line with the ability to pay and the possibilities of leveraging further profit, thus deepening sociospatial inequalities. Critical commentators have homed in on these aspect of smart cities, but there is much more work to be done to understand how the political economy of cities is being affected by smart city efforts.

NG: Given the focus of civic command and control systems on security (Rio de Janeiro's, for example, which emphasizes environmental resiliency, antiterrorism, and the accident-proofing of urban infrastructures) and also the emerging politics of information in the twenty-first century (exemplified by the direct access of government institutions like the US National Security Agency and the UK's Government Communications Headquarters to every aspect of their citizens' lives), how imminent are the threats of surveillance and militarization in the civic space?

RK: I think concerns about the surveillance and militarization of civic and domestic space are absolutely warranted. Vast quantities of data about cities and citizens are being generated daily and used for all kinds of purposes that affect people directly and indirectly. We are coming to live in an age where we are no longer lost in the crowd; our movements, interactions, and transactions are being tracked and traced by various public and private entities. While this data remains mostly in silos (and thus the trails remain disjointed), they are evermore being combined through data aggregators, mined for insights, and used to draw conclusions about people and segment services. Legal provisions concerning data generation and protection are struggling to adapt to the quickly changing terrain. And as the WikiLeaks and Snowden revelations exposed, national governments are at the forefront of mass spying on citizens without their knowledge.

In states with weak forms of democracy, the technologies of the smart city pose many potential concerns to the freedoms and rights of citizens. Interconnected and flattened city systems that can track and trace individuals—through monitoring the locations of their phones (sensing their MAC address), their vehicles (using automatic plate number recognition), their faces (using facial recognition software linked to CCTV), their interactions (their email and phone records), their social media, their household consumption (using smart metering), and so on—open up the potential for an Orwellian-style panopticon. Taken to their logical conclusion, they form the perfect sociotechnical assemblage for a totalitarian state: an all-seeing, all-tracking, all-reacting system that stifles dissent before it has chance to organize. And while governments and companies may reject such an assessment as alarmist or overblown—arguing that they are only trying to improve cities and their economy, transportation, environment, safety, security, and so on for all citizens, mainly using anonymous data or metadata—the empirical evidence reveals that as such technologies are being deployed and massive amounts of data are being generated and conjoined, privacy is being eroded, people are being predictively profiled and socially sorted, software-enabled governance is becoming more routinized and pervasive, and inequalities are widening. I don't think we should lose sight of these issues. Yes, smart city technologies can potentially improve the lives of citizens, but they can also do this in remarkably uneven, unequal, and discriminatory ways, depending upon how those technologies are deployed.

NG: Would you expand on your previous answer and elaborate on the contemporary confidence in democratic and bottom-up social organizations, ranging from grassroots disaster relief to political uprisings? Where do you see the power of public organizations when their intelligence is founded on privatized information platforms and infrastructures?

RK: One has to believe, I think, in the power of democracy and the activism and advocacy of citizens and community organizations to act as a counterweight to statist and corporate power in the age of the smart city. Smart technologies may be tools of control and profit, but they are also the tools of resistance, transgression, and freedom. As tools, technologies can be wielded by many and used and reappropriated in all kinds of ways. And, yes, the power to act in the city might be asymmetrical and divided, and this could become more imbalanced given who owns and controls the technologies, but events such as the Arab Spring and the civil organizing that took place during Hurricane Sandy show how democracy and the public good, by deploying ICTs, can quickly rise up and make a difference, even if they are closed down afterward.

As I've already noted, however, the danger is that citizen engagement and grassroots organizing forms a relatively weak or moribund counterweight to the deep-rooted structural changes taking place with respect to how states and cities are organized and run. Although rolled out as examples of bottom-up citizen participation and democracy, the fundamental changes occur in a different register. In this sense, I do think that those who are concerned about the political ideology and processes at work in many smart city visions need their counterarguments to work at different levels. It is not simply enough to demand open data; it needs to be accompanied by political work around data protection and security, how data is being generated and used, and the political ideology of the neoliberal city. This, I think, is important work in reimagining and recasting what a smart city is and how it can be developed and deployed.

Indeed, I'm not against smart cities per se: clearly networked urbanism has much to offer in terms of aiding how cities are managed, providing solutions to issues such as energy usage and traffic congestion. And they do provide new opportunities for innovation, entrepreneurship, and economic development. But I do think we need to be careful in how we go about creating smart cities. Often the smart city vision is presented as a *fait accompli*, as if how it is currently unfolding is the only, or most logical, or most reasonable, form—that there's a certain immutable path dependency in operation—rather than the vision and ideology underpinning smart city developments being entirely mutable and open to being reconfigured by design decisions, laws and regulations, and so on in line with public opinion. This, I think, is the challenge of creating smart cities, to build them so that they best serve the common good and not simply the market ambitions of companies or the control desires of states.

And that is a big challenge, when technological development and its rolling out and embedding into society is happening so quickly, with the changes new technologies bring rapidly becoming the new norm. Think, for example, about smartphones and how they have become ubiquitous in a very short space of time and, in so doing, how they have reconfigured notions of privacy. The pace of change is such that there isn't sufficient time for reflection and consideration as to their pros and cons. Policy response has become reactive rather than proactive. Somehow we have to find a way to become more proactive, to create smart cities that maximize the benefits while minimizing the negatives.

114

A Cyber-Urban Space Odyssey

The Spatiality of Contemporary Social Movements

Merlyna
Lim

From #egyptrevolution to #occupyhongkong to #black-livesmatter, from the Tahrir Square in Cairo to the Civic Square in Hong Kong to Times Square in New York, we have witnessed numerous protests and mass movements take place across the globe. Although the causes, goals, and relative success or failure of each differ, one to the other, all share two features in common: each event was intricately networked through the use of social media and each materialized in the mass occupation of a public urban space, in the streets or square of a major city. Although these commonalities have been previously noted, the connection between these two features remains inadequately studied. How can we better understand the interplay between social media and the occupation of urban spaces? How do spaces contribute to insurgent activities and social movements? To what extent do contemporary movements need both cyberspace and physical space to assert influence within a political state?

By treating cyberspace as a technical realm separate from physical space, much current research tends to delocalize what are intensely contextually specific

contestations. Disconnecting cyberactivism from its local contexts has led some scholars to view the power of cyber technologies as socially and politically autonomous and space transcending. This, in turn, has suggested a transformation of politics and society both linear and inevitable: it has endowed ordinary people with greater political freedom to create a virtually empowered civil society that can better pursue—and secure—just political outcomes. Over the years, much of the naiveté that characterizes this thinking has been tempered by more nuanced research on limitations as well as potentialities of cyberactivism. However, the volume of writing that implicitly proposes that revolutions can occur principally, if not solely, through cyberactivism is nevertheless now very large.

For its part, the literature of cyberactivism tends to simply assume that urban physical sites of political contestations are unproblematically available. Focused on the virtual realm, it speculates about whether online mobilizations by themselves lead to political change. Without a close reading of online-offline connections, studies in this mode understandably arrive at mixed outcomes, ranging from negative or no impact to complete success. Studies focused on the physical sites of political insurgencies, on the other hand, often fail to factor digital media networks into their analyses. Without explicit consideration of the reflexivity of spatial interactions, these studies fall short of offering insights both specific to a given experience and general to the relationship between society and digital technology.

That said, the past three decades have witnessed a spatial turn—a shift toward geographically sensitive work that is attentive to context, difference, and the pre-eminence of locale. Sociologists of space, such as Georg Simmel, Michel Foucault, Michel de Certeau, and especially Henri Lefebvre, provided the necessary foundation for subsequent work by Marxist thinkers, such as David Harvey, Edward Soja, and Doreen Massey, that reintroduced spatial consciousness into the social sciences and that prominently place spatial analysis within social theory.[01] To extend this line of thinking, I offer a spatial reading and analysis of social movements that incorporates a close reading of the movements' relationship to cyber-urban space. Here I use "cyber-urban space" as an umbrella term to describe the fluid and complex spatial landscape we live in, with its blurred boundaries between cyber and physical space. Today, more than 50 percent of the world population lives in areas characterized as urban; that percentage is projected to increase to 66 percent by 2050.[02] In 2015, around 40 percent (3.1 billion) of the world population has an internet connection and more than 90 percent of this population lives in urban areas.[03]

At the heart of the dichotomy of cyberactivism vs. place-based spatial analysis is the fallacy of spatial dualism, where the online realm—that is, the digital, the cyber, or the virtual—is treated differently than the offline realm—the physical, or the real. This "digital dualist" perspective is undoubtedly rooted in early works on cyberspace, such as Sherry Turkle's *Life on the Screen*,[04] which operates under the assumption that the "digital self" of the "life on the screen" is "second" to the "first self" of the "real life" in the physical world.[05] Much recent empirical research shows, however, that digital media is rooted or embedded in, and entangled with, the physical world. It is imperative to challenge this spatial dualism and abandon the assumption that online and offline, cyber and physical, are separate entities. Instead, cyber-urban space is socially constructed as contemporaneous space in the contemporary world in which we live. It is produced in the interaction of, and within a continuum of, online and offline relations. For those who live in urban areas where everyday experiences are heavily mediated by electronic gadgets and screens, the boundaries between the lives we live digitally and those we live physically are increasingly blurred. With our perpetual connectedness to the Internet, especially through social media, the division of online and offline is rendered meaningless. Rather than oppose the "real," the "virtual" has become part of it—of our "real" lives. Hence, the cyber-urban space is a fluid hybrid within which we live and our social practices take place. Online and offline, digital and physical, virtual and material: no one of these experiences is any more real than the other.

Having rejected the notion of spatial dualism, we can now approach the making of contemporary social movements as a process that takes place within the space-time continuum. Social movements are essentially about people engaging with power; these movements entail social processes and relations that are historical as well as spatial. Power can be understood as the structural capacity of a certain individual or group to impose its will over another's.[06] In this context, social movements thus can be understood as a collective endeavour to resist, challenge, and negotiate the relationship with this structural capacity, or can be termed "counter-power." Power relations, like other social relations, unfold in space. To think about power and counter-power is, therefore, to invoke a set of spatial relations. Space is not merely a location, or a container in which power relations are negotiated, resisted, and challenged. Rather, space frequently constitutes an object of contestation (of power) in its own right. Power works *in* and *over* spaces. Cyber-urban spaces provide sites for contestations of power (and counter-power) and are themselves part of the contests over access, control, and representation.

In order to scrutinize the complex entanglement of cyber-urban spaces in the making and development of contemporary social movements, it is useful to group this analysis under three headings: *imaginaries*, *practices*, and *trajectories*. A social movement can be seen as a composite of abstract and concrete acts from and in space involving corporeal and cognitive bodies. This composite can be traced from its genesis (in the *imaginary* realm) through its successive developments (involving *practices* of participation, organization, protest, and symbolic activities) to its unfolding as interconnected events along a continuum (its *trajectory*), which takes place within multiple spatialities.

The Imaginaries of Social Movements

Imagination is one of the most important mechanisms for drawing together a community as well as for facilitating an expression of collective resistance. Imagination allows the collectives to project themselves beyond the present to envision a different, more desirable future.

118

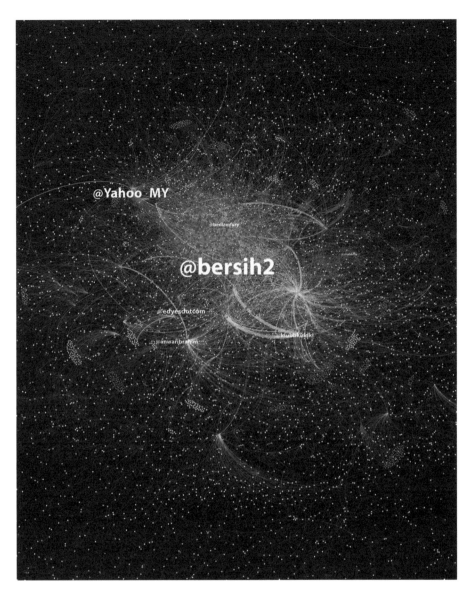

@Yahoo_MY

@bersih2

Connective actions can support collective actions to expand the network of social movement. The map illustrates a form of connective actions facilitated by Twitter that supported and expanded the network of the Malaysian Bersih 3.0 movement. This map was created using Gephi (a social network analytic software) based on tweets generated on the Bersih protest day on April 28, 2012, 1:00 to 7:00 p.m.

Social movements start from this ability to imagine. Alex Khasnabish and Max Haiven argue that such movements are convened by individuals who share a radical understanding and imagination of the world.[07] They contend that radical imagination is the platform upon which to build solidarity and from which to struggle against oppression in the form of robust and resilient movements.[08]

In societies in which people are oppressed or repressed, power is exercised through the propagation of dominant socio-political imaginaries that leave no space for alternative, radical imaginaries to develop. The imaginaries of the State tend to express and re-inscribe power. To radically depart from dominant imaginaries means to have sites for alternative and radical imagination to emerge,

grow, and spread; sites for narratives of resistance to be created, communicated, and practiced. These are sites where adherents ascertain the possibilities of resistance through everyday practices and that allow for interactivity and exchange to take place.

Imagination is a process by which we collectively map the present, narrate it as the result of the past, and then speculate on the future. It is a process that is both cognitive and corporeal that involves the specific (certain political issues) and the mundane (the everyday). By oscillating within a fluid realm between the material and the immaterial, cyber-urban space potentially generates more alternative sites for radical imaginations than either physical space or cyberspace could on its own.

119

Merlyna Lim

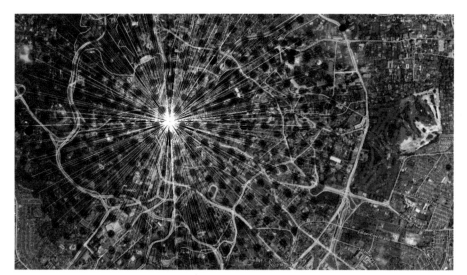

The map illustrates how social space is practiced materially and immaterially. It shows the physical location (geotagged map) of some tweets from April 28, 2012, at 2:00 p.m., during Malaysian Bersih 3.0 protest; there are high concentrations of tweets coming from spots where the protesters congregated in corporeal/material sense.

When traditional civic sites such as mosques and universities are policed and depoliticized and labor unions are destroyed, as was the case in Egypt prior to the 2011 uprisings, social media becomes one initial site where resistance can be fostered and radical imagining can take place.[09] In a different scenario, where the Internet and social media platforms are highly disposed to control and censorship by the State, as was the situation in Hong Kong in 2014, activists make use of traditional sites (school and university classrooms, in this case) to cultivate imaginaries of an alternative future for the society, keeping these brain-storming sessions free of the use of electronic gadgets. Alternative imaginaries become possible not merely through the availability and use of social media, nor through access to less controlled physical sites alone, but because activists can manipulate the power projected in space by effectively navigating between material and immaterial realms. Alternating between the materiality and immateriality of cyber-urban space, the imaginaries of social movements find their place to start and gestate before developing and spreading to wider arenas.

This conceptualization of cyber-urban space as hybrid in nature offers not only more possibilities but also more challenges. With the disappearance of traditional public places in contemporary urban life, social media emerges as new social networks and sociocultural contexts from which radical imagination can emerge. However, social media platforms are neither inherent nor friendly to radical imaginaries projects. Social and cultural spaces of social media are largely dominated by corporations (and other capitalist actors), disposing the take-over by narratives of imagination tailored for the contemporary culture of consumption. The imaginaries that dominate social media are based on simple, simplified, and over-simplified narratives that reduce social and cultural complexities to consumable bytes.[10] Given that the radical imagination is a terrain of political struggle that represents a complex agent-driven collectivism, it is not reducible to ideology and/or narratives in any simplistic sense of consciousness or fetishism.[11] In this regard, social media alone does not provide an autonomous and fertile environment for fomenting the radical imagination. For any radical imaginaries project to prevail in social media, it would require repeatedly "hacking" the dominant consumer culture—that is, invading, subverting, intercepting, and disrupting that culture, such as in a form of culture jamming.

The limitations of social media in facilitating the radical imagination to emerge and grow speak directly to the need for sites where corporeal assemblies can take place. In such assemblies, corporeal bodies would congregate and interact with each other to collectively nurture the imaginaries project. While we use our cognitive minds to imagine, the imagination itself is "corporeal and embodied." As Max Haiven and Khasnabish explain,

> Our imagination is not seated in the mind but involves our senses, feeling and the way we move our bodies in the world. Bodies that are marked, exploited or circumscribed, will imagine the world and their personal and political potentialities very differently than those that "pass" without notice, fear or exploitation in the world.[12]

The Practices of Social Movements

Social movements involve a set of practices that render mobilizations possible and sustain them in various ways.

From the existing literature on social movement theory, we learn that the practices of social movements can be clustered into four categories: participation, organization, protest, and symbolic activities.[13] Participation includes practices through which social movement actors engage other individuals to join in the various stages of the movement; in the early stage, for example, or at the height of mobilization.[14] Organization practices include "social practices through which activists are able to plan meetings, arrange protests, and coordinate actions."[15] Protest practices entail "the performance of public protests," and symbolic practices include "those social practices linked to the development of discourses, meanings and interpretations about contentious issues and protests."[16]

In the predigital era, these practices were clustered based on where social movement actors were physically located. In our contemporary world, the practices of social movements are structured under the logic of network that can transcend the barrier of space and time and thus can challenge space-time-bound relations.[17] And, yet, the logic of network is not placeless. In cyber-urban space, the networks connect practices of social movements in specific places—spaces that acquire meaning through identity politics in certain moments in time—to specific information and communication flows.

In the practices of participation, activists continue to recruit new participants by connecting with traditional civic associations, such as churches, universities, and schools in the initial stage of Hong Kong's Occupy Central movement, and mosques in the Bersih (electoral reform) movement in Malaysia, or with social and cultural clusters, such as soccer fan clubs in Egypt.[18] These practices, however, also extend to new types of social networks facilitated by social media and blogospheres. In the 2011 Egypt uprisings, the April 6 Youth Movement—one of the main organizers of the Tahrir protests—made use of Facebook to expand its recruitment network, while also cultivating its existing network of labor activist composed of textile factory workers.[19] Such practices connecting traditional and new civic spaces pervade today's social movements because social media spaces are now intimately entangled with our everyday social practices—a reality that cannot be separated from the disappearance of public and communal spaces, the deterioration of traditional social networks, and the decline of social capital.[20]

Similar patterns can be found within the practices of organization and protest, even though they sometimes differ from one context to another. In places where the internet population is low and access to social media is unequally distributed, such as in Egypt and Tunisia, meetings and other coordinating actions still need to take advantage of traditional networks, in addition to online social networking platforms. By December 2010, Tunisia counted only one million Facebook users, concentrated in Tunis and the surrounding area.[21] In villages and towns located in the interior regions that lacked internet infrastructure, protests were coordinated over a hybrid network combining mobile phones, pocket cameras, community radios, coffee houses, and face-to-face conversations.[22] The Bersih movement offers a different story. In Malaysia, internet penetration is above 60 percent: in urban areas, where much of the activism of the movement took place, the rate is even higher (in Greater Kuala Lumpur, for example, it is 87 percent). In this movement, nearly all organizational practices were facilitated online.[23] Activists publicized public events on websites and blogs, planned meetings and coordinated actions prior to the protests on Facebook, and used Twitter during the protests as an on-site networking tool.[24]

Since the "Battle of Seattle" in 1999, activists have started extending the philosophy of activism and direct action to "the world of electronic information exchange and communication" by employing a set of tactics called online direct action (ODA).[25] Some earlier forms of ODA (for instance, online petitions, virtual sit-ins, and hacktivism) were developed as digital analogues to traditional tactics (paper petitions, physical sit-ins, and sabotage). As the prevalence of social media increased, practices of protest extended into the spheres of Facebook, Twitter, Instagram, and the like. Currently, one of the most popular types of social media–based protest is "hashtag activism," an effort to collectively curate a massive amount of short statements by using certain hashtags.[26] The new social media terrain offers endless possibilities to facilitate protest and, especially, symbolic activities. By joining in #blacklivesmatter, for example, an individual might participate not only in the protest against the police violence against black youths but also in discourses around relevant issues such as institutionalized racism and state violence. In addition, the individual might also express his or her own interpretation of the issues.

However, physical sites of assembly are still important to the corporeal practices of protest and its symbolism. Staging protests on the main streets and in the public squares of a city is still perceived as the most effective way to collectively express resistance, demonstrate the strength of a movement, and directly challenge the dominant power.[27] Bodies, in their visibility to the public, are central in the struggle for power. The body itself is the site of both subjugation and resistance.[28] Protest is, according to a sociologist Theresa O'Keefe, "intimately connected to corporeal realities whereby the dissenting body disrupts—literally and figuratively—by presence and action."[29] By occupying public spaces with visible bodies, social movements challenge the dominant power both symbolically and corporeally.

Evidently, the practices of contemporary social movements are not removed from the territorial character of momentous movements in the history of humanity. Instead, they extend "from the space of places to the space of flows."[30] In the contemporary social movement, cyber-urban space is not simply a backdrop, a site, or a point of struggle; it is also a *resource* for participation, organization, protest, and symbolic practices.

The Trajectories of Social Movements

Social movements are transient phenomena: they arise, they develop, they interact with power (the authority and/or mainstream politics), they fade, and then they are gone, leaving behind a residue or impact. A social movement therefore encompasses multiple events within its trajectory. These "events"—meaning the various actions enacted by various actors in and around a shared imaginary—do not occur in isolation from each other. They are interconnected, interacting with each other.

The interconnections between events are germane to the life cycles of social movements (also known as "protest cycles").[31] The dynamics of these cycles are complex, influenced by internal and external circumstances including larger economic cycles, and they are beyond the scope of this article.[32] However, the role of space and spatiality in sustaining the life cycle of a social movement at various junctures along its trajectory is important to consider here. Borrowing from Pamela Oliver and Daniel Myers, we can conceive of a social movement as a distribution of events across a population.[33] A social movement starts with an event, is sustained by more events, rises when many events happen involving a large proportion of the population, and fades when it stops generating future events.

In cyber-urban space, events are networked and their boundaries are porous. Through numerous labyrinths of cyber-urban space, information and narrative of resistance as well as their embodied emotion and sentiment can travel and diffuse from one event to another. Contemporary social movements make use of hybrid spatial networks connecting diverse sites and localities, involving traditional and new social linkages, old and new media, and large and small media within the cyber, physical, and interstitial spaces of the cyber-urban milieu. In the event that one media channel becomes blocked, information finds its way through other available channels, like rainwater running on the streets. This is the beauty of the hybrid network. It offers information paths of least resistance. The multitiered system is fully redundant and resilient, ensuring that no information can be halted, even in the case of a technological blackout. In Egypt, when the Mubarak regime cut off virtually all internet access in an effort to contain the protests, Egyptians connected to each other in person and through traditional networks, leading to more participation in the uprisings. In the case of Occupy Central in Hong Kong, when the internet connection was shut down in October 2014, making social media networks defunct, the meshed phone-to-phone network application Firechat was used to revive interconnections between events.

The diffusion of information has a direct consequence on the proliferation of protests. As information easily travels from one place to another, the struggle for justice, freedom, and dignity journey with it; connecting not only one mobile phone to another but also an individual to various networks of individuals and to a network of networks. These hybrid human-communication-information networks in cyber-urban space form connective structures that link one event to another, from the local to the national to the global and vice versa. These connective structures help social movements to generate collective actions in various locales among individuals who share collective identity and act upon it by reproducing the protests. Beyond this, connective structures also help by linking collective actions with individuals who perform connective actions. In contrast to collective actions, where group actions coalesce around collective identities, in connective actions people contribute to movements through personalized expressions facilitated by their online connectivity.[34] Because connective actions rely on loose ties formed by digital communications networks, they are temporal and transient in nature. At times, connective actions can support collective actions to expand the network of social movement. At other times, they can also conflict with collective actions. If connective actions hijack and weaken collective actions, a movement may lose deeper forms of engagement needed to sustain itself.

The redundancy of hybrid networks in cyber-urban space is significant to the trajectories of social movements, particularly for two reasons. First, an ability to move fluidly between the various networks of cyber-urban space (be they physical or virtual) is important for navigating control and hegemony. By being able to appear and disappear, become visible and invisible, be present and hidden from the gaze and control of authority, a social movement can maintain and protect its existence while expanding its participation and replicating its events in multiple sites. Second, by diffusing in multiple networks, the movement can propagate a decentralized and distributed network of resistance, which by its very nature is robust and resilient. In times of crisis, the movement may disappear from the public space, but it may not completely perish. Instead, its roots may grow and start another cycle.

Conclusions

Power is not an easy entity to observe. The act of exercising power, however, is observable as it unfolds in space. Social movements are about the engagement of power by collectivized individuals and, therefore, are most visible as they act toward space: contesting it, occupying it, claiming it. By analyzing social movements spatially, this study has exposed cyber-urban space as not only the *site for* but also a *part of* the contestation of power. This hybrid space has emerged as integral to the initiating and development of contemporary social movements. Its fluidity and resilience suggest that cyber-urban space will continue to be part of any future social movement, presenting new possibilities as well as new complexities and challenges for protests' imaginaries, practices, and trajectories.

01. Georg Simmel, *The Sociology of Georg Simmel*, trans. and ed. Kurt H. Wolff (New York: Simon and Schuster, 1950). Michel Foucault, "Space, Knowledge and Power," in *The Foucault Reader*, ed. Paul Rabinow (New York: Pantheon, 1984), 239–56. Michel de Certeau, *The Practices of Everyday Life*, trans. Steven Rendall (Berkeley: University of California Press, 1984). Henri Lefebvre, *The Production of Space* (Oxford: Blackwell, 1974). David Harvey, *Justice, Nature and the Geography of Difference* (London: Wiley-Blackwell, 1996). Edward W. Soja, *Postmodern Geographies: The Reassertion of Space in Critical Social Theory* (London: Verso, 1989). Doreen Massey, *For Space* (London: Sage, 2005).

02. United Nations, *World Urbanization Prospects: The 2014 Revision, Highlights* (New York: Department of Economic and Social Affairs, 2014), 2.

03. "Internet Users," Internet Live Stats, accessed May 24, 2015, http://www.internetlivestats.com/internet-users.

04. Sherry Turkle, *Life on the Screen: Identity in the Age of the Internet* (New York: Simon and Schuster, 1995).

05. For more on the critique of digital dualism, see Nathan Jurgenson, "Digital Dualism versus Augmented Reality," *Cyborgology*, February 22, 2011, http://thesocietypages.org/cyborgology/2011/02/24/digital-dualism-versus-augmented-reality.

06. Manuel Castells, "Communication, Power and Counter-Power in the Network Society," *International Journal of Communication* 1 (2007): 259.

07. Alex Khasnabish and Max Haiven, "Why Social Movements Need the Radical Imagination," *Tranformation*, July 22, 2014, https://www.opendemocracy.net/transformation/alex-khasnabish-max-haiven/why-social-movements-need-radical-imagination.

08. Ibid.

09. Merlyna Lim, "Seeing Spatially: People, Networks and Movements in Digital and Urban Spaces," *International Development and Planning Review* 36, no. 1 (January 2014): 58–59.

10. Merlyna Lim, "Many Clicks but Little Sticks: Social Media Activism in Indonesia," *Journal of Contemporary Asia* 43, no. 4 (November 2013): 636.

11. Max Haiven and Alex Khasnabish, "What Is the Radical Imagination?," *Affinities* 4, no. 2 (Fall 2010), i–xxxvii.

12. Ibid.

13. Alice Mattoni and Emiliano Trere, "Media Practices, Mediation Processes, and Mediatization in the Study of Social Movements," *Communication Theory* 24, no. 3 (August 2014): 252.

14. Ibid., 259.

15. Ibid.

16. Ibid.

17. Manuel Castells, *The Rise of the Network Society*, vol. 1, *The Information Age: Economy, Society, and Culture* (Oxford: Blackwell, 2000).

18. Merlyna Lim, "Clicks, Cabs, and Coffee Houses: Social Media and Oppositional Movements in Egypt, 2004–2011," *Journal of Communication* 62, no. 2 (April 2012): 242.

19. Ibid., 240.

20. Lim, "Seeing Spatially," 55.

21. "Tunisia," Internet World Stats, February 1, 2011, http://www.internetworldstats.com/africa.htm#tn.

22. Merlyna Lim, "Framing Bouazizi: 'White Lies, Hybrid Network, and Collective/Connective Action in the 2010–2011 Tunisian Uprising," *Journalism: Theory, Practice and Criticism* 14, no. 7 (October 2013): 934.

23. Merlyna Lim, "Digital Media and Malaysia's Electoral Reform Movement," in *Citizenship and Democratization in Postcolonial Southeast Asia*, ed. Ward Berenschot, Henk Schulte Nordholt, and Laurens Bakker (Leiden: Brill Publisher, forthcoming).

24. Ibid.

25. Ricardo Dominguez, "Electronic Disturbance: An Interview," in *Cultural Resistance Reader*, ed. Stephen Duncombe (London: Verso, 2002), 390.

26. A hashtag is a type of metadata consisting of a word or an unspaced phrase prefixed by the hash character (#). It is used to cluster conversations around certain topics on social networking sites.

27. Lim, "Seeing Spatially," 62.

28. Michel Foucault, *The History of Sexuality*, vol. 1, trans. Robert Hurley (New York: Random House, 1978).

29. Theresa O'Keefe, "Power, Body Politics and Dirty Protest" (lecture, Jailers, Prisons, and Prisoners seminar series, Centro de Investigacao e Estudos de Sociologia, Lisbon, March 23, 2012).

30. Manuel Castells, *Networks of Outrage and Hope: Social Movements in the Internet Age* (Cambridge, UK: Polity Press, 2012), 61.

31. Sydney Tarrow, *Power in Movement: Social Movement and Contentious Politics* (Cambridge: Cambridge University Press, 1998).

32. Andre G. Frank and Marta Fuentes, "On Studying the Cycles in Social Movements," *Research in Social Movements, Conflicts and Change* 17 (1994): 173.

33. Pamela E. Oliver and Daniel J. Myers, "Diffusion Models of Cycles of Protest as a Theory of Social Movements" (lecture, Congress of the International Sociological Association, Montreal, July 26, 1998).

34. W. Lance Bennett and Alexandra Segerberg, "The Logic of Connective Action: Digital Media and the Personalization of Contentious Politics," *Information, Communication & Society* 15, no. 5 (2012): 752.

123

Fiber-Optical Illusions
Outwitting the Smart Corridor

Caitlin
Blanchfield

Borders exist across the strata of the real: they are the speech acts that limn geopolitics, the morphologies that mark ecological transition, the apparatuses that measure mobility. They are simultaneously malleable, leveraged, and static. Historically, borders were recorders of data, the boundary survey being just one example of such geographic stocktaking. Yet as the nature of data changes in the twenty-first century—one in which it seems the nation-state is as undermined as it is overdetermined—the border as a concept and as a territorial formation is reconfigured in the shape of a shared public-private authority. It is through the act of data collection, now a primary occupation of both the state and the corporation, and through its mobilization that landscapes of difference emerge. The ethnoscapes, technoscapes, and financescapes that Arjun Appadurai so lucidly describes in *Modernity at Large*, for instance, find their intersection in twenty-first-century border making.[01] The border by extension is a prism, bottleneck, and departure point for lines of flight, according to rubrics like Appadurai's.

Infrastructure transverses and reinforces the marking out of difference, and it transforms it. In an era of free trade, information infrastructure like fiber-optic cable and broadband generally can dictate who gets to move across space and who is afforded access to information. Today, information infrastructure is no different than those systems of physical mobility that preceded it. Infrastructure needs capital in abundant supply. The

American highway system offers a case in point: a configuration that both speaks to and facilitates the conquest of land, the movement of commodities, the creation of a national imaginary. During the 1950s, the highways generated labor and introduced standards for efficient flows of people and products. The national railway system was the highway's precursor and established a cycle of dependency between immigration, labor exploitation, mobility, capital, and resource extraction. As historian Richard White has noted, the railroads collapsed time and space with speed and data. Empirical calculations of the value of goods and the rate of their transport determined where railroads stopped and how often cargo was hauled, conflating cost and distance through a numbers game.[02] Western Union, the telegraph carrier, provides another early instantiation—an analog in terms of colonial expansion, the relay of information, and the conflation of communication and finance. Wiring news gave way to wiring money when the West was no longer a land to conquer but rather one to cultivate.

Networked though these routes were, the history of mobility and communication in the United States generally tracks from East to West, following Manifest Destiny, connecting new centers of population, new markets, and new industries. From the stagecoach to the interstate, the omnibus function of transcontinental infrastructure underscores the inseparability of transportation and information transmission, both ideologically and administratively. In 1920, Frederick Jackson Turner famously noted that, in America, "the slender paths of aboriginal intercourse have been broadened and interwoven into the complex mazes of modern commercial lines ... like the steady growth of a complex nervous system."[03] In language echoing Turner's, Samuel Morse anticipated "those nerves," which were to "diffuse, with the speed of thought, a knowledge of all that is occurring throughout the land."[04] Morse, the semiotician of dots and dashes, envisioned a telegraph system not operated along commercial lines, however, but rather licensed by the government and administered through a federal organization, much like the postal service.[05] His code became the military's default form of communication throughout one civil and two world wars. To command a territory meant not only to physically possess the land but also to oversee it—to know what transpired across the nation and thus be prepared to intervene.

Technology made speedy the transmission of intelligence, but the conduits through which code traveled were still stubbornly grounded and needed to cross the expanse of land their very purpose was to negate. So telegraph lines followed the tracks of the railroad. Rights-of-way were already established along the tracks, and railroad stations (along with hotels) were often the places that both needed and could afford the nascent communication technology. What's more, US Code granted right-of-way to telegraphy, as it had railroads, through any public lands for future development.[06] Since its early history, then, information communications technology (ICT) advanced through public-private partnership in the United States, its infrastructure determined by transportation needs and serving commercial and state interests.

Since the 1990s, however, the spines along which communication and transportation comingle have aligned vertically. Globalization, as we know, engendered new frontiers of international trade, where commodities and concepts were thrust onto open markets. If in the past the railroad and telegraph collapsed time and space, digital communication flattened it. That is, at least, for some.

The laying of fiber-optic cable, the lifeline of late capitalism, can reinforce the trajectories of colonialism, as Keller Easterling and other sociologists and historians have recently pointed out. In *Extrastatecraft*, Easterling makes evident how broadband routing retraces industrial networks of the nineteenth century, established when the United States and Great Britain dominated industrial trade and the telegraph lines on which it ran. The first fiber-optic cable laid in Africa, for instance, connected the port cities of colonial empires—places like Casablanca, Lagos, and Dakar—to Mauritius, India, and then areas further into Asia. The corporations that now broker in broadband and fiber optics are reconfigured alliances of the same industrial powers that abetted empire.[07] Looking at this global context, it seems no coincidence, then, that in the United States, battles over new fiber-optic lines (bundled with plans for freeway expansion and light rail in "smart corridors") are taking place on Native American reservations—the spatial vestiges of the nation's own colonialist past, which encompass much of the remaining open land of the American West.

The glass spindles of fiber optics dictate access to information, ease of communication, and availability of products and services found on the Internet. Their positioning—within locations that the telecommunications companies predict will be lucrative—enables the kind of connectivity that facilitates learning, provides opportunity, widens spheres of influence, and enables all of the time-wasting indulgences housed on the Internet. As a result, it becomes important to ask: Who lays these cables? How is their path determined? Who benefits from their placement? A look at the plans for a "multimodal" highway expansion—a so-called NAFTA superhighway— sheds a little light on these questions.

The Canamex Corridor

The Canamex Corridor is a two-lane highway at its US entrepôt. From the Mexican border, the road, raised and snaking, canopies over the city of Nogales, Sonora, crosses through a checkpoint, and turns into US 19, the main artery for scruffy, sleepy Nogales, Arizona. It is a humble stretch of pavement, yet on paper, the corridor is a formidable thing: a conduit of commerce and tourism that wends from Mexico City to Edmonton, in Alberta, Canada. According to the Arizona Commerce Authority, a private organization working closely with the state's Department of Transportation, it is a "smart corridor," meaning that the roadway will be lined with fiber-optic cable and outfitted for broadband capability.[08] The stated purpose: to allow rapid communication between tax-free inland ports and truck drivers, to ease passage for those truck drivers at special customs stations located fifty miles from the Mexican border, and to bring high-speed internet to rural communities. The reality: to advocate pipe dreams and legislative proposals promoted by and for local congress people and private interest groups.

With its name derived from the countries it connects, the Canamex is a piece of aspirational infrastructure. Conceived in the wake of the 1994 passage of the North American Free Trade Agreement (NAFTA), the plan is now picking up steam in Arizona in particular, as that state makes a bid to become a new center for importing

126

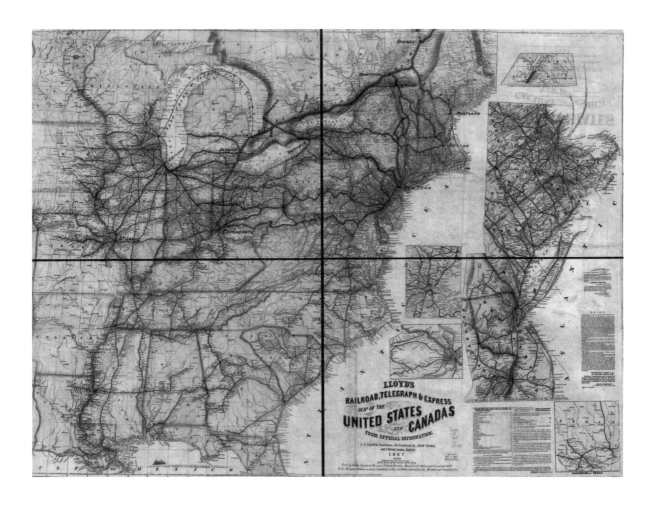

goods from Mexico. But as a framework, and as a set of infrastructure upgrades that will likely happen, it raises some vital concerns for an emerging geography of information. Most important among these is why the federal government is relying on infrastructure upgrades and public-private partnerships to bring information access to rural and sparsely populated areas. What information deserts will this type of approach leave in its wake? What geographies of difference, in terms of technology, does it already reveal?

The quick collusion of extragovernmental organizations like the Arizona Commerce Authority and telecommunications companies underscores the need to remain skeptical of the rhetoric of "access" in service of corporate hegemony. It also indicates the poverty of resources at the state level. The Arizona Commerce Authority was created after the dissolution of the Arizona Department of Commerce. The state government effectively subcontracted the task of stimulating economic growth to an organization whose advisory board is comprised of CEOs from real estate companies, banks, and manufacturing.

Moreover, the commerce authority, which has the power to grant right-of-way to broadband companies, is charged with making the laying of cable palatable to corporations like Comcast, AT&T, and Cox. As is the case with so many government contracts, a public good must be pitched to corporate power, in the language of the private sector. This is one of many reasons why NAFTA has generated such inequality across geopolitical boundaries. The same framework for ICT infrastructure is not available in northern Mexico; the US corporations invited to lay broadband in Arizona, Utah, Nevada, and Montana do not operate in Sonora and Sinaloa. There are no organizations equivalent to the Arizona Commerce Authority in those states. Instead, the uneven deployment of information infrastructure along a free-trade corridor perpetuates the exploitative labor practices that make ferrying goods through Mexico inexpensive. The rapid and efficient access to consumers, enabled by the corridor, makes the United States

127

Above: Lloyd's Railroad, Telegraph & Express Map of the United States and Canadas, 1867.

Caitlin Blanchfield

Canamex
Corridor.

a desirable market.[09] High-speed internet is also used to expedite the off-loading and communication processes in and between Arizona's inland ports. In the global era, roads may seem perversely grounded, but they are also reminders that control of the land is still elemental to the movement of commodities and the creation of wealth—no matter how digital those two things have become. Control over the land equals command of information, so it is important to understand who possesses that control. While the government can lease rights-of-way, the facilitation of development through and alongside these jurisdictional spines is in the hands of the public-private partnership, a murky constellation of advisory CEOs, former government officials, current elected officers, and the corporations that lay cable and build the inland ports that cable connects.

"No Build"

I could expound further on the duplicity of an act that provides high-speed access to commodities and their shepherds while denying it to immigrants seeking work or family in the United States. I could wonder whether, because infrastructure appears invisible, it is easier for the state not to take responsibility for it? I could ask, Shouldn't the government provide internet access to all citizens? Moreover, I could question why it is that fiber optics is only an initiative in the United States stretch of the Canamex, when it could be equally (if not more) useful in rural Mexican villages. These are important issues, but in the interest of resisting the simply critical lens, I want to turn instead to the alternative geographies of information that resistance to this highway has forged

Sells, Arizona.

and strengthened. These are networks of communication that do not rely on existing axes of mobility but instead work within local grassroots networks, across the lines of solidarity of activist bloggers and between the hubs of protest and organization that dot vulnerable landscapes throughout the American West.

Not far off US 19 in southern Arizona is the Tohono O'odham Nation, a staggering landscape of saguaros and ocotillos hemmed in by mountains and sandstone plateaus. Its capital is Sells, a town of just under 3,000. This appears to be the kind of small community that the Canamex broadband initiative would benefit. Instead, it has become a site of resistance against the highway, both of its local expansion and of its broader ideology. Fighting to prevent the creation of Loop 202, a four-lane ring road north of Phoenix that would divert Canamex traffic around the congested city, activists from the Tohono O'odham Nation called on O'odham tribes in Arizona and northern Mexico. Together they petitioned tribal leaders to reject the construction of the freeway on their land, which would have bisected Gila mountain range, a site sacred to the tribe. They allied themselves with other O'odham people in Sonora, Mexico, and throughout Arizona, convening meetings in Sells. They also found partners in the affluent suburb of Laveen, whose NIMBYism they used to leverage a greater platform of protest against the Phoenix city government. They rallied college students to picket and became regular attendees at city council meetings,

besieging representatives with questions and counterproposals. In short, in opposing the Canamex Corridor they constructed their own avenues of communication and solidarity in both digital and physical space. Blogs and email chains with links to articles dispersed research among local O'odham and their allies. The dirt roads of the reservation became the paths by which young activists could connect with the established leaders in the O'odham community who had historical knowledge about development on their land. City hall became a site where Native Americans who historically have felt disenfranchised from electoral politics sat with suburban residents to envision alternative methods of land use. Ultimately this unlikely coalition succeeded in passing a "no build" resolution that barred construction of the highway.

The efforts of the O'odham solidarity network reached beyond the megalopolitan region of Phoenix and Tucson to articulate a broader critique of neoliberalism and free trade to its constituents and to forge reciprocal bonds of knowledge gathering and sharing across the West Coast and Midwest. Alex Soto, one of the group's organizers (and one-half of the hip-hop duo Shining Soul), spoke to me of friends in Chicago conducting research on a similar highway project connecting Laredo, Texas, to Duluth, Minnesota. There they discovered that the lands that the highway would appropriate cut through the territory of a tribe in Kansas that had been relocated to the area from southern Illinois, another region this road (and its

129

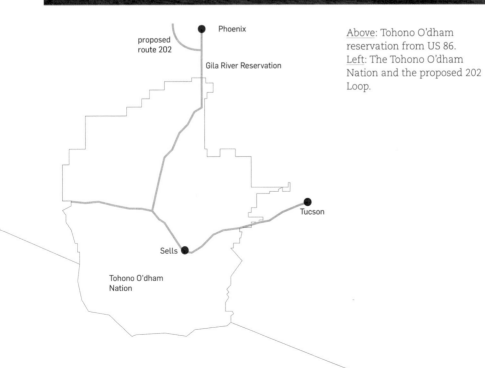

proposed
route 202

Phoenix

Gila River Reservation

Tucson

Sells

Tohono O'dham
Nation

Above: Tohono O'dham
reservation from US 86.
Left: The Tohono O'dham
Nation and the proposed 202
Loop.

sprawling roadside amenities) would bisect. Such circumstances make plain the particularly destructive effect the infrastructure of free trade is having on Native American reservations. Corrupt leadership has led to rapidly sold land rights and the invitation to build the outlet malls, service centers, and lighted billboards that line these corridors. Soto also spoke of his tour down the West Coast from Vancouver to San Francisco, where he was able to educate other politically minded musicians about the corridor and enlist them to help with research. The tour bus became another vehicle of communication and information dissemination, creating friction along the smart corridor. Though the struggle of Alex and his partners had a particular local urgency, efforts to understand the context that gave rise to this highway and to propose an alternative future created a more networked, informed, perhaps even global, tribal region. It also undermined a center periphery divide between Phoenix and the reservation.

Even as it encroached upon the reservation, Loop 202 would have to reinscribe the barrier between the O'odham and metropolitan Phoenix: protesting against it has eroded those barriers and prevented further commercialization of the land.

If the laying of fiber-optic cable often retraces the pathways connecting colonial markets, then can the mapping of alternative networks of information sharing—both digital and physical—open up anticapitalist cartographies; ones that in fact hijack the communicatory fabric of those systems of power they aim to resist? "Multimodality" has become the word of choice for infrastructure expansionists, connoting not just wider roads, selective screenings, and tax-free zones at their margins but also broadband and capacity for high-speed rail. Yet couldn't multimodality also refer to a rhizomatic strategy for contesting hegemonic power, creating alliances across and between borders through research, information sharing, and protest?

01. Arjun Appadurai, *Modernity at Large: Cultural Dimensions of Globalization* (Minneapolis: University of Minnesota Press, 1995), 33.

02. For White's theory of railroads and "absolute space," a hybrid space of physical geography and abstracted calculations of value, see Richard White, *Railroaded: The Transcontinentals and the Making of Modern America* (New York: W.W. Norton & Company, 2011), 144.

03. Frederick Jackson Turner, *The Frontier in American History* (New York: Henry Holt and Company, 1920), 15.

04. Samuel Morse, passage from "Electro-Magnetic Telegraphs," Report No. 753, House of Representatives, 25th Congress, 2nd Session, 8–9, quoted in Joshua D. Wolff, *Western Union and the Creation of the American Corporate Order, 1845–1893* (Cambridge: Cambridge University Press, 2013).

05. Ibid.

06. See *Code of Federal Regulations*, Right of Way through Public Lands Granted to Railroads, title 43, section 934; and *Code of Federal Regulations*, Rights-of-Way for Railway, Telegraph, and Telephone Lines; Town-Site Stations, title 25, section 312. The latter statute reads: "A right of way for a railway, telegraph, and telephone line through any Indian reservation in any State or Territory, except Oklahoma, or through any lands reserved for an Indian agency or for other purposes in connection with the Indian service, or through any lands which have been allotted in severalty to any individual Indian under any law or treaty, but which have not been conveyed to the allottee with full power of alienation, is granted to any railroad company organized under the laws of the United States, or of any State or Territory…"

07. Keller Easterling, *Extrastatecraft: The Power of Infrastructure* (New York: Zone, 2014), 104.

08. "Smart Corridor," Canamex Corridor Coalition: The Safe, Smart, and Secure (S^3) Corridor, http://www.canamex.org/canamex/smart-corridor.

09. According to the Canamex website, the hourly average manufacturing wage in China and India is $0.25, in Mexico it is $2.10, in the United States it is $17.20. "Statistics," Canamex Corridor Coalition, http://www.canamex.org/statistics

Image Credits

127: Library of Congress, Geography and Map Division.

128: Illustration by the author.

129: Photo © AARoads: http://www.aaroads.com/guide.php?page=s0086az.

130: Photo and illustration by the author.

Caitlin Blanchfield

Predictive Geographies

Mark
Shepard

Information today is embedded within and distributed across a variety of urban and exurban geographies. Indeed, it has become difficult to point to situations where information systems *do not* play a direct or indirect role in the disposition of physical features of the city and its surroundings, or of human activity as it affects and is affected by them. On any given day, we gain access to transportation systems using a magnetic strip card or Radio Frequency Identification (RFID) tag to pay a fare. While on the run, we coordinate meeting times and places through SMS text messaging on our mobile phones. We cluster in cafes and parks where Wi-Fi is free to check email on a laptop. We check in at our favorite venues using social media apps and leave tips for strangers about what to do there. We drive cars with onboard navigation systems that map optimal routes to a destination, updating in real time to take into account current traffic congestion, construction activity, and special events. We pass through public spaces blanketed by CCTV surveillance cameras monitored by machine vision systems running advanced facial recognition and object-tracking algorithms.

These geographies of information are increasingly driven by data. Data is the raw material from which they are formed, by which they are constituted, and through which they take shape.[01] This data takes a variety of forms: samples, indexes, measurements, abstractions, and representations of the physical world and the events and activities that transpire within it. It varies in size (big data, small data); is qualitative and quantitative in nature; is structured, semistructured, and unstructured in organization; and may be captured, produced, or derived through a variety of processes and procedures.[02] Our smartphones capture data on where we've been and produce location histories from which our mobility patterns can be derived. Our fitness activity trackers monitor a range of health factors—heart rate, steps taken, floors climbed, calories burned, even sleep quality—and produce representations of our progress toward self-identified goals that are shared and aggregated through online portals.

Data that information systems collect, transmit, and store promises greater control over the performance of urban systems and new insights into how the city is inhabited collectively. Embedded systems monitor, manage, and regulate utility services and critical urban infrastructure. Camera networks monitor street intersections and issue traffic violations using automated license plate recognition software. Social media platforms like Twitter and Foursquare provide new ways of tracking how we move, whom we are with, where we go, and what we think of where we've been. Data on trending venues, popular neighborhoods, peak times, and common frequencies enable us to map patterns of mobility and activity in a more dynamic and fine-grained manner. With the advent of big data, some claim we have the opportunity to connect, aggregate, analyze, and integrate data about the urban environment in ways that enable us to better visualize, model, and predict urban processes; simulate probable outcomes; and lead to more efficient and sustainable cities.[03]

Yet data is relatively meaningless in raw form. From data to information to knowledge to understanding to wisdom: each step up the stack requires some form of processing (correlation, interpretation, abstraction, analysis, reduction, aggregation, etc.) that adds value to the previous step.[04] Small data, such as that produced through surveys, interviews, or methods of direct observation common to the social sciences, has to date been processed primarily by people. Often designed to address specific research questions, small data focuses on specific cases and tells individual, nuanced, and contextual stories.[05] With the advent of big data, algorithms are playing an increasing role in the process by which data becomes information. Data-mining algorithms, for instance, operate on large datasets and look for patterns in data that are not readily apparent to people. As algorithms replace people in the derivation of information from data, the production of knowledge becomes a process shared by human and nonhuman actors.

Algorithms also do work in the world. They play a key role in the constitution of particular physical spaces, such as airport check-in lounges or supermarket check-out aisles, for instance. These kinds of spaces rely on algorithms to perform their basic programmatic functions. When the information systems upon which these spaces depend fail, the spatial program transforms: an airport lounge becomes a waiting room, a supermarket aisle becomes a warehouse.[06] Algorithms also influence the organization of space at urban and regional scales. Consider, for example, the role of high-speed trading algorithms in the reorganization of the financial sector of lower Manhattan. When algorithms running on computers located in high-speed trading hubs compete with each other, the latencies of electronic transactions measured in microseconds become critical. The distance between the servers running these algorithms and the trading hubs can make a difference measured in millions of dollars per second. As face-to-face trading is replaced by electronic trading, the value of location becomes more a function of proximity to high-speed communications backbone infrastructure than to centers of human interaction and exchange.[07]

Matters become more complicated when algorithms gain predictive or anticipatory agency. As we move beyond the initial practices and promises of both the smart city and the smart citizen,[08] we find information-processing capacity approaching a higher order of magnitude. These emerging information systems operate on aggregate datasets using predictive analytics. Predictive analytics refers to a variety of statistical techniques—modeling, machine learning, and data mining—that analyze current and historical facts to make predictions about future events. While predictive analytics is closely entwined with data mining, the inferences derived through predictive analytics extend beyond retrospective pattern analysis to incorporate more prospective and anticipatory postulations.

Where data mining describes the exploratory process of finding patterns and information within data, predictive analytics attempts to leverage that information derived from data to anticipate meaning and make predictions about the future.

Predictive analytics has found widespread application in marketing. The *New York Times* published an article a few years ago that outlined the process by which big-box retailer Target deployed predictive analytics to identify women likely to be in their early stages of pregnancy so that it could target advertising to them before their child was born. The algorithm that was behind the analytics was dubbed the "pregnancy-prediction algorithm."[09] Predictive analytics is also at work in social media. The popular online dating website OkCupid uses a relatively simple algorithm based on self-reported data—how you respond to a question, how you want your prospective partner to respond to the same question, and how important the question is to you—to predict compatible romantic partners. Facebook recently experimented with manipulating the emotional content of more than half a million of its users' news feeds. Through altering the number of positive and negative posts users saw based on a simple sentiment-analysis algorithm, the psychological study examined how emotions could be spread through social media.[10] The study found that sentiment is in fact predictably contagious across social networks, where positive expressions beget positive expressions, and negative beget negative.[11]

Predictive analytics has long played a role in military and intelligence applications. Cybernetics pioneer Norbert Wiener worked on predicting flight paths and evasive maneuvers of German warplanes in World War II to assist in their targeting. Today, ArcGIS, a leading software platform for working with Geographic Information Systems (GIS), offers the Predictive Analysis Tools Add-In that provides drone operators with the ability to query digital aerial photographs, imagery from satellites, digital pictures, or even scanned maps to build predictive targeting models from environmental datasets, known parameters, or historic sightings.[12] This tool enables the prediction of targets based on doctrine (established rules for identifying target locations); when a clear doctrine is absent, it uses evidence based on Signals Intelligence (SIGINT)[13] and the like to construct a doctrine based on locations the target has been known to frequent. It is interesting to note that while the military historically has been the originator of technology transfer for commercial applications—GPS technology or the Internet, for example—for ArcGIS it has become just another market segment for their spatial analysis and prediction products, alongside government agencies, real estate developers, and urban-planning firms.

These predictive processes take on qualities of what I have described elsewhere as sentience.[14] The term "sentient" foregrounds the subjective relations that underlie technologies currently being promoted by the marketing departments of high-tech firms as "smart."[15] Sentience, derived from the Latin word *sentire*, refers to the ability to feel or perceive subjectively but does not necessarily include human faculties of reasoning or self-awareness. This is to say, the possession of "sapience," meaning "knowledge," is not required for something to be sentient. Here it is important to differentiate between the act of sensing and that of having a sensation. Sensing, the thinking goes, is something animals, some plants, and some machines can do. It involves a sensing organ or device that enables the organic or inorganic system of which it is a part to actively respond to things happening around it. An organism or system may sense heat, light, sound, or the presence of rain, for example. Yet having a sensation or a feeling is something that goes beyond mere sensing, for it involves an internal state in which information about the environment is processed by that organism or system so that it comes to have a subjective character. "Qualia" is the philosophical term for this, which Daniel Dennett defines as "an unfamiliar term for something that could not be more familiar to each of us: the ways things seem to us."[16]

The capacity for predictive analytics to process data in ways that lend it subjective qualities—this customer *seems* pregnant, this couple *seems* like a good match, this location *seems* like a good one for a new store, this caravan of pickup trucks *seems* like a good target—upends Cartesian distinctions between human and nonhuman beings.[17] Here questions of agency are foregrounded. If a predictive model developed by a hedge fund for high-frequency trading crashes the market, who's to be held accountable? Who, or perhaps more precisely *what*, is responsible when a drone strike on a target identified using predictive analytics is made in error? Does the responsibility lie with the person who developed the predictive model? The agency that provided the data upon which the model was developed? The organization that chose to apply that model to a specific situation? These questions are compounded when algorithms operate at levels of abstraction that exceed the ability of the people who wrote them to understand the high-level descriptors that indicate the likelihood of a future event occurring or not occurring. Here, nonhuman subjectivity becomes a black box of the first order.

When applied to geographies of information, the notion of sentience affords thinking of information systems and infrastructures as complex sociotechnical entanglements of people, data, and space that come into being through a mutually constitutive process. These geographies need to be understood ontogenetically, as something continually

Above: Systemic anomalies: image from Clement Valla's "Postcards from Google Earth" series.

Mark Shepard

brought into being through specific practices that alter the conditions under which space itself is (re)produced. Whereas predictive models indicate the probability of individual action, agency in this context is distributed across a range of human and nonhuman actors and is understood in more collective terms. Consider for example the assemblage of drivers, passengers, smartphones, apps, networks, city streets, fare models, policies, regulations, investors, employees, and so on that constitute the urban car service Uber. When demand is high at a given location, a mechanism called "surge pricing" kicks in, by which the standard fare for a ride is multiplied by a factor proportional to the degree of scarcity of available cars nearby. This inflated fare—which can often rise to at least eight times the standard fare—is intended to incentivize drivers to migrate in the direction of that scarcity. Here the spatial distribution of resources (available cars) is balanced through an economic incentive (surge pricing) based on real-time analytics of fine-grained, geo-located demand (passengers).[18]

This has implications for how we think about not only the material basis of urban form but also the theater of operations for practices that seek to engage urban life within these hybrid conditions. The notion of a gated community (or office tower) changes when access to physical space can be granted or denied in real time based on what an algorithm anticipates an individual may or may not do. Predictive models alter how policies are formulated and decisions are made regarding the distribution of urban services and resources such as the locations of parks and hospitals, or the strategic prepositioning of ambulances and police cars. New global connections between locales, cities, and regions alike are created when passenger airlines dynamically determine flight routes based on emerging markets predicted by algorithms. When historical facts and probable futures converge in an algorithmic present, acting upon the spatial organization and material disposition of these diverse conditions becomes a question of negotiating relations between people, data, code, and space across a range of scales and durations.

Finally, we might address conditions of error within these new geographies. Within the field of predictive analytics, it is standard practice for statisticians to conduct tests in order to determine whether or not a speculative hypothesis concerning observed phenomena of the world (or its inhabitants) can be supported. The results of such testing determine whether a particular set of results agrees reasonably (or does not agree) with the speculated hypothesis. In experimental science, the null

Above: Kangbashi New Area, Ordos, China.

hypothesis—*the hypothesis to be tested*—is generally a statement that there is *no* relationship between the value of a particular measured variable and that of an experimental prediction. The accuracy of such predictions is measured as a percentage of false positive (or false negative) results. A false positive is considered an error of the first order in statistical analysis (a type I error), where the error leads one to conclude that a supposed relationship between two entities exists when in fact it does not. It is the incorrect rejection of a true *null hypothesis*.

What will we make of geographies produced through false positives? One could look to the geographies of foreclosure emerging in the wake of the 2008 financial crisis for clues. As predictive analytics plays an increasing role in real estate development—anticipating desirable neighborhoods and markets[19]—we will inevitably see new patterns of both density and vacancy emerge. When algorithms that can predict the crime rate of a neighborhood using Google Street View are added to the feature list, errors in Neighborhood Home Price Indexes and Automated Valuation Models could lead to new cycles of real estate booms and busts.[20] With the occasional predictive failure in audience-level targeting and hyperlocal demand generation, we can look forward not only to inexplicable microislands of density but also to ghost streets, buildings, and individual homes cropping up in odd and unexpected places. Given the highly optimized, evermore efficient and overcoded nature of these new geographies, it is perhaps within their unintended anomalies that we'll find the more interesting terrain for thought and action.

01. For a historical perspective on how data came to be understood as preanalytical and prefactual, existing prior to interpretation and argument, see Daniel Rosenberg, "Data before the Fact," in *"Raw Data" Is an Oxymoron*, ed. Lisa Gitelman (Cambridge, MA: MIT Press, 2013), 15–39. For an overview of how this understanding has evolved recently in considering how data is constitutive of the ideas, techniques, technologies, people, systems, and contexts that conceive, produce, process, manage, and analyze it, see Rob Kitchin and Tracey P. Lauriault, "Towards Critical Data Studies: Charting and Unpacking Data Assemblages and Their Work," *The Programmable City Working Paper* 2 (July 30, 2014), http://ssrn.com/abstract=2474112.

02. Rob Kitchin, *The Data Revolution: Big Data, Open Data, Data Infrastructures and Their Consequences* (London: Sage, 2014).

03. Rob Kitchin, "The Real-Time City? Big Data and Smart Urbanism," *GeoJournal* 79, no. 1 (2014): 1–14.

04. Kitchin, *The Data Revolution*.

05. Rob Kitchin and Tracey P. Lauriault, "Small Data, Data Infrastructures and Big Data," *The Programmable City Working Paper* 1 (January 8, 2014), http://papers.ssrn.com/sol3/papers.cfm?abstract_id=2376148.

06. Rob Kitchin and Martin Dodge, *Code/Space: Software and Everyday Life* (Cambridge, MA: MIT Press, 2011).

07. Kazys Varnelis, "The Architecture of Financialization," *Perspecta* 47 (2014): 185–94.

08. Mark Shepard, "Beyond the Smart City: Everyday Entanglements of Technology and Urban Life," *Harvard Design Magazine* 37 (Winter 2014): 18–23.

09. Research shows that if you capture customers prior to the birth of a child, they are far more likely to purchase all of the various items they will need from you. See Charles Duhigg, "How Companies Learn Your Secrets," *New York Times Magazine*, February 16, 2012, http://www.nytimes.com/2012/02/19/magazine/shopping-habits.html.

10. Vindu Goel, "Facebook Tinkers with Users' Emotions in News Feed Experiment, Stirring Outcry," *New York Times*, June 29, 2014, http://www.nytimes.com/2014/06/30/technology/facebook-tinkers-with-users-emotions-in-news-feed-experiment-stirring-outcry.html.

11. Adam D. I. Kramer, Jamie E. Guillory, and Jeffrey T. Hancock, "Experimental Evidence of Massive-Scale Emotional Contagion through Social Networks," *Proceedings of the National Academy of Sciences* 111, no. 24 (2014): 8788–90.

12. See ArcGIS for the Military, http://solutions.arcgis.com/military.

13. For more on how mobile phone SIM cards are currently used by the US military for locating targets, see Jeremy Scahill and Glenn Greenwald, "The NSA's Secret Role in the U.S. Assassination Program," *The Intercept*, February 10, 2014, https://firstlook.org/theintercept/2014/02/10/the-nsas-secret-role.

14. Mark Shepard, *Sentient City: Ubiquitous Computing, Architecture, and the Future of Urban Space* (New York: Architectural League of New York; Cambridge, MA: MIT Press, 2011).

15. See, for example, IBM's Smarter Planet initiative, http://www.ibm.com/smarterplanet/us/en.

16. Daniel C. Dennett, "Quining Qualia," in *Consciousness and Contemporary Science*, eds. A. Marcel and E. Bisiach (Oxford: Oxford University Press, 1988).

17. René Descartes argues in *Meditations on First Philosophy* (1641) that sentience was an essential human capacity, whereas the behavior of animals, for instance, could be accounted for by purely physical processes involved in mere sensing.

18. It didn't take long for people to figure out how to out-smart the algorithm, however. If one waited five minutes or so, the system would balance itself and the fare price would return to normal. Uber itself publicly announced this way of hacking its surge-pricing system in response to strong reactions to what was widely perceived as price gouging.

19. See, for example, smartzip's predictive analytics services, http://www.smartzip.com/data.

20. See, for example, research by MIT's Computer Science and Artificial Intelligence Laboratory as reported in Luke Dormehl, "This Algorithm Predicts a Neighborhood's Crime Rate Using Google Street View," Co.Labs, http://www.fastcolabs.com/3036677/this-algorithm-knows-your-neighborhood-better-than-you-do.

Image Credits

135: Photo by Clement Valla.

136: Photo by Tim Franco.

137

Mark Shepard

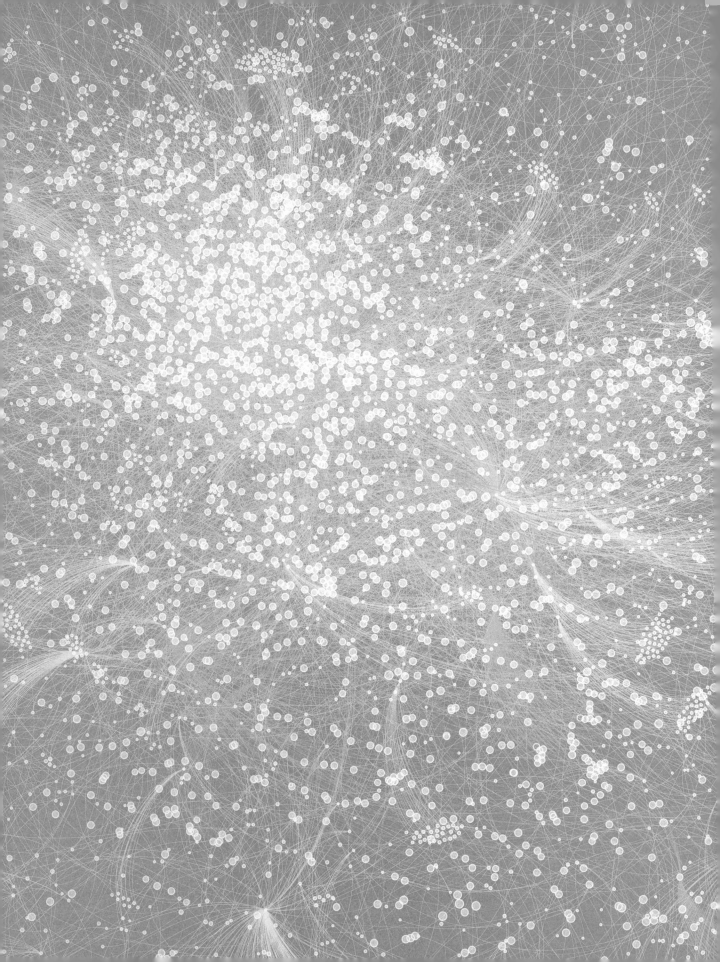

Urbanizing Military Information Technology
Interview with Jennifer Light

New Geographies: To begin, can you elaborate a little bit on the motives behind your work on the evolving role of information and communications technologies within the urban landscape of post–World War II America?

Jennifer Light: The growth of the Internet, and of the attendant geographical and architectural metaphors for the online world (cyberspace, home page, information superhighway, chat room), was the initial spark that ignited my interest in thinking geographically about the history of information and communications technologies, a topic I had studied as a graduate student in the history and sociology of science and technology. I was struck, as I followed this interest into readings in urban studies and the history of US cities, how few scholars were writing about the military-industrial complex. Historians and sociologists of American science, social science, and technology recognize military and national security concerns as a dominant influence on scientific and technological development in the second half of the twentieth century—shaping the trajectories of knowledge and practice in these fields and sponsoring the creation of many innovations that found their way into civilian life. To be sure, urban historians had examined military influences on the landscape in studies of civil defense and the role of the defense industry in regional economic development.[01] But the complementary story of how these larger forces shaped urban knowledge production and innovation (what I describe as "techniques and technologies") had yet to be told.

Initially, it was not so obvious whether the lack of prior coverage reflected the absence of similar influences on urban theory and practice, on account of the many public statements by city officials such as New York Mayor John Lindsay, who criticized excessive spending on the Vietnam War and the Apollo program, and called for similar investments in US cities. But after some poking around—and particularly after discovering how Lindsay, despite such criticisms, was simultaneously cultivating relationships with RAND Corporation consultants and inviting former NASA employees to advise him on technologies for urban management—it became clear that there were some interesting connections to explore. I was especially fascinated that the transfer of ideas and innovations went beyond the most obvious points of connection, such as policing and transportation, into social and economic planning; these more unexpected connections became the focus of my book. *From Warfare to Welfare* was thus my effort to reread American urban history through the lens of the history and sociology of science and technology.[02]

I blend methods from intellectual and technical history with methods from the sociology of knowledge to lay out the many ties that existed between the military-industrial complex and the ideas and innovations applied to addressing city problems in the 1960s and 1970s, and to explain why these collaborations took shape during the Cold War. The interest in metaphor that initially sparked my interest in thinking geographically about the histories of information and communications technologies carried through here because analogical thinking—whether about cities as communications systems or the urban crisis as a national security crisis—laid critical groundwork for the movement of expertise and innovations from the defense and aerospace industries to US cities. This mix of methods has proven to be a productive route to understanding the significance of technicians and their tools in American urban history, which I've applied in subsequent projects on the historical geography of information in earlier periods.

NG: In your work, especially in *From Warfare to Welfare*, you have highlighted the role of military research in the formation of cybernetic systems of command and control, and in the development of postwar communications and information technologies. Can you expand on the agency of war and the military in giving rise not only to these technologies but also to the theoretical underpinnings of their application?

JL: The linkages between cybernetics and the military are ones that many historians and sociologists of science and technology had established before I embarked on this project. Studies such as Paul Edwards's *The Closed World* (1996) lay the necessary intellectual groundwork for my explorations of the many ideas, technologies, and people moving from defense and aerospace contexts into urban settings.[03]

It's worth noting some differences in emphasis, however, between military and urban applications of this scientific field's belief that humans, animals, machines, and organizations all constituted systems of communication and control. In military contexts, the notion that humans were machinelike and machines were humanlike paved the way for projects such as Norbert Wiener's antiaircraft work and the SAGE air defense system. It also shaped the fields of cognitive psychology and artificial intelligence, which were indebted to military sponsors.

Cybernetics' analogical understanding of humans, animals, machines, and organizations did similarly important work in urban contexts, but themes of human-machine integration were less prominent. Instead, one finds more general claims that cities are "communication systems," or "systems of subsystems," like the complex systems managed by defense and aerospace communities—claims that lay the conceptual and rhetorical groundwork for the transfer of expertise and innovations.

140

NG: A set of new expertise emerged in the mid-twentieth century at the intersection of new information technologies, warfare industries, and the built environment. We can trace the impact of military practices on planning research and education (through systems thinking and computer-generated models), the professional practice of planning (introduction of the planning command center), and the spatial organization of American cities (decentralization and suburbanization). Can you elaborate on the links between information technologies, warfare industries, and the emergence of a new form of expertise in the built environment within the context of the Cold War and explain how they fed one another? What new institutions and expert communities developed as a result of this linkage?

JL: In the 1950s prominent voices from the defense industry at institutions such as RAND and TRW began publishing articles in the *Journal of the American Institute of Planners* suggesting how, in light of these similarities, their technological tools might assist planners' work. Although collaborations got underway before the major period of civil disorder in the 1960s, urban violence cemented the link between the two communities. Institutions including RAND, Lockheed, and SDC created new urban and civil systems divisions to facilitate technology transfer. New organizations such as Urban Systems Associates (USA Inc.), founded by General Bernard Adolph Schriever (retired former chief of the Air Force Systems Command and head of the Intercontinental Ballistic Missile program), were also established. It was with the assistance of such firms that cities including New York and Los Angeles subsequently set out to construct new crisis anticipation systems, computer databases with modeling capabilities to predict and forestall future conflict. The US Department of Housing and Urban Development and other federal agencies provided financial support for some of these efforts.

The participation of academics alongside city officials and defense intellectuals at gatherings such as "Space, Science, and Urban Life" and "Applications of Computers to the Problems of Urban Society" (meetings that helped to sustain the confidence in analogical thinking) points to a parallel story in schools of planning and public administration. These institutions witnessed an influx of faculty and students with ties to the defense and aerospace industries during this period, as well as new sources of funding from the national security establishment. Courses such as "Systems Analysis and Urban Planning" and "Cybernetics and Urban Analysis" became part of the curriculum in this period, many initially taught by individuals who had honed their skills on defense projects. The federal Office of Naval Research offered early funding for faculty work on geographic information systems, for example, sponsoring the Harvard Design School team developing SYMAP. In addition, defense and aerospace workers interested in retraining for careers in city planning and management could enroll in executive education courses such as Project ADAPT at MIT's Department of Urban Studies and Planning and the Aerospace Employment Project at UC Berkeley's Extension School and College of Environmental Design.

NG: After World War II, urban problems of poverty, crime, overpopulation, and traffic offered a platform for the transference of techniques, technologies, and methodologies of the military and aerospace industries. What were the ideological and sociopolitical incentives behind this? Why did the methodologies and management practices of the military appear so appealing in addressing the postwar socioeconomic issues of the urban environment? What role did military institutions such as RAND play in this process?

JL: This is a fascinating episode in the political economy of the professions. By that I mean that both defense intellectuals and city planners/managers were in need of resources that, at least temporarily, the other professional community could supply. Defense intellectuals at RAND, Lockheed, and elsewhere were anxious about finding civilian markets for their expertise and innovations in light of possible reductions to future defense and aerospace spending. Many considered themselves to be sympathetic to the needs of city residents and were eager to apply their expertise to making urban environments better places to live. City planners and managers, who had lost face in the wake of the failures of renewal, were seeking new approaches to establishing order in cities and new ways of legitimating urban affairs on the national stage. In an era of public esteem for science and engineering, they hoped to use new mathematical approaches, new scientific theories about cities, and new technological tools to organize "space age cities." Both communities were optimistic that, together, these

141

Jennifer Light

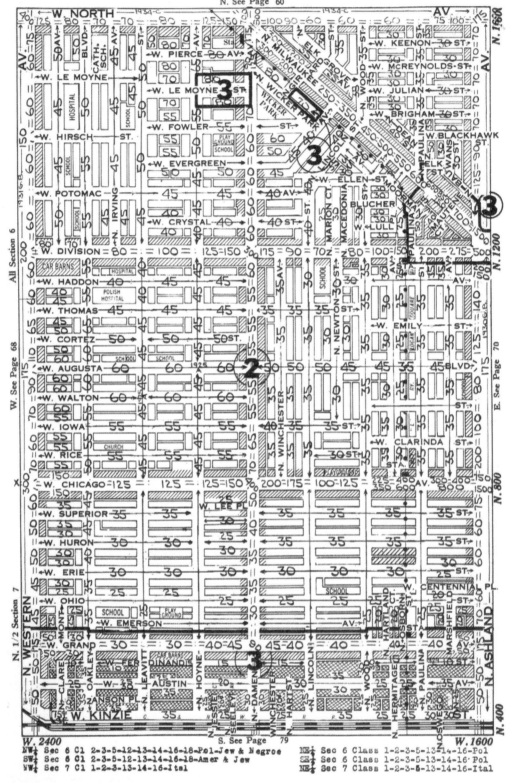

NG07—Geographies of Information

conceptual and technological innovations would make it possible to model and predict the outcomes of multiple policy alternatives and subsequently identify the optimal choice—leading to a new generation of urban policies above politics.

The two communities of experts had, in fact, previously come together for discussions about civil defense planning. These included conversations about "defensive dispersal," whose significance lay less in any transformations to the nation's landscape than in how they brought the two groups into conversation about the future of the nation's cities. These conversations smoothed the way for later collaborations around the shared image of the city as a communication system.

There is another equally critical factor in the convergence of defense intellectuals and city planners/managers around urban problem solving. At the same time that local governments were moving away from the physical planning of the renewal era to undertake programs that also prioritized social and economic planning (for example, the Community Renewal Program), the defense and aerospace communities were turning their attention to socioeconomic data gathering and analysis. Institutions like RAND increasingly hired social scientists to staff their pursuit of what Amrom Katz called "interdisciplinary war."[04] From the computer systems recording social and economic data as part of the effort to win hearts and minds in Vietnam, to the attempts to discern socioeconomic information about enemy populations from satellite imagery, the new focus within the national security establishment called attention to social and economic planning in ways that, at least rhetorically, mapped onto the concerns of urban professionals.

The enthusiasm that accompanied early collaborations (for example, at the RAND Corporation's New York City branch, or at NASA's Jet Propulsion Laboratory in Los Angeles) receded, however, as the limits of analogical thinking became clear. Planners' social objectives such as "quality of life" were not easily quantified. Counterintuitive policy solutions, which excited systems thinkers such as MIT's Jay Forrester, failed to gain political support. Cities lacked on-site technical expertise, making them beholden to outside consultants. The organizational culture and financial resources that enabled military agencies to plan for the long term and to execute orders from the top had no equivalent in cities.

NG: Within the planning and design discourse of the day, cities and urbanization were understood as "organisms," "communication networks," or "systems of self-organizing subsystems." Can you please elaborate on the postwar origin of these organic and technological metaphors? What was the role of science culture in perpetuating the perception of the urbanized landscape as a communication network?

Opposite: Chicago, Illinois. A typical page from *Olcott's Land Values Blue Book of Chicago* (Chicago: George C. Olcott, 1935). Note the numbers and text at the bottom referring to types of buildings and predominant population groups in each half-mile section.

JL: In fact, thinking about cities as organisms or organic systems has a long history, as does the city as machine.[05] In a study that served as a prequel to *From Warfare to Welfare*, I discussed the early twentieth-century belief that cities were "ecologies." Urban professionals sought insights in expert knowledge about the natural world.[06] During this earlier period, concerns about rural areas dominated land use planning programs, and the conservation movement provided a conceptual and organizational model for urban professionals seeking to mobilize public support for action on city problems.

The Cold War vision of cities as cybernetic systems departed from this tradition by merging organic interpretations with machine interpretations, but—consistent with earlier examples of organic and technological metaphors applied to cities—we find close ties between the dominant image of the city, the kinds of methods employed for urban data gathering and analysis, and the ultimate decisions about how best to insure order in cities. Relations between scientists and engineers and urban professionals in

143

the early twentieth century were more distant than they were in the Cold War era, when numerous defense and aerospace industry scientists and engineers participated on urban problem-solving projects. Nonetheless, both abstract techniques and tangible technologies for representing complex systems migrated across professional domains, in this case from ecology to urban studies and from natural resources planning to urban planning. Land use patterns over time were seen as life cycles that could be scientifically managed, and thematic and statistical maps representing these life cycles were used to facilitate land management.

The extent to which midcentury defense intellectuals and city planners were aware of these precedents is unclear. Regardless, they frequently drew connections to the history of planning in other ways. In particular, planners' prior work with tools to manage geographic information, from maps to 3-D models to aerial photography, became fodder for the argument that city governments seeking space-age cities should adopt new technologies including computer simulations, satellite images, and GIS. According to this view, such Cold War innovations were merely more advanced ways for planners to do what they had always done—with the advantage that, for example, they could now create dynamic digital models that could be continuously updated, or forecast future urban conditions under different policy regimes.

NG: What were some of the means of urban intelligence gathering that emerged in the latter half of the twentieth century? And how do you think these practices influenced the planning and spatial organization of cities?

JL: It is worth describing the deeper historical context for midcentury interest in using satellites and other forms of remote sensing for urban "intelligence gathering," because this context explains both the era's enthusiasm for new technologies and the nonadoption of satellites and remote sensing in the longer term.

City planners, housing officials, real estate professionals, and others had long fantasized about applying new technologies to make the process of collecting and analyzing geographic information both faster and cheaper. The dominant methods in the early twentieth century, which included housing censuses and real property inventories, were exceptionally time consuming and labor intensive, on account of the field research and data processing they required. From local realtors' land value atlases to the multiple listing service to aerial photography, a number of efforts to reduce the time and cost associated with geographic information gathering and processing emerged even before World War II. George Olcott's *Land Values Blue Book of Chicago and Suburbs*, for example, explicitly billed itself as turning appraisal into a "desk job." Olcott sent a team of real estate agents to survey the region, gathering information on housing types and population groups, transportation access, age of paving, and other details, so that instead of visiting a neighborhood, appraisers could just read his book.

During this earlier period, statistical maps supplied the most sophisticated tools for working with geographic information. Maps came to be understood as computational devices that could function as aids to statistical analysis, devices for simulating the future, tools for the quantitative modeling of complex phenomena, instruments for automating human labor, and databases for storing geographic information. Especially noteworthy were the risk-rating studies of US cities prepared by the Federal Housing Administration. Originally planned as labor-saving tools, these studies replaced the initial field survey. Although scholars associate them with the origins of federal housing discrimination on account of the unequal access to mortgage insurance that followed, they were initially adopted to provide a more objective route to urban decision making.[07] Their quantitative approach to "computing" the quality of neighborhoods was

144

intended to eliminate the subjectivity of surveyors' judgments. Notably, the map overlay techniques employed here were eventually integrated into GIS.

Although federal and local officials planned to update their information and regularly revise the maps, the discontinuation of real property inventories made this a difficult task. Nevertheless, with access to data gathered locally, these map-based methods were subsequently applied to "computing" blighted areas as a composite statistic in the urban renewal program, a program that similarly aspired to eliminate politics from the decision-making process.[08]

Such projects provide important background for analyzing urban intelligence gathering during the Cold War because they lent credence to claims from technology enthusiasts that these new tools would help planners achieve their long-standing goals by automating the collection and continuous updating of geographic information. Unfortunately, the limited resolution of Landsat, NASA's civilian satellite, rendered it unsuitable for cities.[09] Aerial photography (a technology itself transferred from the military experience in World War I) proved a better match for urban users. In contrast to the sustained use of computer technologies during this period, then, which led to the creation of new divisions in city planning departments devoted to data processing or mathematical modeling, there was no equivalent in the area of satellite imaging and remote sensing.

NG: What dynamics existed between public opinion and expert planning practices that emerged out of systems engineering and operation research in the 1960s and 1970s? Would you please situate expert knowledge within the ideal democratic systems of the time, assuming that professionalization of the language in these emerging practices could potentially lead to the exclusion of public opinion in decision-making processes?

JL: Public opinion in general and citizen participation in particular were very much on the minds of city officials in the 1960s and 1970s. The urban renewal program had ostensibly required citizen input into decision making about neighborhood demolition and rehabilitation, and indeed the "conservation" of neighborhoods depended on participation from local residents. But many cities complied with these federal requirements in only limited ways. The Community Action Program that followed as a response allowed citizens so much voice that program administrators found it difficult to get anything done.

Public opinion and citizen participation were also on the minds of defense intellectuals as military agencies turned their attention to interdisciplinary war. The effort to reduce counterinsurgency through modernization in the pacification program in Vietnam and in programs such as the Peace Corps exemplify these professionals' awareness that opportunities for marginalized populations to express themselves in limited ways could complement strategies for security planning organized around top-down control.

The two communities of experts thus agreed that citizen participation and public opinion sharing should be increased to maintain control and stability in political systems, whether abroad or at home. This shared outlook sparked new kinds of collaborations. With support from city governments, defense intellectuals such as RAND's Herbert Dordick, who had previously explored the role of communications technologies in development and modernization abroad, later applied similar ideas to planning cable communications in cities as tools for citizen expression. The cybernetic notion that cities were systems suggested in turn that urban problems were communications problems, lending support to the idea that cable infrastructure accessible to citizens, alongside computers and satellites used by experts, would help to prevent future disorders in city streets.

As your question suggests, these emerging practices were increasingly technical, presenting obstacles to citizen engagement. In the case of cable, both professional communities together with many community groups organized educational projects to train citizens in video production. The recognition that the language of urban problem solving in the period was difficult for nonexperts to understand sparked other collaborations as well; most notably, the effort to teach the residents of America's inner cities about systems thinking using simulation games. In yet another example of how the tools used to manage military geographic information moved into urban contexts, gaming simulations became a fixture in the federal Model Cities program.[10] War games, which were among the tools used for geographic information and analysis at RAND, had begun to appear in the curriculum at schools of planning and public administration in the mid-1960s. Thanks to the academic orientation of the Model Cities program, they subsequently found their way into the hands of citizens as well. CONSAD and Abt Associates, two defense contractors that had developed military simulation games and computer simulations, won federal contracts to devise games to teach Model Cities residents the language of systems so that they could "game out" the consequences of alternative policy choices.[11]

When compared to other games of the period, Model Cities fits squarely within the military's tradition of "limited modernization," encouraging citizens to maintain the stability of the system rather than destroy it. Residents were educated to debate the political choices offered by the game but not to question the models of urban systems themselves. Model Cities departed from more academic games in that it encouraged players to collaborate rather than compete. By manipulating the game's outcome it suggested the ultimate fairness of "the system." This outcome, in other words, had as much to do with the designers' assumptions as it did with how citizens played. Regardless of the extent to which these projects promoted community participation, however, collaborations around cable and games ultimately fell apart, due primarily to economic issues.

NG: How do you see the future of "big data" and smart cities in relation to sociopolitical problems? Do you think that these new technologies can be effective in solving societal issues?

JL: Witnessing the unfolding discussions about big data and smart cities, I am struck by the reappearance of familiar themes, now linked to new technological tools. Contemporary visions of the possibility of comprehensive information gathering, continuous monitoring, and policymaking by algorithm update longtime fantasies of mastering cities through technology. So, too, many of the discussions about engaging citizens in local decision making using Public Participation GIS or online games update approaches to public participation focused on training "participants" to choose among options within the frameworks of a particular model of the issue at hand, rather than question the models' assumptions themselves.

The continuities between past and present invite us to ask hard questions about why earlier technologies disappointed, and about why the belief in technological solutions to political problems persists. To be sure, there are important distinctions between the technologies of the contemporary moment and those of earlier periods. For example, computers are vastly more powerful, and the resolution of civilian satellite images has improved. From citizen mapping projects such as the Detroit Geographic Expedition to the field of critical GIS, previous generations called attention to the limits of earlier technologies in ways that shaped the development of new tools, including Public Participation GIS.

Yet, if there is a single conclusion to draw from the history of geographic information, it is that technical improvements alone do not guarantee the solution of complex problems facing cities and regions. Technological solutions redefine political problems, from the notion of "quality of life" to the meaning of citizen participation. Howard Gardner's critique of previously narrow definitions of human intelligence—and his proposal for multiple intelligences—has relevance here, in light of the varied individuals and institutions poised to gain from the application of a new generation of tools.[12] What exactly is a "smart" city? Whose definition of "smart" prevails? What cannot be captured by "big" data gathering and processing tools?

Taken together, my work on the Cold War and earlier periods showcases the important if underappreciated work of technicians and their tools in shaping American urban history, in particular through the conceptual and technical models of cities they devised.[13] My hope is that, in an era when a new generation of people and technologies is in the public eye, such historical evidence prompts skepticism about the future they promise, and underscores the growing need for alternative approaches to civic education that demystify the models shaping our daily lives.

Acknowledgments: The editors would like to thank Ghazal Jafari for her role in initiating and composing the interview.

01. Kenneth D. Rose, *One Nation Underground: The Fallout Shelter in American Culture* (New York: New York University, 2001); Ann Markusen, et al., *The Rise of the Gunbelt: The Military Remapping of Industrial America* (New York: Oxford University Press, 1991); Michael Dudley, "Sprawl as Strategy: City Planners Face the Bomb," *Journal of Planning Education and Research* 21, no.1 (2001): 52–63.

02. Jennifer S. Light, *From Warfare to Welfare: Defense Intellectuals and Urban Problems in Cold War America* (Baltimore: Johns Hopkins University Press, 2003).

03. Paul Edwards, *The Closed World: Computers and the Politics of Discourse in Cold War America* (Cambridge, MA: MIT Press, 1996).

04. Amrom Katz, *The Short Run and the Long Walk* (Santa Monica: RAND, 1966), 4.

05. For precedents of the city as machine, see John M. Jordan, *Machine-Age Ideology: Social Engineering and American Liberalism, 1911–1939* (Chapel Hill, NC: University of North Carolina Press, 1994).

06. Jennifer S. Light, *The Nature of Cities: Ecological Visions and the American Urban Professions, 1920–1960* (Baltimore: Johns Hopkins University Press, 2009).

07. See Jennifer Light, "Discriminating Appraisals: Cartography, Computation, and Access to Federal Mortgage Insurance in the 1930s," *Technology and Culture* 52, no. 3 (July 2011): 485–522.

08. I am currently conducting a GIS analysis of this work to explore the politics of blight determination using methods similar to those used in another paper on the earlier neighborhood risk-rating program. See Jennifer S. Light, "Nationality and Neighborhood Risk at the Origins of FHA Underwriting," *Journal of Urban History* 36, no. 5 (September 2010): 634–71.

09. Landsat did prove useful for natural resource planners, for example, as part of LUNR, an early geographic information system for New York State.

10. Jennifer Light, "Taking Games Seriously," *Technology and Culture* 49, no. 2 (April 2008): 347–75.

11. CONSAD had also developed information systems for Pittsburgh and New York City.

12. Howard Gardner, *Frames of Mind: The Theory of Multiple Intelligences* (New York: Basic Books, 1983).

13. No doubt sometimes such quantitative work served as window dressing for predetermined political outcomes, and there are examples of this across the historical periods on which I've worked.

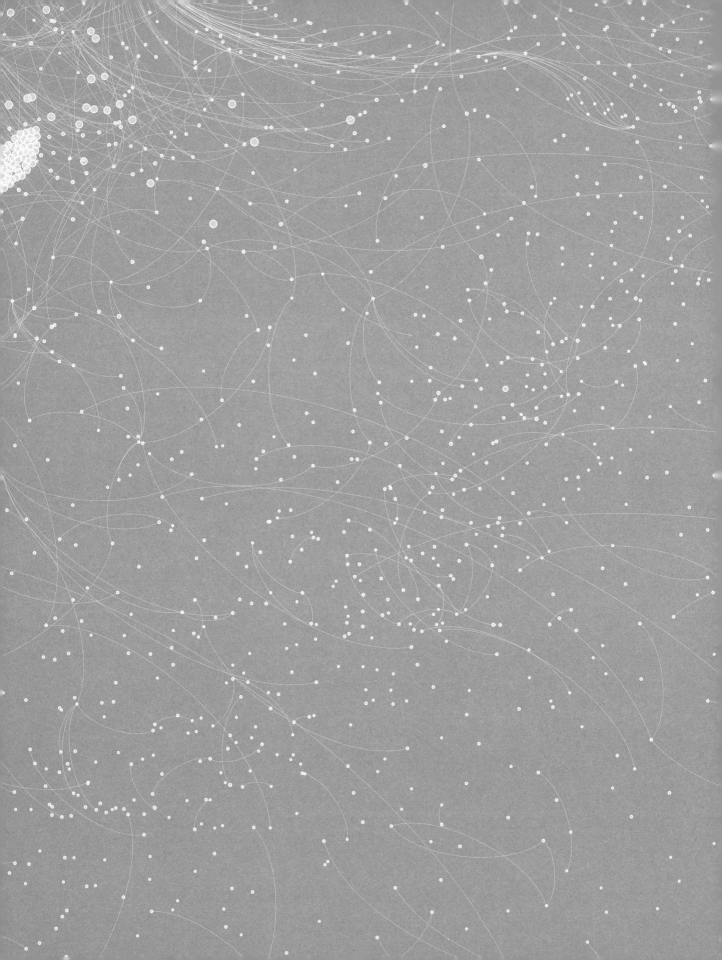

Pavlov's Cube(s)
An Architecture for the Soviet Computer Network

Evangelos
Kotsioris

In 1966, nearly three years after the Advanced Research Projects Agency Network (ARPANET) was conceptualized in the United States, the Central Committee and the Council of Ministers of the USSR declared their intention to form a nationwide information-management and computer-based, decision-making system called OGAS. This small acronym of a rather colossal project stands for All-State System for the Collection and Processing of Information for Reporting, Planning, and Management of the National Economy.[01] In a centrally planned economy such as that of the USSR, the search for the "optimum performance" and ideal allocation of scarce resources would be able to be computed for each sector of the economy separately, as well as for the economy of the Union in its totality.

The mastermind behind OGAS was academician Victor M. Glushkov, director of the Institute of Cybernetics in Kiev, Ukraine. OGAS would electronically connect information systems in all state enterprises and industrial branch ministries across a vast geographical territory. This included the fifteen Soviet republics that famously amounted to more than "one-sixth of the Earth's land area."[02] According to a map with a scheme for the OGAS network, projected for completion by 1990, Moscow would be connected directly with Leningrad and strategic inland centers like Sverdlovsk (Yekaterinburg), Novosibirsk and Kuybyshev. On the west, the links would thread state capitals such as those of the Baltic States (Tallinn, Riga, Vilnius), Minsk

and continue through Kiev, Kishinev (Chișinău), Tbilisi, and Baku. Eastern outposts would stretch as far such as Irkutsk and Khabarovsk, all the way to Petropavlovsk on the Pacific coast of the Kamchatka Peninsula, after passing through the Central Asian capitals of Tashkent, Alma-Ata (Almaty), and Dushanbe.

Soviet officials envisioned OGAS as the Cold War equivalent of the Roman road network: a vital connective infrastructure that would decisively modernize the oversight, management, and control of a geographically vast "empire." By gathering together economic information from nearly all edges of the Union and communicating it to Moscow, the city would be advantageously positioned to financially surveil and direct industrial production throughout the Soviet republics. The network would shrink the immense topography of the Union to create both a new internal administrative geography and a new global geopolitical reality.

Western media was quick to call attention to the dangers of such a "system of total management," insisting that it could easily envelope every aspect of social and political life as well.[03] According to Glushkov's proposal, the geography of physical space would be mapped onto the virtual space of OGAS. The interconnected computing centers dispersed in key Soviet cities would "[contain] in their memory every street, every house, every apartment … and the like."[04] The US press looked at the Orwellian scenario of generalized citizen surveillance through a computerized network as the ultimate fulfillment of totalitarianism.[05]

Glushkov's Roman metaphor of choice for OGAS was not infrastructural but rather architectural. He imagined OGAS evolving into a virtual space of multilateral communication for Soviet citizens and compared it to the ancient Roman Forum: a dematerialized edifice of democratization for the exchange of opinions. One could describe it as a precursor of early online bulletin boards and internet forums or, in Glushkov's own words, "something like a general assembly of the country's whole population—what's more, one that would be permanently in session."[06]

Whether it would evolve into an innocuous discourse platform or transfigure into a dystopian surveillance apparatus, the sheer scale and complexity of OGAS required an unprecedented physical technoscape of computer equipment, telecommunication lines and specialized buildings—a sea of practically thousands of Computer Centers (VTs) at every node of the idealized map of OGAS. The beating heart of this new topology of economical governance, management, and control would be situated in the center of the Russian capital, about a mile away from the Kremlin, at the new Main Computing Center (MCC) of the USSR State Planning Committee (commonly called Gosplan).[07]

Experience with Soviet bureaucracy suggested that such a system would (fatally) mirror the hierarchical diagram of other existing administrative institutions that—oriented top-down—radiated out from Moscow. Instead, Glushkov conceived of OGAS as a continuous two-way channel that would allow the bottom-up electronic transmission of economic data from state enterprises to their respective ministries, then to regional state Gosplan offices, and finally to the MCC of the USSR Gosplan in Moscow.[08] In reversing the flow of information and by eliminating local filtering and cooking of economic data, Glushkov aspired to create the ultimate administrative device.

Gosplan acquired data through a vast array of affiliated state research institutes, such as the Central Statistical Administration (TsSU),[09] in order to centrally allocate resources and compute production targets for State enterprises. The work of Soviet mathematicians and economists like Leonid V. Kantorovich implied that "perfect planning"[10] could be achieved through the adoption of mathematical models of optimization, such as linear programming.[11] Such techno-utopian beliefs would be realized by Gosplan, and would be complemented with custom calculative and decision-making algorithms developed by partner institutions, such as the Central Economic Mathematical Institute of the USSR Academy of Sciences (TsEMI).[12] These algorithms for economic planning and management would

be based on the Soviet versions of cybernetic theory that flourished during the 1960s.[13]

After years of speculation, the Central Committee of the Communist Party of the Soviet Union (CPSU) and the Council of Ministers of the USSR issued a semi-public resolution in 1963 formalizing the decision to initiate the implementation of OGAS. Later archived under a secret inventory number, the resolution also included a list of possible mainframe computers to be purchased. Impressively enough, the very first architecture of OGAS was "hardcoded" in the resolution as well. The document concluded with the decision to erect a new 8,000-square-meter building for the MCC in Moscow, an expected date of construction between 1964 and 1965 and a building budget of 75,000 rubles.[14] Leonid Pavlov, head architect of Workshop No. 11 at the city design office Mosproekt-2, was shortly after appointed as the designer of the very first building for OGAS;[15] by extension, he was entrusted to devise the set of design principles of a wholly new architectural typology—that of the Soviet networked computing center.[16]

The MCC of the USSR Gosplan was part of a large number of high-profile building complexes planned for Novokirovskii Avenue. The two-and-a-half-kilometer traffic artery jetted out northeast from Moscow's Boulevard Ring, which defined the borders of the historical White City. Cut decisively through the city, Novokirovskii Avenue was planned to be lined up with trees, landscaping, and freestanding buildings that housed administrative bodies, scientific institutes, banks, and other significant state-related organizations.

As part of a later phase for the design, Pavlov provisioned the physical connection of the MCC with Le Corbusier's Tsentrosoyuz Building situated less than 200 meters away southwest. A perspective drawing illustrating a pedestrian-level view of the Novokirovskii Avenue (today Academician Sakharov Avenue) looking northeast depicts the Tsentrosoyuz Building and the MCC, with an additional slab building in between and a taller square-planned tower barely discernible in the background. Representationally, Pavlov's proposals clearly take a backseat to Corbusier's building that Pavlov greatly admired.

The Tsentrosoyuz Building had been completed in 1936 as the offices for the Central Union of Consumer Cooperatives.[17] Yet, in the late 1950s it was repurposed as the seat of the Central Statistical Administration of the USSR—the primary statistical organization of the Soviet Union. Given the latter's key role in economic planning and management, it made perfect sense to offer a link with its premises. Pavlov's decision to break down the MCC complex into a series of interconnected prisms—

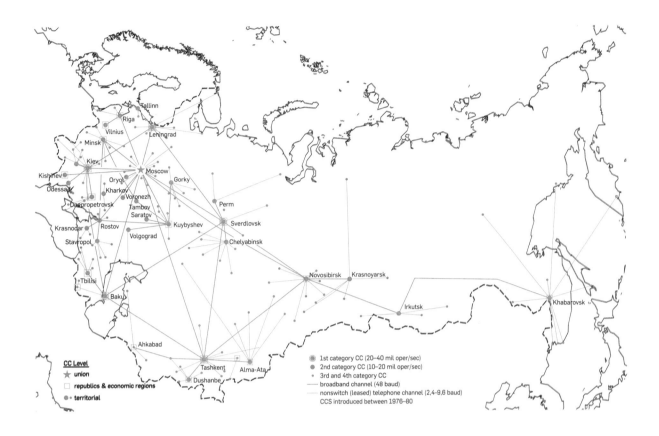

CC Level
★ union
☐ republics & economic regions
● · territorial

◉ 1st category CC (20–40 mil oper/sec)
● 2nd category CC (10–20 mil oper/sec)
· 3rd and 4th category CC
— broadband channel (48 baud)
— nonswitch (leased) telephone channel (2,4-9,6 baud)
CCS introduced between 1976–80

the number of which could increase over time—certainly echoed Le Corbusier's compositional strategy for the massive program of the Tsentrosoyuz. Only Pavlov's articulation strategy for the networked computer center of the MCC extended beyond the scale of the singular building, suggesting an administrative architecture that would eventually become a network in itself.

The MCC of the USSR Gosplan became the first realized example of a networked computing center for OGAS in Moscow.[18] Pavlov's austere scheme for the building comprised a "light-washed" volume that balanced precariously over a narrower, oblong plinth. The glazed, slightly squeezed "cube" measuring 36 × 42 × 42 meters was dynamically positioned off center on a horizontally expanding prism along the avenue. In a crisp, modernist fashion, Pavlov strived to match the spectrum of technical requirements of the architectural program with a variety of contrasting spatial conditions: free plan, high ceiling, ventilated halls for the computer rooms; intimate compartments for staff offices; and easily accessible, large span spaces for the auditorium, the dining hall, and the cafeteria.

The correspondence of program and materials was rather inverted. The twelve-story, transparent cube contained the more private functions and restricted areas (such as computer rooms or directors' offices), while the

fortress-like, single-story podium on the ground floor housed the more public functions (including a foyer and a library). Geometrically speaking, the figure of the cube is more congruent with notions of compactness and introversion, as it constitutes the regular prism with the smallest ratio of external surface (of facades) to internal volume (or "program"). It is through this contrast of material treatment and geometrical articulation that the glass cube of Gosplan's MCC was elevated to a prominent position, both visually (as experienced from the street) and symbolically.

The total floor surface of the MCC was rather small, especially considering the scope of its central positioning for the OGAS network. Even if the realized version of Pavlov's scheme was more than two and a half times larger than the initially planned 8,000 square meters, it could still accommodate a mere of five mainframe computer systems with peripheral units. Confronted with the budgetary restrictions of the project, Pavlov's design inventively "hacked" the aesthetic rigidity of generic construction panel systems for housing (II-60, in this case)

Above: Projective map of the OGAS network by 1990 across the Soviet Union, c. 1980. The backbone of the project would have consisted of approximately 200 centralized, 2,500 branch, and 22,500 individual computing centers stretching across the entire territory of the Soviet Union.

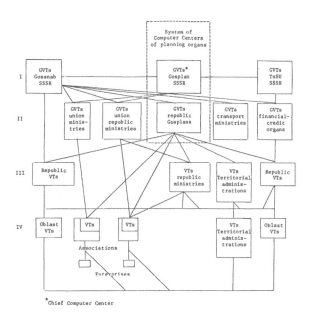

by combining prefabricated concrete modules of the former with ad hoc designed components.[19] Attired in glass, travertine, granite, natural wood, and perforated aluminum panels, the inexpensive "back end" of the building's makeup remained tactfully concealed.

The greatest technical ingenuity of the MCC building, perhaps, lay in its transversal section. Every two of the equal-height floors devoted to human occupants of the building correspond to two uneven floors devoted to computers. A short service floor above each of the five high-ceiling computer halls accommodated the vast supplies of ventilation and electricity needed. This internal organizing principle was expressed on the facades through the alternation of solid bands of panels that capped the projections of the floor slabs on the building envelope.

The twelfth floor of the cube presented the only exception to this rule, as it contained on all sides of its perimeter the most restricted administrative spaces: the directors' offices, deputy halls, meeting rooms, lecture halls, secretary rooms, typing rooms, accounting offices, and rooms for "special departments." Pavlov designed the protected central core of this floor as a safeguarded space for the electronic storage devices that could be accessed from the floors below. This architectural distinction between spaces for storage of economic data and spaces of computation echoed the modular nature of the computer, where different functions take place in discrete interconnected units. The MCC building was a rather sophisticated example of what one might call "computer architecture," an architecture in which the built armature of the computer constituted an integral part of its extended hardware.

Pavlov's MCC building served as a showpiece of technological progress. A *Wunderkammer* of Soviet computerization, it was unveiled to socialist leaders aligned with Soviet policy. Access to the building was reserved for prized invitees, visiting allies, and accredited press delegations. About a year after its completion, in April of 1971, a delegation of the Socialist Unity Party of Germany, headed by the first secretary of the party's Central Committee, State Council Chairman Walter Ulbricht, and First Secretary Erich Honecker, made a much-publicized visit to the MCC a few days before the conclusion of the Twenty-Fourth Congress of the Communist Party of the Soviet Union in Moscow. In June of 1972, on the occasion of Cuba joining the Council for Mutual Economic Assistance, Fidel Castro also toured Pavlov's building as first secretary of the Central Committee of the Cuban Communist Party and prime minister of Cuba.

The typical floor plan of each of the cube levels was divided into three zones: a large band of free plan for the computer halls looking over Novokirovskii Avenue, a narrow strip of solid spaces dedicated to vertical communications and services, and a less visible anterior zone for offices, conference halls, and other administrative spaces. Considered volumetrically, thus, the cube was divided into areas designed to elicit the optimal performance of machines and humans, while organizing the

Above, left: Chart diagram depicting the hierarchical levels of the structure of OGAS and the central position of the MCC of Gosplan in Moscow ("GVts Goslpan SSSR"), 1977. Above, right: Leonid Pavlov, Main Computing Center of the USSR State Planning Committee (Gosplan), Moscow, 1966–74.

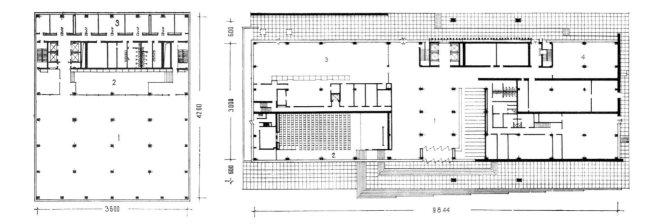

interfacing of the two. Slotted between the zones of the computer halls and the vertical core, an elevated platform served as an observation deck that allowed the act of computer-aided planning to be visually perceived. From this advantageous point, MCC's directors and their guests were afforded an almost aerial overview of the computer room of each floor.

This enactment was made possible through the use of a floor-to-ceiling window-wall that separated the relaxed, smoky area of the observation decks from the ionized, heavily air-conditioned atmosphere of the computer rooms. It was the architectural surface of this visual interface that also dictated the dress code of human agents: formal suits for the audience, scientists' lab coats for the performers. One could argue that the setup alluded to an architecture intended for theatrical performance. In this particular case, however, the actors' stage and audience seating were inverted. The miniaturized "urbanism" of freestanding consoles, central processor units, card readers, tape units, and line printers acted as a perpetually animated set. All the operable "facades" of the computer deliberately faced the observation deck. Indicator lights went on and off, magnetic tapes spun, and printers inscribed, delivering a mesmerizing performance of Muscovite virtuosity.[20]

Beyond its physical presence in Moscow, the MCC building was aestheticized in newspapers, newsreels, films, journals, and books and mediatized as an existing first step toward Soviet computerization and the fulfillment of OGAS. The architectural image of the MCC was often instrumentalized to communicate tangible progress toward that end. Pavlov's building was translated into a recognizable pictogram in popular cybernetics books, even before its structure was complete. One such illustration was included in the widely circulated *Small Encyclopedia of Great Cybernetics*, written for high school children in 1970.[21]

In a chapter called "Cybernetics in the Economy," a cartoon-like aerial perspective of the Pavlov Gosplan cube appears. Black arrows symbolizing state directives emanate from the cube. Contradicting Glushkov's vision for a series of cybernetic loops of information, the arrows here are sketched according to the only familiar planning paradigm—Gosplan's centralized plans and targets delivered to six major pillars of the Soviet economy: trade, transport, industry, energy, agriculture, and construction. The accompanying text confidently announces: "This will be the All-Union Center for the collection, storage, processing and transmission of economic information." In its graphical simplicity and diagrammatic quality, such graphic devices familiarized a future generation with an incomplete project: it rendered the opaque and still-unimplemented processes of Soviet computerization as both accessible and real.

In 1971, the interior of the MCC of the USSR Gosplan was revealed in the color documentary *Plans and Life*, commissioned by Central Television of the USSR.[22] "What has been given to the Soviet people during the past eight five-year plans? And what will be the ninth?" asks the narrator. A camera dolly slides smoothly on its rail along one of the observation decks, overlooking one of the glass-encased computer rooms. Line printers frantically output results as piles of fanfold paper. Economic specialists work at their desks, have breakout meetings, lean over spreadsheets. Inside the transparent computer hall, equipment units appear dramatically uplit with spotlight brought in specially for the occasion. A male operator is sitting at the operating console. His female colleague leans over momentarily, before performing a scripted choreography

Above, left: Typical floor plan of the MCC "cube": (1) computer hall; (2) observation deck; (3) offices. Above, right: Ground floor plan of the plinth: (1) entrance hall and cloakroom, lounge; (2) auditorium; (3) dining hall; (4) library.

153

154

on the machine floor to graciously activate a series of magnetic tape units of an ICL System 4-70 digital computer.[23]

Similar scenes unfold in the newsreel *Moscow—Capital of the USSR* filmed a year later, in 1972.[24] Computer operators dedicated to scientific planning are seen again in white lab coats. One of the bustling blonde female workers, previously spotted in press photos of Fidel Castro's visit, makes a brief reappearance. Only this time she holds the role of the protagonist, embodying the figure of the untroubled socialist worker of the electronic age. She wanders among the freestanding computer modules of the free-plan computer floor, examines data printouts, pushes blinking square buttons on control panels, takes handwritten notes.

Did the newsreel's audience understand what was going on in these images? Was what was depicted actually what was going on within Pavlov's pristine cube? That is, did the Soviet-acquired computers actually fulfill the planning tasks of Gosplan? Did the MCC of the USSR Gosplan succeed in its mission to channel the flow of economic information and achieve the sought-after optimization of Soviet planning? In many ways none of this mattered. Through various mass media, the fantasy of the networked computer at work was seductively communicated not only for the Soviet people but also for allied nations and observing opponents. The imagery of the computer at work aimed at suturing the schism between the imaginary of total computerization and lived reality of the Soviet computer industry. The clean-cut, modernist interiors of Pavlov's MCC building served as the perfect backdrop for the Soviet version of the Cold War "electric drama," a drama that lived "mythically and in depth."[25]

By the early 1970s, the articulation of cybernetic principles on a national or territorial scale had seduced technocrats and officials of central governments in places far beyond the United States and the Soviet Union.[26] Computer networks had already started forging new material and political geographies. In contrast to ARPANET's slow but steady expansion across American universities and government institutions, though, the realization of large-scale networks in other geographic contexts was often limited to the prototyping of an architectural image of centralized control.[27]

In the case of Gosplan's MCC in Moscow, architecture functioned for years as a surrogate for the often missing advancements in state computerization. As a circulating symbol, Gosplan's MCC operated as a synecdoche for the computing power and connectivity that it was supposed to instantiate. Pavlov struggled to define the physical, spatial typology of the seemingly immaterial, dimensionless network node; to articulate pointed concentrations of matter as parts of a larger, invisible constellation; to both fulfill the mundane functional demands of the computer's operation while simultaneously devising a photogenic architecture for it.

155

Glushkov, in parallel, campaigned passionately for the realization of OGAS until the end of his life. In a series of

Opposite, above: Fidel Castro (third from left) on tour at the MCC of Gosplan during his visit to the Soviet Union on the occasion of Cuba joining the COMECON, June 28, 1972. Opposite, below: View from the observation deck into the computer room. Media-covered visit of officials to the MCC of Gosplan, September 1, 1973. Above: Stills from the newsreel film *Moscow—Capital of the USSR* (*Moskva—Stolitsa SSSR*), 1972.

articles in scientific journals and interviews to newspapers like *Pravda*, he regularly advocated for the administrative and economical benefits of what turned out to be his lifetime project. Fully aware of the scale and ambition of the endeavor, he compared OGAS to Lenin's titanic plan for the electrification of Russia.[28] Even if the full implementation of the fifteen-year plan for OGAS was estimated to cost 20 billion rubles, Glushkov anticipated that the optimization of economic planning would spare the state a five-fold of that staggering amount during the same period.[29] The fulfillment of his proposal, though, proved more than challenging in gaining consistent governmental support. Ultimately, Glushkov's death in 1982 brought discussions for a Soviet computer network to a (temporary) halt.

Cold War "computer architectures," as that of Gosplan's MCC, did not merely function as buildings with an amplified iconic performance in mass media. Rather, they constituted key nodes of larger mediatic networks invented for the organization and distribution of information. One could argue, thus, that the typology of the networked computer center was not simply an architectural one. It was rather a transmedial one. Undoubtedly, such architectures organized relationships between human subjects and intricate pieces of electronic equipment—in this case between economists, mathematicians, programmers, and electronic computers. But as transmedial mechanisms in themselves they also synchronously organized the hetereogenous sets of linked-up media across which they participated as both form and content.

01. In Russian, *Obschegosydarstvennaia automatizirovannaia sistema ucheta i obrabotki informatsii*.

02. "One-Sixth of the Earth," *Life*, March 29, 1943, 61–63. Even if the exact proportion changed multiple times throughout the history of the Soviet Union, popular articles like this helped perpetuate the term.

03. Victor Zorza, "Computer Bank May Help Kremlin Keep Tighter Control," *The Guardian*, May 6, 1971, 2.

04. Moev, V. Cheloveku—chelovecheskoe, mashine—mashinnoe [To man—human, to machine—machine], *Literaturnaia gazeta*, April 21, 1971, 12; Zorza, "Computer Bank May Help Kremlin Keep Tighter Control," 2; and Zorza, "Kremlin Planning for 1984; Kremlin Prepares for a Computerized 1984," *Washington Post*, July 25, 1971, B4.

05. Victor Zorza, "Kremlin Planning for 1984."

06. Victor M. Glushkov, quoted ibid., B4.

07. Short for *Gosudarstvennyi planovyy komitet*, commonly translated in English as State Planning Committee, State Plan Commission, or Central Planning Agency.

08. Kathryn M. Bartol, "Soviet Computer Centres: Network or Tangle?," *Soviet Studies* 23, no. 4 (April 1972): 612.

09. Short for Central Statistical Administration of the Council of Ministers of the USSR (*Tsentral'noe statisticheskoe upravlenie pri Sovete Ministrov SSSR*).

10. A. Kosygin, "Ob Uluchshenii Upravleniia Promyshlennostiu Sovershenvovanii Planirovania i Usilenia Ekonomicheskovo Stimularovanii Promyshennovo Proisvodsta [On Improving Industrial Management, Perfect Planning and Increasing Economic Incentives for Industrial Production]," *Pravda*, September 28, 1965.

11. Kantorovich famously developed his theory of linear programming in the late 1930s. Leonid V. Kantorovich, "Ob Odnom Effektivnom Metode Resheniya Nekotorykh Klassov Ekstremal'nykh Problem [A New Method of Solving Some Classes of Extremal Problems]," *Doklady A.N. SSSR* 28, no. 3 (1940): 212–15. For his work on optimal allocation of resources he was awarded the Nobel Prize in Economics in 1975.

12. Short for *Tsentral'nyi ekonomiko-matematicheskii institute Akademii nauk SSSR*. Slava Gerovitch, *From Newspeak to Cyberspeak: A History of Soviet Cybernetics* (Cambridge: MIT Press, 2004), 272.

13. Ibid., 280. For a brief overview of Soviet cybernetics and their interpretation on Norbert Wiener's foundational work, see also Loren R. Graham, "Cybernetics and Computers," in *Science, Philosophy, and Human Behavior in the Soviet Union* (New York: Columbia University Press, 1987), 266–93; Viktor M. Glushkov, *Vvedenie v Kibernetiku* (Kiev: Izdatel'stvo Akademii Nauk Ukrainskoi, 1964), published in English as Viktor M. Glushkov, *Introduction to Cybernetics*, trans. Scripta Technica, Inc. and George M. Kranc (New York: Academic Press, 1966).

14. The budget is equivalent to a modest $67,500 (figured on exchange rates for 1963 provided by the Central Bank of the Russian Federation) for a building of 84,100 square feet. Tsentralnii Komitet KPCC i Soveta Ministrov SSSR, "Postanovlenie No. 564: Ob uluchshenii rukovodstva vnedreniem vychislitel'noi tekhniki i avtomatizirovannykh sistem upravleniia v narodnoe khoziaistvo [Resolution No. 564: On the Improvement of Directorship in the Introduction of Computer Technology and Automated Systems of Management in the National Economy]," resolution of the Central Committee of the Communist Party of the Soviet Union, May 21, 1963, 11–12, f. 5446, op. 106, d. 1324. l. 160-172, State Archive of the Russian Federation (GARF).

15. Project architects L. Pavlov, L. Gonchar, A. Semenov, O. Trubnikova; engineers L. Muromtsev, V. Trostin. Mosproekt was the design institute established in 1930 for the development of architectural and urban projects pertaining primarily to Moscow and its suburbs.

16. Pavlov also led the design investigations for other institutions in Moscow: examples include the Main Computing Centers for the Central Statistical Administration of the USSR in Izmailovo Av. (1968–80) and the State Bank of the USSR on Svobody St. (1974–96). In addition, he designed unrealized schemes for the Computing Center for the Ministry of Agriculture

156

(early 1970s) and a complex of computing centers on Sheremet'evo St. (mid-1970s).

17. On the "epic" of the Tsentrosoyuz Building, see Jean-Louis Cohen, "L'épopée de Centrosojuz," in *Le Corbusier et la Mystique de l'URSS: Théories et Projets pour Moscou, 1928–1936* (Paris: Pierre Mardaga Éditeur, 1988), 87–137; translated in English as Jean-Louis Cohen, "The Centrosoyuz Adventure," in *Le Corbusier and the Mystique of the USSR: Theories and Projects for Moscow, 1928–1936* (Princeton, NJ: Princeton University Press, 1992), 60–105.

18. N. Pekareva, "Glavnyi vychislitel'nyi tsentr Gosplana SSSR [Main Computing Center of Gosplan CCCP]," *Stroitel'stvo i arkhitektura Moskvy*, no. 3 (March 1973): 17.

19. Pekareva, "Glavnyi vychislitel'nyi tsentr Gosplana SSSR," 19.

20. Live theater or dance performances were almost always included on the visiting schedules of officials invited by the Kremlin. On the evening of the computer "performance" at Gosplan, Fidel Castro was escorted by Brezhnev, Kosygin, and the rest of the Kremlin delegation to a ballet performance of Cervantes's *Don Quixote*.

21. The book explains in simple terms concepts and terms related to the "new science" of cybernetics, such as feedback, automation, algorithms, programming, bionics, and computers and computing centers. It discusses the practical uses of mathematical methods in the optimization of planning and central management of production executed with the help of computers—"the golden key to pen the door into the mysterious realm of the economy." Viktor D. Pekelis, *Malen'kaia entsiklopediia o bol'soi kibernetike* [Small Encyclopedia of Great Cybernetics] (Moscow: Detskaia literatura, 1970), 147.

22. L. Kristi, *Plany i zhizn'* [Plans and Life] (Moscow: Tsentral'noe televidenie SSSR, 1971), documentary film, from Net-Film: Russian Archive of Documentary Films and Newsreels, 54:02, http://www.net-film.ru/film-7063.

23. The British-manufactured ICL System 4-70 computer was acquired by the Gosplan of USSR in 1969, after the approval of the Coordinating Committee for Multilateral Export Controls (CoCom) and the US Departments of State, Commerce, and Defense. It had a bus rate of 70 mil. bits/sec. On US intelligence and the approval of this acquisition, see Central Intelligence Agency, *ICL Computers for the U.S.S.R.*, secret report (Langley, VA, February 22, 1971, declassified August 31, 2010), 13; Boris Nikolaevich Malinovsky, *Pioneers of Soviet Computing*, ed. Anne Fitzpatrick, trans. Emmanuel Aronie (SIGCIS, 2010), 128–32, http://www.sigcis.org/files/SIGCISMC2010_001.pdf, originally published in Russian as Boris Nikolaevich Malinovsky, *Istoriia Vychislitel'noi Texniki v Litsakh* [The History of Computing in Personalities] (Kiev: KIT; A.S.K., 1995); Frank Cain, *Economic Statecraft during the Cold War: European Responses to the US Trade Embargo* (London: Routledge, 2007), 128–32, 137–39.

24. V. Skitovich, *Moskva 1972, No. 2: Moskva—Stolitsa SSSR* [Moscow 1972, No. 2: Moscow—Capital of the USSR], (Moscow: Tsentral'naia studiia dokumental'nykh fil'mov, 1972), newsreel film, from Net-Film: Russian Archive of Documentary Films and Newsreels, 9:47, http://www.net-film.ru/film-12596.

25. Marshall McLuhan and Quentin Fiore, *The Medium Is the Massage* (Berkeley: Gingko Press, 2001 [1967]), 9–10.

26. Eden Medina, for example, provides a fascinating account of the Project Cybersyn developed between 1971 and 1973 in Allende's Chile. Eden Medina, *Cybernetic Revolutionaries: Technology and Politics in Allende's Chile* (Cambridge, MA: MIT Press, 2011).

27. The Operations Room designed for Project Cybersyn would be a paradigmatic example.

28. O. Gusev, "Tvorit'—znachit Vnedriat'… [To Create, Is to Implement]," *Pravda*, February 12, 1971; on Lenin's GOELRO plan of electrification, see Jonathan Coopersmith, *The Electrification of Russia, 1880–1926* (Ithaca, NY: Cornell University Press, 1992).

29. V. S. Mikhalevich, "Academician Viktor Mikhailovich Glushkov," *Cybernetics and Systems Analysis* 29, no. 3 (June 1993): 306.

Information Geographies and Geographies of Information

Mark
Graham

Human geographies are infused with information. Information is created, processed, and used in places. It is stored in places, moves across places, and ultimately annotates and augments places.

Until relatively recently, however, much of the world's geographic information was tethered to particular parts of the world. Some of it passed orally, from person to person. Information, or content (for instance, directions, a description, a story), was stuck to its container (the person who spoke about it, who heard about it). As a result it was necessarily mutable. Information mutated or changed as it moved from person to person.

Mass media such as books, radio, and television allowed information to become immutable while remaining mobile.[01] Information was still stuck to its container (words were printed onto a book's pages), but that information could move around the world without significantly changing. This fundamentally altered the political economy of geographic information. Immutable but mobile geographic information could be employed to exert power in economic, social, and political spheres of

life and governance. This meant that those in control of the means of informational production (publishers, printers, media companies, governments, and censors) could wield enormous influence over how places came to be represented.[02]

But the digital moment has brought about a fundamentally different relationship between content and its container.[03] Information now can be separated from its container and yet still remain immutable. This ability to detach content from its container has massively lowered the barriers to entry associated with earlier media production (the hand-copied manuscript, for example, and the first television sets). This has led many commentators to point to the possibility of more democratized information geographies. The digital moment therefore offers the potential for a radically different political economy of geographic information:[04] the potential for broad-based participation and representation that can circumvent traditional mediators of information; and the potential for citizens to play a greater role in shaping the immutable geographic information that plays such an important

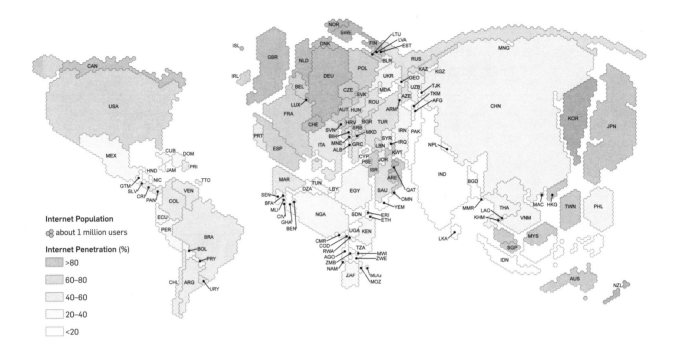

Internet Population
🌐 about 1 million users

Internet Penetration (%)
▉ >80
▓ 60–80
▒ 40–60
░ 20–40
☐ <20

role in everyday life.[05] By exploring a few examples of the global geographies of information, some empirical evidence may be brought to bear on those promises.

Here it is relevant to point out an important difference between "information geographies" and "geographies of information," as I see them. The former is a way of signifying concern about the augmented or saturated nature of places with information. Because places are ontogenetic (that is, in a state of becoming that emerges through practices), talking about already existing information geographies poses a challenge.[06] In the same way that a walk through Osaka draws upon and brings into being very different geographies for me than it would for an Osakan, information geographies likewise have no ontological stability or fixity. "Geographies of information" instead refers to the geographic distribution of information: sometimes treating information as representative of some other underlying phenomena and sometimes treating it as a phenomenon itself.[07] This paper explores geographies of information, but it does so as a starting point to understand one crucial facet of information geographies.[08]

Three categories of information seem especially worthy of consideration: geographies of access and enablement, geographies of participation, and geographies of representation. The goal of this investigation it is to identify some of the key contours of unevenness, barriers to participation, and concentrations of content or representation that exist today and influence the overall political economy of information. In particular, access to the Internet (as an example of access and enablement), contributions to Wikipedia (as an example of participation), and content on Wikivoyage (as an example of representation) will be explored. Although information geographies as seen through the lens of these three distinct datasets may not prove in any way representative of other digitally mediated practices, the mode of analysis undertaken in this essay offers a guide for the type of questioning we may want to pursue when looking at other datasets related to information geographies.

Internet Access

When reflecting on the geography of access, disconnectivity, and enablement, it is crucial to begin with basic internet access, a prerequisite for most types of digital engagement. Data from 2013 collected by the World Bank and International Telecommunications Union records internet use among the total world population.[09] The data is mapped as a cartogram in which the size of each country represents its population of internet users, with each hexagon on the map symbolizing one-third of a million internet users.[10] Shading on the map is used to represent each country's internet penetration rate, with darker shades symbolizing higher levels of internet usage among the population.

Above: Map showing average number of edits to Wikipedia.
Opposite: Map showing internet population and penetration.

Average number of edits
over three months
■ >1,000,000
■ 500,001–1,000,000
■ 100,001–500,000
□ 50,001–100,000
□ 10,001–50,000
□ 1–10,000

The map paints a revealing picture about human digital activity. The world's largest internet population (over half a billion connected people) lives in China. Indeed, 42 percent of the world's internet users now live in Asia: China, India, and Japan alone are home to more internet users than all of Europe and North America combined.[11] Few countries, however, can count a majority of their populations as internet users: India, for instance, falls into the lowest category of penetration, at less than 20 percent. This is not to suggest that significant change is not occurring. Between 2011 and 2014, some African countries experienced staggering growth in internet penetration: almost all North African countries doubled their internet population (Algeria being the exception). Kenya, Nigeria, and South Africa also saw significant growth. Other countries, however, have seen little change, with more than twenty countries located in sub-Saharan African having internet penetration of less than 10 percent in 2013, and exhibiting very little growth since then.

Looking at this data as a starting point, therefore, reminds us that despite the massive impacts that the Internet has on everyday life for many people, there remain starkly uneven geographies of access. The majority of humanity has never used the Internet.

Contributions to Wikipedia

Wikipedia is one of the most visible components of digital information geographies. It contains 32 million articles and exists in more than 200 languages. Fifteen percent of all internet users access it on any given day. Content on the platform thus plays an important role in annotating parts of our world.[12] Wikipedia operates using a digital architecture that, in theory, allows anyone with an internet connection to contribute content: indeed, the platform's strapline is "the free encyclopedia that anyone can edit." In practice, however, the geography of participation is highly geographically uneven, as demonstrated by mapping data related to Wikipedia editing activity over time.

Quarterly data regarding the total number of edits to all Wikipedia versions that emerged from any territory (that is, the amount of content people producing in each country) was averaged over a two-year period (2010–2011) and plotted on the world map.[13] Inequalities in the amount of content produced are stark: the United States, Germany, the United Kingdom, and France all have on average over a million edits each quarter. Most countries in Africa and the Middle East, in contrast, register only a few thousand edits per quarter. Interestingly, more edits originate in Hong Kong each quarter than within the entire continent of Africa.

Some of this variation can be explained by internet population: generally, the more internet users in a country, the more edits originated there. However, even adjusting for their small internet populations, most Middle Eastern and African countries still register far fewer edits than would be expected when internet penetration is considered.[14]

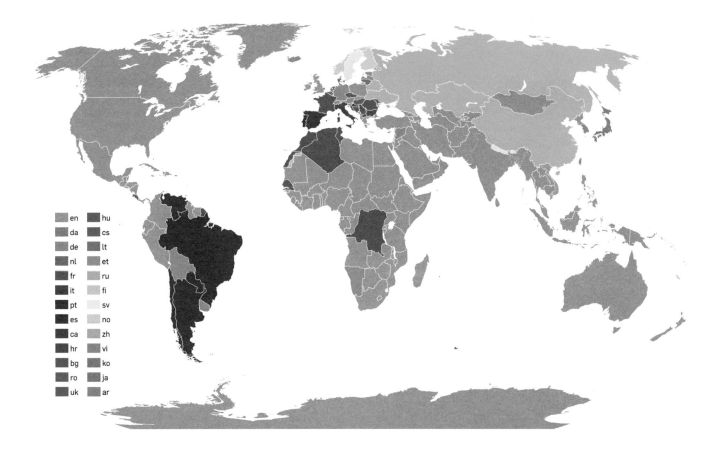

en	hu
da	cs
de	lt
nl	et
fr	ru
it	fi
pt	sv
es	no
ca	zh
hr	vi
bg	ko
ro	ja
uk	ar

These uneven geographies of participation cannot be simply explained by considering internet access. Something else is at play. Said plainly, geographies of participation are heavily skewed in favour of internet users in high-income countries. Interviews and focus groups involving Wikipedians revealed that a number of other circumstances also affected participation. The availability of reliable infrastructure (such as power supply), a broad ecosystem of local information, and an educated and tech-literate population that included both men and women were all found to be significant enabling factors, as was the prevailing belief that the internet could be trusted rather than feared as an arm of surveillance by the state. Having the critical mass for local-language tools, platforms, and communities was also identified as a significant factor enabling participation.[15]

The massively uneven rates of participation on Wikipedia manifest themselves in other patterns as well. One such pattern involves the varying amounts of information about a country that appear in different languages—most notably, in languages other than that country's dominant one. There are more articles about France in French, for example, than in any other language. Mapping statistics related to the entire world reveals that almost every European country has more articles about itself written in its own dominant language than in any other language: more articles about Finland in Finnish than in English or German or Russian, and so on.

But that pattern is not replicated across many low-income parts of the world. English emerges as the dominant language of digital content in much of Africa, the Middle East, South and East Asia, and even parts of South and Central America. French and German are similarly dominant in a few other countries scattered around the world.

The scale of these differences results in some implausible comparisons. For instance, not only are there more Wikipedia articles in English than Arabic about almost every Arabic-speaking country in the Middle East, but there are even more English articles about North Korea than there are articles in Arabic about Saudi Arabia, Libya, the United Arab Emirates, and many other countries in the region. These patterns illustrate one way that uneven rates of participation manifest. Some parts of the world are well represented by locals, while others are largely defined by people with few ties to those places.

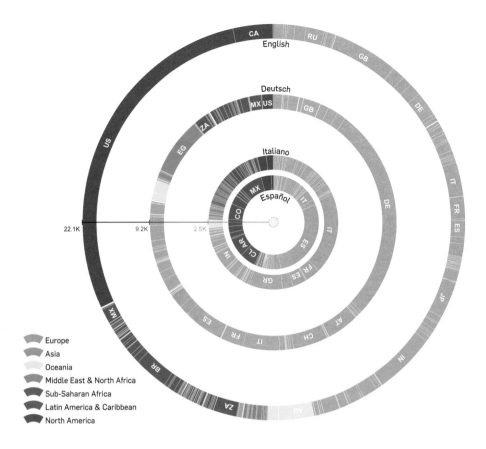

Right: Geographic coverage of Wikivoyage. Opposite: Wikipedia articles by country (depicting dominant language).

Europe
Asia
Oceania
Middle East & North Africa
Sub-Saharan Africa
Latin America & Caribbean
North America

Content on Wikivoyage

Entirely user-generated, Wikivoyage is one of the Internet's most accessed travel guides. Like many other platforms, such as Wikipedia, Twitter, and OpenStreetMap, it displays significantly uneven geographies of content. But Wikivoyage is particularly notable because the presence or absence of content on the site has an obvious and direct link to economic and cultural geographies.[16]

Data for 2013, which is freely available from the Wikimedia Downloads website, compares English, German, Italian, and Spanish content.[17] These languages represent the largest subprojects and provide examples of both geographically concentrated and dispersed languages. Each circular ring in the Wikivoyage infographic above represents one of four languages and is sized in relation to the number of articles present on Wikivoyage in that language. Each section of a ring represents a country—or more specifically, the number of articles in that language about a country.

The graphic reveals the selective picture of the world offered in Wikivoyage. We see that there is a large amount of self-focus in each language version of the travel guides

on the website. English-speaking countries account for about half of the pages written in English; the same holds true for Spanish-speaking countries. German-speaking countries account for only about one-third of the German platform, whereas the Italian edition dedicates about one-fifth of its content to Italy. This is particularly notable because, unlike other platforms that rely on user-generated content (Wikipedia and OpenStreetMap, for example), Wikivoyage is a project designed to explicitly facilitate writing about distant parts of the world. But even under those preconditions, contributors still tend to be more inclined to focus on local topics. This is important, because—as demonstrated in the previous section—participation has its own, uneven geography.

We therefore see that low-income countries are particularly underrepresented by the English, German, and Italian projects, with only about one-third of articles in those languages dedicated to countries outside the Global North. The Spanish version understandably contains more content about South America, but with only 0.1 percent of the guides about sub-Saharan Africa, it practically ignores that region.

Mark Graham

Information Geographies

As the sections above have demonstrated, not only are the geographies of access uneven but so too are patterns of participation and representation: producing geographies of information characterized by data shadows and digital divisions of labor that are heavily concentrated in global economic cores. Furthermore, the broadening of internet access (with more than 3 billion people able to be counted as users today) does not seem to have resulted in any significant leveling of the playing field.

As human societies became exponentially more complex, moving from preindustrial to industrial to postindustrial modes of economic organization, the reliance on geographic information that is both immutable and mobile grew evermore pronounced. But the digital moment has offered the potential for something different. Geographic information can remain immutable, but unlike in previous eras content now can be more easily separated from its container. This matters because geographic information becomes simultaneously influential in the ways that it can travel around the web and often becomes untraceable to particular organizations or people. For instance, think how a Wikipedia article on London or OpenStreetMap edits in Edinburgh can impact a multitude of other sites and services that use that content; yet the conditions under which that information was produced (who created the content, why they chose to highlight some elements and omit others, etc.) remain relatively opaque and often untraceable when accessed through those third-party users. The removal of the tether between content and container does not untether that geographic information from the very geography that it represents; rather, it untethers it from the digital contexts of its genesis and production.

This tethered yet untethered geographic information is essential to critically understanding information geographies. At a time when an increasing amount of everyday life is mediated by the digital, we need to better understand both the political economy of, and the forms of power that produce particular information geographies. And because immutable geographic information is becoming increasingly untethered from its contexts and containers, we face more complexity at a moment in which we really need opacity.

The uneven geographies of information outlined above can profoundly impact economic, social, and political life. Geography is fundamentally informational, and that information has its own geography. Yet as information infrastructures and the political economy of digital information shift into a digital era, it has become ever harder to map, understand, and critique those geographies.

This piece has sought to explore a few examples of the geographies of information in order to attempt a better understanding of how we might interrogate one important facet of contemporary information geographies. As content separates from its containers, as more complex relationships between mutable, immutable, fixed, and mobile information are brought into being, as creative destruction ceaselessly creates ever more information infrastructures, and as geographic information is increasingly governed by a diverse array of political economic configurations, we need to ask what rights should be expected in the contexts of our immersive information geographies.

What sort of information opacity should be a right? What sort of privacy should be a right? What sort of access to digital information should be a right? And what sort of voice and speech within the contexts of information geographies should be a right? Legal scholars, philosophers, and computer scientists engage in rich debates about rights, privacy, transparency, and access. What can we as geographers add to the debate? I would argue that productive questions sit at the intersection of research about uneven geographies of information (access, production, and representation) and power within information geographies. We currently know too little about how people are empowered or disempowered within information geographies; how some circumvent some forms of power; how some forms of power are reinforced and amplified. As more collections like this one on the geographies of information are assembled, we may more productively turn the theoretical and methodological tools of geography into information geographies.

Acknowledgments: This paper is an abridged and amended version of: M. Graham, S. De Sabbata, M. Zook, "Towards a Study of Information Geographies: (Im)mutable augmentations and a Mapping of the Geographies of Information," *Geo: Geography and Environment* (2015). I wish to give special thanks to Stefano De Sabbata whose work on the images on pages 160 and 163, as well as our broader Information Geographies project (geography.oii.ox.ac.uk), has been invaluable. I am also grateful for the help of numerous people who collaborated on a multiyear effort to map and measure the geographies of Wikipedia. In particular I would like to thank Bernie Hogan, Ralph Straumann, and Ahmed Medhat. This work was also made possible by research grants from the International Development Research Centre and the European Research Council under the European Union's Seventh Framework Programme for Research and Technological Development (FP/2007–2013) / ERC Grant Agreement n. 335716.

01. Bruno Latour, "Visualization and Cognition: Thinking with Eyes and Hands," *Knowledge and Society: Studies in the Sociology of Culture Past and Present* 6 (1986), 1–40.

02. Ernesto Laclau and Chantal Mouffe, *Hegemony and Socialist Strategy: Towards a Radical Democratic Politics* (London: Verso, 1985).

03. David M. Berry, *Critical Theory and the Digital* (New York: Bloomsbury Academic, 2014); Heather Ford and Mark Graham, "Semantic Cities: Coded Geopolitics and the Rise of the Semantic City" (unpublished manuscript, 2015).

04. Lawrence Lessig, "An Information Society: Free or Feudal?" (lecture, World Summit on the Information Society, Geneva, Switzerland, 2003); Yochai Benkler, *The Wealth of Networks: How Social Production Transforms Markets and Freedom* (New Haven, CT: Yale University Press, 2006); Axel Bruns, *Blogs, Wikipedia, Second Life, and Beyond: From Production to Produsage* (New York: Peter Lang, 2008); Henry Jenkins, *Convergence Culture: Where Old and New Media Collide* (New York: New York University Press, 2006).

05. Daniel Sui and Michael Goodchild, "The Convergence of GIS and Social Media: Challenges for GIScience," *International Journal of Geographical Information Science* 25, no. 11 (November 2011): 1737–48.

06. Rob Kitchin and Martin Dodge, "Rethinking Maps," *Progress in Human Geography* 31, no. 3 (2007): 331–44; Rob Kitchin and Martin Dodge, *Code/Space: Software and Everyday Life* (Cambridge, MA: MIT Press, 2011).

07. Matthew W. Wilson, "Morgan Freeman is Dead and Other Big Data Stories," *Cultural Geographies* 22, no. 2 (April, 2015), 345–49.

08. In other words, the goal of my own empirical project is to understand power in digitally augmented places. I approach this through two lenses: (1) how information geographies are augmented (what they contain, who they serve, etc.); (2) whose voices get to shape information geographies (and who gets left out). Geographies of information necessarily only offer a selective lens on one important facet of information geographies. Geographies of information tell us little about the various ways that geographies are variably performed and enacted, but they do reveal some of the informational raw material for those performances; they reveal whether some of the necessary, rather than sufficient, conditions are in place for inclusive, participatory, and representative information geographies.

09. At the time of publication, 2011 data was the most complete dataset available. For an older but more detailed discussion of these patterns, see M. Graham, S. Hale, and M. Stephens, "Digital Divide: The Geography of Internet Access," *Environment and Planning A* 44, no. 5 (2012), 1009–10.

10. Countries with fewer than that number are not included on the map.

11. India has the world's third largest Internet population, and Japan has the fourth largest.

12. For similar arguments about geographic imbalances in digital participation, see M. Haklay, "Neogeography and the Delusion of Democratisation," *Environment and Planning A* 45 (2013), 55–69, in which the author argues about a 'delusion of democratization'; see also Mark Graham, "Internet Geographies: Data Shadows and Digital Divisions of Labour," in *Society and the Internet: How Networks of Information and Communication are Changing our Lives*, eds. Mark Graham and William H. Dutton (Oxford: Oxford University Press, 2014), 99–116, with a focus on "digital divisions of labour"; or Monica Stephens, "Gender and the GeoWeb: Divisions in the Production of User-Generated Cartographic Information," *GeoJournal* 78, no. 6 (August 2013), with a focus on the gendered nature of user-generated content.

13. This data was obtained from "Wikimedia Traffic Analysis Report—Page Edits," Wikimedia, http://stats.wikimedia.org/wikimedia/squids/SquidReportsCountriesLanguagesVisitsEdits.htm.

14. For detailed statistical analyses on the topic, see M. Graham, S. Hale, and D. Gaffney, "Where in the World Are You? Geolocation and Language Identification in Twitter," *Professional Geographer* 66, no. 4 (2014), 568–78.

15. See Mark Graham, "Inequitable Distributions in Internet Geographies: The Global South is Gaining Access but Lags in Local Content," *Innovations* 9, nos. 3–4 (December 2014): 17–34.

16. For an anlaysis of Wikipedia, see Mark Graham, "Wiki Space: Palimpsests and the Politics of Exclusion," in *Critical Point of View: A Wikipedia Reader*, eds. Geert Lovink and Nathaniel Tkacz (Amsterdam: Institute of Network Cultures, 2011), 269–82; for an analysis of Twitter, see Graham, Hale, and Gaffney, "Where in the World Are You?," 568–78; for an analysis of OpenStreetMap, see M. Haklay, "How Good is Volunteered Geographical Information? A Comparative Study of OpenStreetMap and Ordnance Survey Datasets," *Environment and Planning B: Planning and Design* 37, no. 4 (July 2010): 682–703.

17. "Wikimedia Downloads," Wikimedia, http://dumps.wikimedia.org/backup-index.html.

Image Credits

160: Mark Graham and Stefano De Sabbata. Internet Geographies at the Oxford Internet Institute, October 2013. Data source: World Bank 2011.

161: Mark Graham, Bernie Hogan, Ahmed Mohammed, and Richard Farmbrough. Oxford Internet Institute, 2015. In collaboration with Ilhem Allagui and Ali Frihida. Support provided by IDRC. Data obtained from Wikipedia in January 2012, averages taken from the 2011–2012 period.

162: Mark Graham, Bernie Hogan, Ahmed Medhat, and David Palfrey. Oxford Internet Institute Support provided by the IDRC. Data obtained from Wikilocation and the Toolserver in July 2012. Four million georeferenced articles analyzed in 42 languages.

163: Mark Graham and Stefano De Sabbata. Data source: Wikivoyage.org.

165

Governing Planetary Skin
Energy as Information Geography

Benjamin H.
Bratton

The Stack is the accidental megastructure that we continue to build through planetary-scale computation and in its image.[01] It is at once a technical apparatus, a political institutional form, and a geographic model. At its base an earth layer provides the source minerals and energy that power the whole, including cloud computing platforms and global cities. In the transposition of biology, chemistry, and ecology into information, it is also a critical site for emerging forms of computational governance. Put differently, for the holistic totalizing views of curatorial ecology and geoengineering (from early Holocene agriculture to early Anthropocene genomic technologies) there is, finally, no biopolitics that is not first a politics of energy. For our contemporary model allegories and infrastructures drawn for and by planetary-scale computation, both biology and energy are quanta to be *sensed*, *visualized*, and *optimized* at the same global scale as their integrated effects. As these operations attempt to rationalize the political economy matter, they also spawn unforeseeable accidents that may ultimately prove to be both dangerous and/or fortuitous.

The Stack's visual geography amplifies economies of mutual simulation between land, image, and interface by redefining the *surface* of the earth as a living and governable epidermis, and recomposing that skin as a bio-informational matrix enrolled into hard and soft systems. As a landscaping machine, planetary-scale computation twists and combs settled areas into freshly churned ground, enumerating input and output points and rendering them as glassy planes of pure logistics. It wraps the globe in wires, making it into a knotty, incomplete ball of glass and copper twine. It activates the electromagnetic spectrum overhead as another drawing medium, making it visible and interactive, limning the sky with colorful blinking aeroglyphs.[02] The Stack walls off whole layers of that spectrum for private purposes by optimizing it through finer and finer atmospheric grids, turning location into geolocation and geolocation into application engineering.

The image-of-infrastructure and an infrastructure-of-the-image flip-flop their respective works, repositioning geoscopy as geoaeshetics and geoaesthtics as geoeconomics. For example, the earth layer also situates a network of telescopes "looking out" into space from many positions at once, so as create a composite "false" image of a portion of the universe. This technique, known as Very Long Baseline Interferometry (VLBI), creates a single discontiguous machine distributed among many countries, only useful if it is used across multiple time zones at once. As a Stack geographic machine, Google Earth can be thought of as an inverse of VLBI, in that it looks inward instead of outward to create a composite false image of the distributed surface of the earth by integrating the perspectives of multiple orbital satellite perspectives into an (interactive) visual totality, and as it stands for a global domain drawn in place, this mosaic draws Earth's skin as an island to be measured and mastered. As it builds on the Apollo 8 image of figure and void, Google Earth amplifies it into a general-purpose application interface through which the user layer and earth layer of the Stack seem to inform one another directly.[03] Here the geoaesthetics of Stack geography displays ecology as an archive, to be indexed, catalogued, and sorted, and only then acted upon.[04]

Such Stack geographies both complicate and clarify the design of platform sovereignty, as much for what they make possible as for what they disrupt. Google's motto, "to organize the world's information and to make it useful," changes meaning when the world itself is seen as *being* information, such that to organize all the information is to organize all the world. Furthermore, synthetic computation expands what is sensed, measured, calculated, communicated, stored, and worked upon. That is, the ascendance of digital computing from a narrowly deployed, elite scientific-military instrument into a general-purpose planetary-scale consumer infrastructure transforming what states (and other systems of governance) can see, know and affect, reforms it into an organ of organizational cognition. As sensing extends to all specific surfaces—no longer dumb but rather affective—the net sum of what is opened up or closed off by computation largely defines what it is that any governance platform now chooses to sense and not to sense in general. The information that is sensed and sensible is, more often that not, on the surface of the territory, and this intensifies governmental focus on them. Skin is the largest sensory organ of any animal body, composed of numerous dermal and epidermal layers holding organs together and mediating multiple layers of individual interiority and exteriority.[05] The extrapolation of planetary surfaces as epidermis has been inextricably linked with the conceptualization of climatic measurement and prediction. Global climate and weather systems have long been driving applications for planetary instrumentation and the understanding of the globe as a "vast machine."[06]

The interdependence of the image-of-infrastructure and the infrastructure-of-the-interfacial-image is exemplified as the systems logic of a geographic, bio-informational, planetary-scale epidermal sensing and computation

megastructure by—who else?—the Planetary Skin Institute. For this project, the living and breathing geoepidermis is surveyed through a proposed metainstrumentation of the biosphere into a totally available, archived present, open to interested intervention, collaborative management, and quantified governance. Originally launched cooperatively in 2009 by NASA and Cisco Systems, and now an independent nonprofit research and development platform, Planetary Skin sought to integrate data from many sources into a single, branded geoadministrative mechanism. An internal Cisco white paper describes Planetary Skin as "an open network platform for real-time, highly distributed mass remote sensing, authentication, risk-profiling, certification, and monitoring of carbon stocks and flows that generates trust and enables collaboration among the players in all sectors [industry, government, academia]."[07] Its ultimate ambition is to provide an open and comprehensive multiconstituent platform for monitoring and governing planetary biological-ecological systems, with particular emphasis on water distribution and carbon quantification (ultimately to support pricing of these reserve currencies, one would imagine). One early pilot project, *Rainforest Skin*, would measure the total quantity of carbon contained within the planet's rain forests, perhaps the most immediately leverageable carbon governance opportunity, and where CO_2 sinks are concentrated but threatened by land use. The project would combine datasets drawn from "geo-referenced satellite[s], unmanned aerial vehicle[s], and multiple ground-based sensor networks to estimate the forest's carbon stock and flow dynamics, and then to allow for trading—and risk management of—this new commodity."[08] Stack-scale initiatives such as Planetary Skin (and there are many others) frame the earth as a total field in which to identify and track strategic chemical subroutines, such as carbon flows, and to present these totalities back to the whole. This sort of speculative megacomputation is but one way that geoscopy, geography, and geopolitics blur and blend into amalgamated images, territories, and governmental techniques. It is but one way that the Stack composes the earth layer.

The Planetary Skin Institute's tagline, "you can't monitor what you can't measure," is a good motto for the big data society, should it ever be clarified at some point in the process who is and isn't "you." As Planetary Skin describes its plans, the "you" are likely drawn from the usual stakeholders—technocrats, academics, NGOs, consultants, and so on.[09] The likely effect of this initiative, however, were it or something like it ever fully realized, would not merely extend or consolidate the arrangement of zero-sum governance as we currently know it but would inevitably introduce other compound subjects and objects, some human and some not, and elevate them from object to subject in uncertain ways. A benefit of these initiatives would not only be to quantify a *status quo* but, ultimately, to break ground for alternative norms and to constitute (or at least support) another medium of governance over the biosystems that it ("we") can measure and monitor. Planetary Skin, or some similar descendent platform, might connect with existing governmental and nongovernmental biopolititcal authorities, supporting, augmenting, and eventually superseding them. Through ecumenical platform interoperability, this platform would ultimately become itself a governing authority. Through "neutral" simulation-visualization of ground-level patterns upon which any large-scale carbon trading markets would depend, a platform like this could quantify the carbon stocks that might be traded or sequestered as well as validate treaty verifications or violations. This would in turn help convert matter into money by providing a kind of "financial" transparency, in this case of financialized molecules. Such platform projects emblematic of the Stack's incorporation of the earth as a layer, would convene political authority not by starting from scratch but by remeasuring, reframing, and reinstrumentalizing some already existing geographic whole. They generate comprehensive quantifications of processes and patterns that, to the extent that they operate as intended, also take on an effective force of law within an expanded ecopolitical jurisdiction, even if their claims are not ratified by states (Westphalian or post-Westphalian) to do so. Further, as these metatechnologies of ecological observation become necessary to even perceive the contours of ecological risk, they enter directly into the programmatic center of governance as such. This is not internationalism, however. The force of platforms is different, for example, from the ecoglobalism feared by conspiratorial isolationists, all spittle-lipped over UN Agenda 21, in that there is, according to design at least, no central commanding body outside the architecture of the platform itself.[10] Such platforms in principle may even work, for better or worse, to undermine political centralization that they themselves do not or cannot calculate or articulate. That said, nothing is certain. A transference of sovereignty from the declared self-interest of whoever counts as a citizen to the calculation of carbon and energy binds one inhale with another exhale across continents, and so guarantees at the very least indecipherable accounting paradoxes.

Computation is training governance to see the world as it does, and to be blind like it is. If, over time, something sees *for* the State, *on behalf of* the State, *in place of* the State, it does so by seeing *as* the State, or by seeing as something the State has not yet become but would become once it was trained by these same new tools of perception and blindness. As the State incorporates new techniques into itself, those techniques absorb, displace, and diminish the State by controlling access to unique jurisdictions that the State cannot otherwise possibly comprehend without their help. As the Stack extends its jurisdiction it also confiscates and multiplies it. It does not merely accelerate or open-up governance as presently configured; it invents substitutions as alternate jurisdictions appear, linking cellular biology to macroecologies to computational geopolitics. Some of these substitutions last for seconds; others will endure perhaps for many centuries. Macroscopic platforms such as Planetary Skin frame Earth as a competitive archive sorted into a quantifiable past, an atemporal surficial now, and a predictive virtualization of futures, from which models and simulations—their preferred instruments of governance—can be derived.

Through this process, opacity and privacy are redefined by a spectacle of transparency. A platform's authority is based on the quantity and quality of its data, together with the means at its disposal to translate that stash into instrumental simulations of error-corrected pasts, presents, and futures. Cisco, NASA, Google, and the like make data available for free or on a subscription basis. They invite users to innovate vertical markets through the use of their datasets and tools. Because geoepidermal megastructures realize their political value through immediate and potential events, they can sense their economic value through the currencies they can verify for their users, and they are themselves dependent on enabling users to actively engage platform interfaces and to *act back* upon the materials they represent. A platform is a machine as well as map, "an engine, not a camera."[11] Platforms are tools to compose things, not just to measure them, and so the slogan "you can't monitor what you can't measure" may require the Foucaultian revision, "you can't modify what you can't monitor," or even "you can't *not* modify whatever it is that you sense."

Today, this and other geoscopic situations are provided to us by Stack infrastructures of orbiting satellites—artificial constellations—and the terrestrial grids connecting them to terrestrial networks. Instrumenting the planet in this way has not only allowed for a more finely grained *geo-graphy*, it has also physically altered the very scale of Earth's gradient body—altered what it measures as the Holocene atmospheric membrane, now augmented by a crust of smart satellites and dumb garbage. The planet's "natural" equatorial diameter is 12,756 kilometers, and if one were to include the celestial atmospheric firmament,

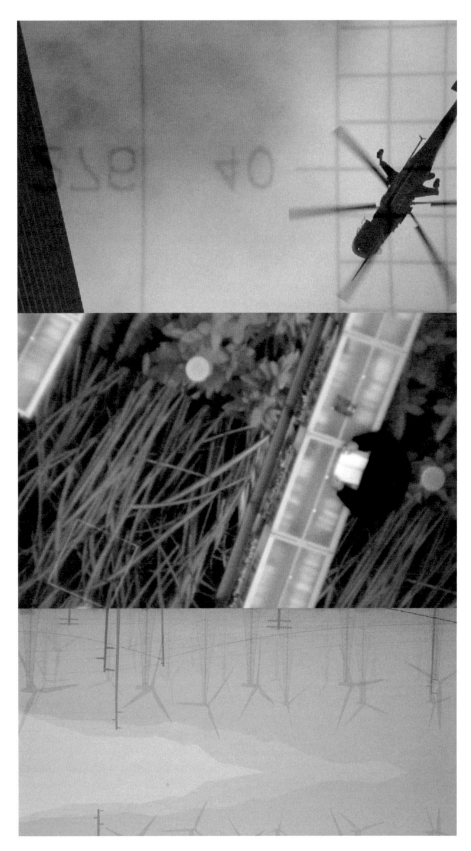

Machine sensing.

that number would swell to almost 13,000 kilometers. The ring of communications technologies, however, geosynchronously orbiting Earth every twenty-four hours, linking together points on its surface, and locating the whole sphere within its lonely void, forms another outer membrane, extending the measurement to 36,000 kilometers. Are they not also part of Earth's body?

Generally speaking, satellite observation technology has vastly inflated the physical geometrics of the observed planet, but it has compressed the conceptual spaces of relative distance as well. As surely as the Stack generates new spaces, does it also ensure a certain erasure of other worlds? This is a common refrain within critiques of modernity from both the right and the left, providing a negative apologetics of globalization and the subsumption of the continuity of the earth into the omnivorous universalisms of cyberinfrastructure. For some, the "world" is a tragic casualty of its appearance in digital images of itself.[12] It cannot survive this manner of testimony. It is shrunken, eaten, defamed by its reduction to a plateau of digitalized time. Whereas difference and analogy are natural functions of distance, in the instantaneousness of global information, the landscape of distances has collapsed, and so in some critiques, digital space is a form of dark matter, but a form that, instead of expanding and elongating real distances, flattens the space of analogy into the simultaneity of network time.

There are other, and better, judgments of these accelerations, displacements, elongations, migrations, vectors, lines, and links. Can they be drawn without replicating the terms of reduction that any truly living image would need to escape? Is that what is most starkly absent from Google Earth's transformation of the map into an interface? In that the diagrams and visualizations of the networked totality are also, to varying degrees, cosmograms—figures of the whole of the universe and earthly situation—what intrinsic violence does the speed of interactivity do to the depth, or depthlessness, of the global space that it models? What can we do with these pictures of the data that the world secretes, and what do they want from us ultimately?

These questions are themselves some of the productive "accidents" of the Stack's earth layer. The technologies we use to measure and monitor the earth have increased the objective scale of the planet and have shown us real pictures of the cosmic abyss, which crack open our little primate skulls; but in doing so, they have also collapsed the phenomenal scale of our sense of habitat. In its paired world-making and world-erasure projects, the earth layer of the Stack will have introduced equal measures of numinous insight and atonal banality.[13] Our inclination,

however, is that, like the turn away from geocentrism and toward heliocentrism (still very much an incomplete turn as measured against the superstitious norms of humanist geopolitics), the platformization of the earth will, in net sum, provide for greater "worlds" than it erases.

That said, the engineering program ahead will be full of twists and turns, many of which will involve sourcing the power to continue the evolution of the Stack itself. The Cloud layer, located just above the earth layer in the Stack, makes epic, rapidly expanding energy demands and so risk is not hard to find.[14] Data centers are located to mitigate cost and uncertainty, away from likely natural disasters and in proximity of cheap and/or clean energy sources, diverse power-grid interconnects, favorable land-use zoning, inexpensive intermediate bandwidth, etc.[15] Because there is no planetary computational economy that is not first a planetary energy economy, the limits to growth for the Stack are not only governed by Moore's Law and Shannon's Law (accelerating the speed of processors and squeezing more information into existing channels) but also, and perhaps more importantly, by the need to secure the energy required to power those data centers, smart cities, homes, cars, roads, smart objects, and phones. The real costs (or benefits) of doing so must necessarily be calculated at the expense of other infrastructure, like new roads and buildings.[16] In principle, there is potentially a virtuous correlation at work for innovation across computation and energy sectors, and the gamble on that potential is another generative accident of the earth layer. The continuing growth of the Stack and of the computationally intensive transformation of energy sourcing and distribution infrastructures upon which it depends likely cannot occur without one another.

The architectures of new energy-information networks, including so-called smart grids, require pervasive computational systems to realize necessary gains in the timely, efficient, and equitable distribution of watts of energy across networks. For this, each point in the grid that might produce or consume energy (which in principle includes pretty much anywhere and anyone) must not only be able to store or transmit that energy but also to calculate and communicate its activities to platforms that steer the whole. All electrons must pass through the angelic regime of recording and optimization, but today such grids are slow to come online.[17] Their politics are filled with inertia and gamesmanship, and moreover, the underlying physics are uncooperative; electrons do not work "like bits" no matter what your Smart City Consultants are telling you. At the same time, the Stack itself depends upon new energy grids to feed and undergird its growth. It requires a conjoined-twin energy-information network that can generate, calculate, and allocate those usable electrons point-to-point. Absent the deus ex machina of a radical relaxation of energy scarcity by renewable sources, the fine-grained electron sorting between points of production and consumption must be realized at global scale or the growth of planetary-scale computation will hit physical energy limits and will stall.[18] A more scalable grid of electrons needs to be wrapped inside and around the Stack's earth layer. In short, planetary-scale computation needs smart grids to grow, and for smart grids to grow they need more ubiquitous computation. The computational future of energy and the infrastructural program of computation form such a coil, one end feeding on the other like Ouroboros, the snake eating its own tail.

01. The term "The Stack" comes from my book *The Stack: On Software and Sovereignty* (Cambridge, MA: MIT Press, forthcoming).

02. Consider, for example, Usman Haque's SkyEar: "Sky Ear is a non-rigid carbon-fibre 'cloud,' embedded with one thousand glowing helium balloons and several dozen mobile phones. The balloons contain miniature sensor circuits that respond to electromagnetic fields, particularly those of mobile phones. When activated, the sensor circuits co-ordinate to cause ultra-bright coloured LEDs to illuminate. The 30m cloud glows and flickers brightly as it floats across the sky." Usman Haque, "Sky Ear," Haque Design + Research, http://www.haque.co.uk/skyear.php.

03. Mark Dorrian, "On Google Earth," *New Geographies* 04: *Scales of the Earth*, ed. El Hadi Jazairy and Melissa Vaughn (2011): 164–70.

04. That archive is also made into an interface *toward itself*, provoking user-initiated feedback loops between icons and events. On this idea, see my chapter "Interface," in *The Stack*.

05. The question of "skin" shows up in cultural theory in a variety of ways. In addition to the obvious connotations for theories of race and racism, see also Mark C. Taylor, *Hiding* (Chicago: University of Chicago Press, 1998); Nicholas de Monchaux, *Spacesuit: Fashioning Apollo* (Cambridge, MA: MIT Press, 2011); and Peter Sloterdijk, *Bubbles*, vol. 1, *Spheres: Microspherology* (Los Angeles: Semiotext(e), 2011). The governance of skin figures prominently in the "City" chapter of *The Stack*, in this case, as urban skin.

06. Paul N. Edwards, *A Vast Machine: Computer Models, Climate Data, and the Politics of Global Warming* (Cambridge, MA: MIT Press, 2010).

07. Juan Carlos Castilla-Rubio and Simon Willis, "Planetary Skin: A Global Platform for a New Era of Collaboration," Cisco Systems internal white paper, March 2009, http://newsroom.cisco.com/dlls/2009/ekits/Planetary_Skin_POV_vFINAL_spw_jc.pdf.

08. Ibid.

09. Some descriptive detail from the Planetary Skin website informs this assumption: "It is supported by joint policy programs that extend the model of planetary instrumentalization to the political realm through open and collaborative, if also expert-piloted, forums. These include theconnectedrepublic.org, connectedcommons.org, and connectedurbandevelopment.org, and it also extends to include tools for the integration of actors into common parliamentarian media, largely identical to those in development and deployment under the rubric of E-Government (digitalization of governmental processes) and Government 2.0 (employment of open social media channels and tools to support self-governance)." The white paper reads, "The Planetary Skin platform can be thought of as a globally pervasive 'nervous system,' assimilating disparate and siloed data sets held in public and private enterprise resource planning (ERP) systems. It also analyzes data originating from airborne and terrestrial sensor networks located around the world (*SensorFabric*). These, in turn, are connected to a Web 2.0 mashup of decision-support tools (*DecisionSpaces*). These tools facilitate proactive management of resources, risks, and new environmental markets, enabling innovation by private sector entrepreneurs, next-generation regulatory agencies, and social entrepreneurs (*CommonSpaces*)." Castilla-Rubio and Willis, "A Global Platform."

10. See Glenn Beck and Harriet Parke, *Agenda 21* (New York: Pocket Books, 2012).

11. Donald A. MacKenzie, *An Engine, Not a Camera: How Financial Models Shape Markets* (Cambridge, MA: MIT Press, 2006).

12. Raymond Depardon and Paul Virilio, *Native Land, Stop Eject* (Paris: Fondation Cartier pour l'art contemporain, 2008).

13. See Benjamin H. Bratton, "What We Do Is Secrete: On Virilio, Planetarity and Data Visualisation," in *Virilio and Visual Culture*, ed. John Armitage and Ryan Bishop (Edinburgh: Edinburgh University Press, 2013).

14. The total carbon footprint of the world's data centers is presumed to surpass that of the airline industry and to quadruple by 2020. See William Forest, James Kaplan, and Noah Kindler, *Data Centers: How to Cut Carbon Emissions and Costs* (New York: McKinsey & Company, 2008), http://www.mckinsey.com/clientservice/bto/pointofview/pdf/BT_Data_Center.pdf.

15. Data center and fiber-switch installations are an avant-garde of secret urbanism and subterranean architecture. See Bratton, "Cloud" and "City," in *The Stack*.

16. "The Shannon-Hartley theorem bounds the maximum rate at which information can be transmitted over a Gaussian channel in terms of the ratio of the signal to noise power." Eric Price and David P. Woodruff, "Applications of the Shannon-Hartley Theorem to Data Streams and Sparse Recovery," technical paper, 2012, http://www.cs.utexas.edu/~ecprice/papers/isit.pdf.

17. The smart grid, as theological technology, is a recording medium for

172

the direction representation of all things, passing through significatinon, to enable a perfected harmony of things. See Sol Yurick, *Metatron: The Recording Angel* (Los Angeles: Semtiotext(e), 1985).

18. The weight of virtual systems is amplified by the weight of virtual systems that monitor and mediate virtual systems. Consider the impact of Bitcoin and coin mining.

The key innovation is that "the work needed to commit a fraud is set to be higher in electricity costs than the economic benefit derived from it." Mark Gimein, "Virtual Bitcoin Mining Is a Real-World Environmental Disaster," *Bloomberg Business*, April 12, 2013, http://www.bloomberg.com/news/articles/2013-04-12/virtual-bitcoin-mining-is-a-real-world-environmental-disaster; and Rohan Pearce, "Cloud's Real Ecological Timebomb: Wireless, Not Data Centres," *Computerworld*, April 09, 2013, http://www.computerworld.com.au/article/458439/cloud_real_ecological_timebomb_wireless_data_centres.

OXAV

Matthew W. Wilson

Although the distortions on the peripheries of the orthographic view may be extreme, we perceive the correct proportions because we visualize a three-dimensional body instead of a flat map. The use of these projections is limited to illustrative and educational maps, and in many cases the results will be amusing rather than of practical value, yet they open up a new avenue of experimentation, the end of which has not yet been seen.

— Erwin Raisz, 1943[01]

It will usually be necessary for the map designer to make a conscious choice between generalization and particularization. Each has its value, but if the main goal is good overall comprehension, we will usually need to generalize to a substantial degree. ... No method has ever been invented which is capable of optimally serving both goals simultaneously.

— Howard T. Fisher, 1982[02]

The pages of *New Geographies* are undoubtedly filled with contemporary examples of experimentation in geographic representation. Stroke widths, object alignments, and typographic stylization dominate the fine, last-minute adjustments made in illustration software. And while these visual works likely share little in common with their predecessors from a century prior, that moment of experimental tinkering with a drawing binds these practices. What follows is a brief rumination on one of the first computer maps, articulated as an extension of early twentieth-century experimental methods in mapmaking,

designed to provoke reflection on the current status of such experimentation in geographic representation today.

The ability to see the world as it unfolds around us is inherent in the mapmaker's craft. Erwin Raisz (1893–1968) and Howard T. Fisher (1903–1979), both Harvard cartographers, employed different techniques to shape what was possible in mapmaking. Their two quotes in the epigraph and their two related figures deliberately connect two experimental processes of crafting a vision of the world. I title this rumination on experimental mapping methods "OXAV," a midcentury shorthand for printing method, the provenance of which I outline below. More than method, then, OXAV marks a "make-do" attitude in the 1960s advent of the digital map—to take what was perfectly adequate in one domain and apply it, make more of it, in another domain. Fisher and his team of programmers decided to use this overprinting of characters to produce visual densities. Central to this kind of digital experimentation was an interest in the projection of a three-dimensional image across a flat medium—an interest well established in the history of cartographic expression. The work of geographic representation, as Raisz's words suggest, was considered largely perceptual, a persistent condition to this day. While he would witness the beginning of a new mapmaking method at Harvard, Raisz's work would challenge geographic representation in traditional, manual methods as in later digital ones, which were ascending at the end of his life.

This experimental spirit at Harvard was born from a series of events that connect the campus of the mid-1960s to the broader revolutionary stirrings in the spatial sciences

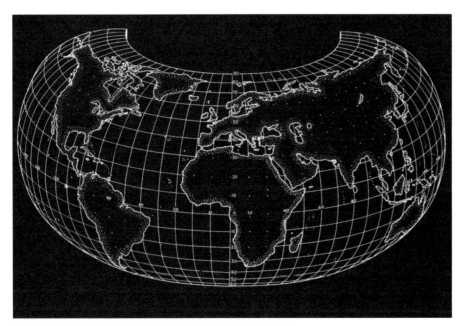

Left: Armadillo map projection. Raisz experimented with graphic techniques that would allow a lay public to see the curved Earth, to make visible the cartographer's craft.
Below left: OXAV. Fisher experimented with the use of overlapping symbols and photographic scaling to produce representations of surfaces.

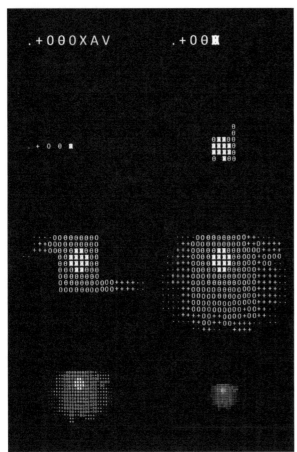

across North America. On a Saturday in 1963 on the campus of Northwestern University, Howard Fisher (then a lecturer there) attended a workshop led by Ed Horwood, a faculty member in the department of Civil Engineering at the University of Washington. Horwood, who had studied under Lewis Mumford at the University of Pennsylvania, developed a program called CARD MAPPING, which produced digital maps of numbers: areas were assigned numbers at their centroid representing the frequency of a specific phenomenon. Importantly, Horwood's research assistants at Washington in the late 1950s and early 1960s included a number of graduate students in geography studying under Bill Garrison. Many of these students would become proponents of a theoretical and quantitative variant of geographic scholarship.

One of the students, Bill Bunge, discusses this emerging approach to analyzing complex social and spatial phenomena, and the representation of such analyses, in his dissertation:

> The exact distinction between the map as a logical system and the map as a framework for theory is murky, but it is of the utmost importance since theory can only be as powerful as the underlying logic. For this reason cartography is placed in company with mathematics.[03]

For these midcentury geographers, the map was burdened by both the particularity of observable facts and the theorization of geographic phenomena (here understood as map abstraction or generalization). An epistemological turn was afoot, driven by the use of the computer in spatial analysis. A new language to express geographic relationships required a revolutionary method for expressing these relationships.

Students of Horwood and Garrison, such as Waldo Tobler and Brian Berry, became key resources for Howard Fisher as he innovated within the CARD MAPPING program. With the assistance of a programmer named Betty Benson, Fisher produced a procedure called the Synagraphic Mapping program (SYMAP). SYMAP was a revision of the Horwood process of printing out a field of numbers, creating representations of surfaces by overprinting characters using technology that was generally available at major computing centers. The overprinting of characters O, X, A, and V created a visual solid that, when placed near other symbols, created gradation. With photographic scaling, these individual characters could be perceived as a mapped surface.

Shortly after developing the first version of SYMAP, Howard was hired by the Harvard Graduate School of Design, where in 1965 he founded the Laboratory of Computer Graphics (LCG). His earliest work on SYMAP and the OXAV method focused on comprehensibility—refining a representational technique to allow a user to directly and efficiently connect the representation with reality. Howard assembled a team of developers to expand the routines available within SYMAP. One student from his freshman seminar, Donald Shepard, revised the interpolation method, allowing a more efficient computation of map surfaces.

Like Raisz's tinkering with map projections in prior decades, these experimentations intended to expand the possibility of observing a changing planet. Far from requiring scientific expertise in interpreting geographic representations, these drawings sought to make the world viewable—and therefore accessible—to a public eager to understand the planet's spatial dynamics. The computer, for Fisher, did change the game in thematic cartography. Perhaps more importantly, however, the new capabilities offered by the digital map raised concerns for general comprehensibility.

In the fifty years since the founding of the LCG, the practices of geographic representation have changed both in speed and in volume, whereas the model of map communication and interaction has largely remained the same. Maps are envisioned as documents that, when designed with great efficiency, effectively communicate information about a variety of spatial phenomena. As a method to collect, analyze, and represent geographies of information, mapmaking is burdened by the weight of these models of correspondence and comprehensibility, establishing a particular register within which information about the world is to be viewed. Contemporary techniques in geographic representation, sometimes termed geovisualizations, consider the map as perhaps just another informational graphic. Here, it is appropriate to reconsider those same interests in mapmaking of a century ago. When reflecting on her interview with Richard Edes Harrison (1901–1994), a contemporary of Raisz, Susan Schulten reminds us of the visual effect of early twentieth-century mapmaking: "When I interviewed Harrison in New York at the end of his life in 1993, he still insisted that I call him an artist rather than a cartographer, for he disdained the constricted techniques of mapmakers who were hidebound by convention."[04] The gloss, or patina, of contemporary geovisualizations breaks with one key commitment of early to mid-twentieth-century geographic representations: as the work of Raisz and Harrison highlights, a commitment to the wide participation of a map-reading audience. Here, the map, as a vehicle for representation was a kind of fantasy, a creation, vernacular yet artisanal, grounded yet imaginative.

OXAV reminds us of a culturally conditioned comprehensibility, where correspondence between reality and map figures the map reader more deeply into the representation, to make interpretations and draw strong conclusions. These experimentations, to "make do" with available technologies, should inspire contemporary cartographic work. How might design practice resist the gloss of spectacle and elevate slow mapmaking, where representation intervenes in the known? How might the fine adjustments made in design software further disguise the mechanics of representation from a public? How might cartographic experimentation forego the rush toward a faddish polishing of infographics, and instead amplify the disruptive potential of geographic representation?

01. Erwin Raisz, "Orthoapsidal World Maps," *Geographical Review* 33, no. 1 (January 1943): 132–34.

02. Howard T. Fisher, *Mapping Information: The Graphic Display of Quantitative Information*, ed. Jacqueline Anna Cohen (Cambridge, MA: Abt Associates, 1982), 26–27.

03. William Bunge, "Theoretical Geography" (PhD diss., University of Washington, 1960).

04. Susan Schulten, "World War II Led to a Revolution in Cartography. These Amazing Maps Are Its Legacy.," *New Republic*, May 20, 2014, http://www.newrepublic.com/article/117835/richard-edes-harrison-reinvented-mapmaking-world-war-2-americans.

Personal Remote Sensing
Computer Vision
Landscapes

Michalis Pirokka,
Erle C. Ellis &
Peter Del Tredici

Since the invention of aerial photography, remote sensing has played a significant role in efforts to map the ecology of landscapes.[01] Owing to technological innovations, a wide variety of remote sensing techniques are now available to enhance these mapping efforts. Specifically, this article will engage new techniques of mapping ecological and surface structures across landscapes that have been made possible by the combination of lightweight, inexpensive, and publicly available Unmanned Aerial Vehicles (UAV) with computer vision algorithms.[02] These technologies now enable "personal" remote sensing on demand by landscape and planning professionals to generate high-resolution 2-D and 3-D maps in both visible and near-infrared spectrums for multiple uses, from initial site assessments to sophisticated landscape analyses supporting coastal erosion control, forestry, and habitat management.[03]

First from balloons and kites, and later with manned aircraft, satellites, and UAVs, new platforms and techniques for remote sensing and mapping have continued to transform the efforts and the thinking of ecologists, landscape planners, and environmental activists. Now, innovative UAV remote sensing and mapping techniques are entering the design discourse, opening new associations, shifting modes of thinking, and potentially altering the trajectories of the theory, history, and cartography discourses within the design profession.

Remote sensing can be a keystone linking the work of designers, urbanists, and ecologists as it employs a visual language and a mode of representation that can immediately be understood across specialization, especially when it accurately replicates real-time dynamics in the physical characteristics of a site. With remote sensing, precise data can be generated to represent both permanent and ephemeral characteristics of a site, offering opportunities for more grounded design development. With remote sensing mapping, terrain becomes more than topography, it becomes a tangible amalgamation of elements, a layering of time, space, and ecology, and the basis for a real-world design process. At multiple levels, the point cloud topographic model produced by remote sensing technology provides a more holistic view of reality than a conventional layered plan.[04]

On Methods

The introduction of UAVs and 3-D mapping is revolutionizing ecology, allowing a more comprehensive grasp of ecological pattern and process than any prior geospatial methodology.[05] Spatially precise and temporally dynamic, 3-D data enables structural observations to be related to ecological functions, opening up novel spatiotemporal views of ecological phenomena across landscapes. The dramatic evolution in the platforms and flight control of UAVs, their coupling with computer vision, and their migration from military secret to smartphone app have put remote sensing into the hands of those who seek the view from above, from technology enthusiasts to journalists, to environmental professionals, transforming ecological mapping and automating site-specific environmental monitoring.[06]

UAVs enable inexpensive, scale-appropriate image acquisition with resolutions defined more by the application than by technological limits. There has never been a lower cost platform for consistent, site-specific 3-D aerial mapping of environmental phenomena to monitor change either in a single visit or over time. The UAV brings four operational advantages as a mapping tool beyond its relatively low cost of operation: deployment on demand, easy repetition as conditions change, the ability to fly under cloud cover (UAVs fly low and slow), and precision-automated flight plans enabling the acquisition of highly overlapping aerial images needed to support both 3-D reconstructions and "perfect" orthorectified photo mosaics (buildings and trees are seen only from the top, free of lens and height distortions). Data gathered by UAVs at local scales can be georeferenced and integrated with data obtained from traditional maps as well as spaceborne remote sensing tools, seamlessly integrating views and data from local, regional, and global scales.

From the overlapping images collected during a UAV flight, a color-referenced 3-D point cloud, a 3-D landscape geometry, can be generated using "structure from motion" algorithms. Compared with simple, 2-D layers, these 3-D data products, with their more realistic data-rich representation, push scientific studies toward a deeper and more accurate understanding of ecological characteristics.[07]

During the past year, a pilot project at the Harvard Graduate School of Design tested the application of UAV technology at Arnold Arboretum of Harvard University in Boston and Harvard Forest in Petersham, Massachusetts.[08]

Typical UAV-based surveys resulted in the production of color-referenced point clouds, orthomosaics, tree canopy height projections, and vegetation maps detailed enough to allow for the identification of plant species. The application of this technology in these two projects revealed the potential for this methodology to become an integral part of landscape analysis. By returning to the site during different seasons of the year, when species can be readily distinguished from one another based on leaf-out times, flowering, and autumnal coloration, an even more finely grained understanding of present conditions of a site and its possible future trajectories were obtained. Given this realization, the central question of this project became, "How can data obtained by remote sensing be best understood, valued, and deployed by designers and planners?"

To date, UAV and computer vision technology—the cornerstones of personal remote sensing—have been applied successfully in population ecology, vegetation dynamics, precision agriculture, archaeology, forestry, and habitat management. These are fields that are best informed through the gathering of precise information in both horizontal and vertical domains, not unlike the information demands of designers working at large scale. The question then becomes, "Can these emerging functionalities shape new and more 'informed' forms of design, especially in the fields of landscape architecture and urban design?"[09]

On Design

The design disciplines negotiate precise scales that often can be best addressed through personal remote sensing. The use of remote sensing in design and the friction between the two fields can revolutionize the process of gathering and monitoring spatial data that can be used to inform design development. As a modeling tool of extraordinary precision, it can expose the "tectonics" of a site. In combination with other techniques of observation and analysis, it can project a new, more up-to-date direction for design.

Design aims to give form and lend shape to all elements that influence a site. Typically, however, design lacks a fine scale of time. This can be a crucial factor, as landscape architecture interventions (like ecology itself) are inseparably bound up with time. Can analysis informed by remote sensing be the method that narrows the gap between reality and design? Surely, it takes design a step closer to reality just by sheer virtue of its ability to enable precise understanding of the physical reality of terrain and vegetation across large sites. The potentials of this method within design lay in its ability

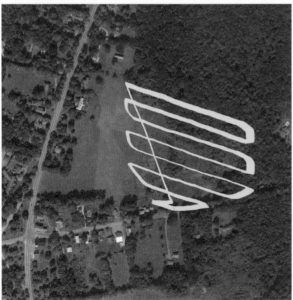

Above: Point cloud aerial perspective, Common Meadow, Petersham, Massachusetts, October 2014. Left: Flight path for an automated flight, Common Meadow, Petersham, Massachusetts, October 2014.

Michalis Pirokka, Erle C. Ellis & Peter Del Tredici

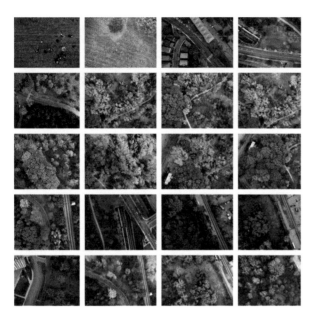

to identify and correlate up-to-date land use and land cover classifications at both the local and regional scales.

Ease of data collection is a major operational advantage that UAV mapping brings to the table for designers. Low operation cost and user-controlled scanning enables repetitive point cloud acquisitions many times across a site on the same day or at least many times per season. By simply associating multiple point clouds with their geolocation, 3-D datasets transform into 4-D datasets, as the variable of time is added to the design equation. This generates the potential for mapping the ephemeral characteristics of a site and, through modeling, of evaluating the specific changes and processes that take place within that site, such as the ebb and flow of tidal waters, seasonal plant changes, animal migration patterns, or the spread of plant pathogens across a landscape, thereby resulting in new associations during design development. With personal remote sensing, we now have the capacity to design for the temporal: this radically shifts the thinking that has characterized design discourse up until this date.

Aerial images traditionally have been crucial for understanding and negotiating landscape and urban scales.[10] But can architects and planners produce credible results when feeding their designs directly into a point cloud? Is this to become a new testing method for design interventions? Personal remote sensing can combine the best aspirations of the design discipline with the best ambitions of mapping, imposing scale-appropriate, efficient, and systemized thought and action. It might even support a new conception of sustainable design, as dynamic

elements of a site can now be registered and ephemeral ecological associations can now influence the scale and form of a design.

By modeling and evaluating the dynamic and the ephemeral, designers can better understand the physicality of the landscape. We are in need of the spatial and temporal precision offered by these new methods: we can no longer afford to ignore the reality of the terrain or to get carried away by intellectual concepts that are independent of the site.[11] Remote sensing can become a significant research topic within design-related disciplines. It is a topic that can be placed in between territory, site design, and ecology, with the perception of geography always present. It is time to bring remote sensing into design and thereby reshape both.

The fields of landscape ecology, landscape architecture, urban planning, and urban design stand at a juncture where innovative technologies provide new methods of site analysis that must be dealt with through emerging, new representational techniques. Traditionally designers dealt with ecology and landscape through the static means of the master plan, with a layering of predefined (and most of the time outdated) datasets. Might we now design in near-real-time frameworks, incorporating datasets updated on demand as the design process unfolds? Potentially these technologies will offer new dynamic tools for the practice of design, bringing us one step closer to realizing the "informed" landscape that fully expresses

Above: Images collected through UAV Technology (left), and Tree Canopy Height DEM (right), Bussey Brook Meadow, Arnold Arboretum of Harvard University, October 2013.

the dynamic articulation of ecological and human processes on a given area of interest.[12]

These new mapping techniques differ from earlier practices. Personal remote sensing is an operational methodology that brings the designer into the physical site, back to fieldwork, whether directly or virtually through 3-D reconstructions.[13] And as a methodology, it has the capacity to question and challenge the techniques and toolsets inherited from the past, just by injecting realistic site data and visualization into the praxis. No longer purely speculative, these new mapping techniques help designers go beyond simply portraying preliminary scenarios to conceiving of credible concepts.

A mixture of remote sensing and traditional mapping techniques has the potential to produce more interesting results and more workable data than either method by itself. Scale thinking based on mapping can alter the typical priorities that drive design, thereby generating new links between design and cartography and, depending on the scale, new connections between architecture, geography, and ecology. Whereas the images generated from a point cloud can be aesthetically pleasing, their true value resides in the data on actual surface cover that they contain and in their ability to enrich the abstract information found in planning documents and maps that have governed design decisions up until now.

On Potentials
The conversation currently taking place within the design discourse will no doubt uncover some critical questions related to the usefulness of remote sensing to the field.

We anticipate accelerating advances in the monitoring, modeling, and representational techniques related to the ecologies of disturbance, density, complexity, and flux, all at the scale of cities, landscapes, ecosystems, and isolated projects. Any misgivings will be revisited in the course of time, as academics and professionals alike become more familiar with—and more dependent upon—these new tools. But it is clear that spatial modeling has the potential to offer designers a unique reading of urban environments.

Remote sensing should never be conceived as a standalone operation: rather, it should always be used to support the design and planning processes as part of a larger context. The greatest potential for further introduction of these tools in the design discipline lies beyond the technological innovation of UAVs. The reprocessing and reinterpretation of raw digital imaging and other data can become a framework for reexamining the use of aerial images in the world of design, and data availability can become a decisive rather than a limiting factor in any future application of remote sensing in the design discipline.

Numerous types of accurate, up-to-date, and high-resolution remotely sensed data can be readily accessible and can be integrated in open-source geospatial libraries (for example, the geospatial libraries linked to each figure in this text). The availability and distribution of data can enhance the collective and communal nature of the

183

Above: Pixel comparison. The images reveal that the end user can define the resolution and the precision of the point cloud. Point cloud perspective, Harvard Forest, Petersham, Massachusetts, October 2014.

Michalis Pirokka, Erle C. Ellis & Peter Del Tredici

Right: Point Cloud Perspective, Brooklyn Bridge Park, Brooklyn, New York, March 2015. As this perspective image reveals, the resolution that a point cloud carries qualifies it as a valuable tool for land use and land cover classification. Below: Pier 1, Brooklyn Bridge Park, Brooklyn, New York, March 2015. Five years after the opening of the park, Michael Van Valkenburgh Associates can use this image to evaluate the success of their design implementation. Opposite: Property Map, Vegetation and Ecological Functioning Units, Bussey Brook Meadow, Arnold Arboretum of Harvard University October 2013. By observing the true orthographic aerial photograph one can start identifying ecological and human processes that take place within the area of interest.

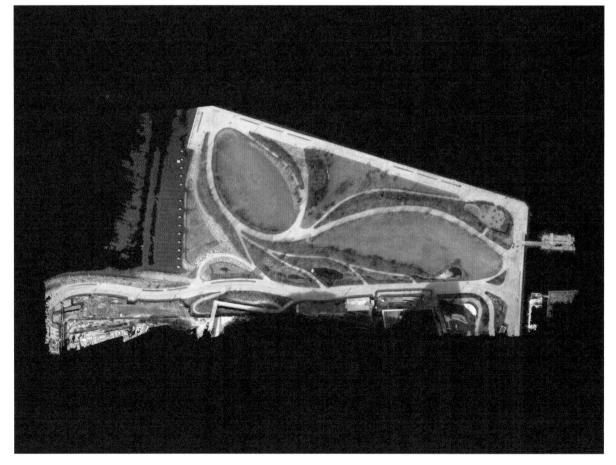

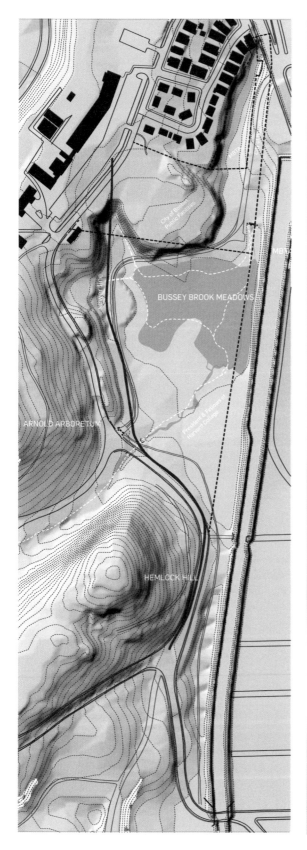

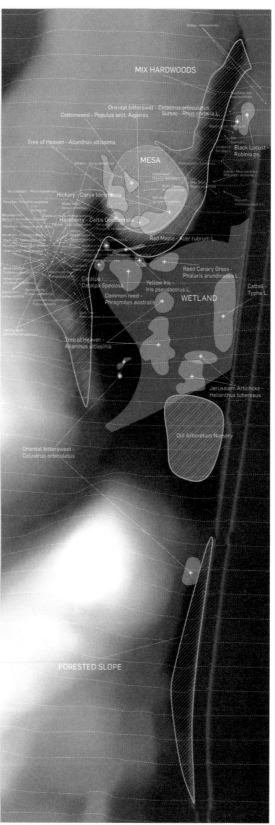

ARNOLD ARBORETUM

BUSSEY BROOK MEADOWS

City of Boston
Public Facilities

Freeman & Hallowell
Herbert College

HEMLOCK HILL

MIX HARDWOODS

Oriental bittersweet - Celastrus orbiculatus
Cottonwood - Populus sect. Aigeiros
Sumac - Rhus coriaria L.

Tree of Heaven - Ailanthus altissima

MESA

Black Locust -
Robinia ps.

Hickory - Carya tomentosa

Hackberry - Celtis Occidentalis

Red Maple - Acer rubrum L.

Reed Canary Grass -
Phalaris arundinacea L.

Catalpa -
Catalpa Speciosa

Yellow Iris -
Iris pseudacorus L.

Cattail -
Typha L.

Common reed -
Phragmites australis

WETLAND

Tree of Heaven -
Ailanthus altissima

Jerusalem Artichoke -
Helianthus tuberosus

Old Arboretum Nursery

Oriental bittersweet -
Celastrus orbiculatus

FORESTED SLOPE

185

Michalis Pirokka, Erle C. Ellis & Peter Del Tredici

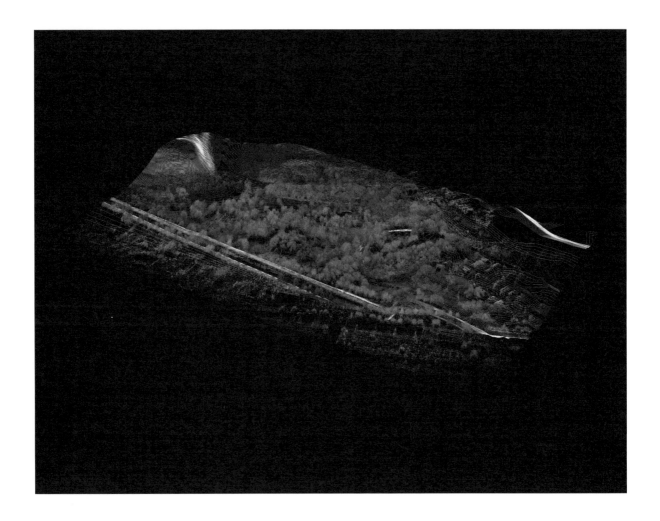

design discipline. This shifts the conversation toward the importance of effective data management and archiving. Due to their large size, UAV data products generate limitations in data sharing. Future efforts must be focused on increasing not only the accuracy but also the availability of datasets for designers. By creating data repositories that can often be managed by libraries, the process of data sharing can be smoothed, enhancing the exchange of research methodologies and ideas.

By increasing the availability of practicable and user-friendly datasets, designers can standardize and automate a process of design analysis that will convert remote sensing into a more effective tool for identifying landscape patterns related to form, use, and cover.[14] Remote sensing reveals potentials related to the observation, design, and maintenance of ecological systems and strategies for landscape development. There is an urgent need for in-depth process understanding and for a more profound, precise, and time-based knowledge of land use decisions that drive the urban structure. To fulfill this need, it is likely that novel approaches toward an increasingly "interactive remote sensing" will become a reality. Monitoring might even happen at the scale of the individual landowner to solve the problem of site accessibility.[15] The designer, as well as other end users will benefit from this. They will be able to update and monitor shared collaborative datasets at any given time, for a close-to-optimal design development process. This interactive form of mapping will be critical for evaluating the success of site restoration and design implementation, cultivating spatial intelligence that helps people better understand and share information about places, and ultimately will transform design information in ways that promote more effective collaboration.

Above: Overlaying site topography with point cloud, Bussey Brook Meadow, Arnold Arboretum of Harvard University October 2013.

An online library including all geospatial data from the scanned sites can be found at: https://dataverse.harvard.edu/dataverse/gsd_designdata.

01. On the use of aerial photography to map landscape ecology, see Olaf Bastian and Uta Steinhardt, eds., *Development and Perspectives of Landscape Ecology* (Dordrecht: Kluwer Academic Publishers, 2002); and Ronen Kadmon and Ruthie Harari-Kremer, "Studying Long-Term Vegetation Dynamics Using Digital Processing of Historical Aerial Photographs," *Remote Sensing of Environment* 68, no. 2 (May 1999): 164–76.

02. For UAV definition, see Karen Anderson and Kevin J. Gaston, "Lightweight Unmanned Aerial Vehicles Will Revolutionize Spatial Ecology," *Frontiers in Ecology and the Environment* 11, no. 3 (April 2013): 138–46. The flight path of a UAV is controlled either autonomously by computers in the vehicle or under the remote control of a pilot on the ground or in another vehicle. Unmanned aircraft are typically launched and recovered by an automatic system or an external operator on the ground. On computer vision algorithms, see N. Snavely, I. Simon, M. Goesele, R. Szeliski, and S. M. Seitz, "Scene Reconstruction and Visualization from Community Photo Collections," *Proceedings of the IEEE* 98, no. 8 (August 2010): 1370–90. See also Jonathan P. Dandois and Erle C. Ellis, "High Spatial Resolution Three-Dimensional Mapping of Vegetation Spectral Dynamics Using Computer Vision," *Remote Sensing of Environment* 136 (September 2013): 259–76.

03. For remote sensing mapping applications, see Anderson and Gaston, "Lightweight Unmanned Aerial Vehicles"; R. Brumana, D. Oreni, M. Alba, L. Barazzetti, B. Cuca, and M. Scaioni, "Panoramic UAV Views for Landscape Heritage Analysis Integrated with Historical Maps Atlases," *XXIII CIPA Symposium*, Prague, Czech Republic (September 2011): 12–16; Dandois and Ellis, "High Spatial Resolution"; Woody Turner, "Sensing Biodiversity," *Science* 346, no. 6207 (October 2014): 301–02; M. J. Westoby, J. Brasington, N. F. Glasser, M. J. Hambrey, and J. M. Reynolds, "'Structure-from-Motion' Photogrammetry: A Low-Cost, Effective Tool for Geoscience Applications," *Geomorphology* 179 (2012): 300–14; and R. Zahawi, J. P. Dandois, K. D. Holl, D. Nadwodny, L. J. Reid, and E. C. Ellis, "Using Lightweight Unmanned Aerial Vehicles to Monitor Tropical Forest Recovery," *Biological Conservation* 186 (2015): 287–95.

04. A point cloud is a set of data points in a specific coordinate system. In a 3-D coordinate system, these points are usually defined by X, Y, and Z coordinates and are often intended to represent the external surface of an object.

05. Anderson and Gaston, "Lightweight Unmanned Aerial Vehicles"; Dandois and Ellis, "High Spatial Resolution Three-Dimensional Mapping"; Woody Turner, "Sensing Biodiversity."

06. With regard to the military uses of remote sensing technology, see Laura Kurgan, *Close Up at a Distance: Mapping, Technology, and Politics* (Brooklyn, NY: Zone Books, 2013), 482.

07. A color-referenced point cloud is one where, in addition to having X, Y, and Z coordinates, has RGB values, which are carried by each point. For "Structure from motion" and 3-D Visualization, see Snavely et al., "Scene Reconstruction and Visualization from Community Photo Collections"; Dandois and Ellis, "High Spatial Resolution"; Gregory P. Asner, Roberta E. Martin, Christopher B. Anderson, and David E. Knapp, "Quantifying Forest Canopy Traits: Imaging Spectroscopy versus Field Survey," *Remote Sensing of Environment* 158 (2015): 15–27.

08. The project began as part of Peter Del Tredici's fall 2014 Research Seminar in Urban Ecology. The work received the Penny White Project Fund award, which allowed students to travel to Baltimore to train at Ecosynth, a lab led by Erle C. Ellis that specializes in UAV remote sensing. During the development of the pilot project, students and their advisors collaborated closely with Janina Mueller, Data Librarian of the Frances Loeb Library. The Ecosynth team at UMBC (http://ecosynth.org) was supported by NSF grant DBI 11-47089.

09. For remote sensing in agriculture, see Jennifer L. R. Jensen and Adam J. Mathews, "Visualizing and Quantifying Vineyard Canopy LAI Using an Unmanned Aerial Vehicle (UAV) Collected High Density Structure from Motion Point Cloud," *Remote Sensing* 5, no. 5 (May 2013): 2164–83. For UAVs in archaeology, see M. Brutto, A. Borruso, and A. D'Argenio, "UAV Systems for Photogrammetric Data Acquisition of Archaeological Sites," *International Journal of Heritage in the Digital Era* 1 (January 2012): 7–14. For forestry and habitat management, see Dandois and Ellis, "High Spatial Resolution"; Asner et al., "Quantifying Forest Canopy Traits."

10. Bastian and Steinhardt, *Development and Perspectives of Landscape Ecology*.

11. Christophe Girot, "The Elegance of Topology," in *Topology: Topical Thoughts on the Contemporary Landscape*, ed. Christophe Girot, Anette Freytag, Albert Kirchengast, and Dunja Richter (2013): 79–115.

12. Wilfried Endlicher, ed., *Perspectives in Urban Ecology: Ecosystems and Interactions between Humans and Nature in the Metropolis of Berlin* (Berlin and Heidelberg: Springer Verlag, 2011).

13. Erle C. Ellis et al., "Measuring Long-Term Ecological Changes in Densely Populated Landscapes Using Current and Historical High Resolution Imagery," *Remote Sensing of Environment* 100, no. 4 (February 28, 2006): 457–73.

14. Ibid.

15. Kit Eaton, "Civilian Photography, Now Rising to New Level," *New York Times*, January 2, 2014.

Image Credits

181, 182 (left), 183: Erle C. Ellis, Peter Del Tredici, Janina Mueller, Hector Tarrido-Picart, and Michalis Pirokka.

182 (right), 186: Peter Del Tredici, Erle C. Ellis, Dana Boswell, Manuel Colon-Amador, Hector Tarrido-Picart, and Michalis Pirokka.

184: Michael Van Valkenburgh Associates, processing and mapping by Janina Mueller and Michalis Pirokka.

185: Peter Del Tredici, Manuel Colon-Amador, Hector Tarrido-Picart, and Michalis Pirokka.

Jean-François Blanchette is associate professor in the Department of Information Studies at the University of California, Los Angeles. He holds degrees in computer science from the Université de Montréal and in science and technology studies from Rensselaer Polytechnic Institute. He is the author of *Burdens of Proof: Cryptographic Culture and Evidence Law in the Age of Electronic Documents* (MIT Press, 2012), *Running on Bare Metal: A Material History of Bits* (University of Chicago Press, forthcoming), and coeditor with Christopher Yoo of *Regulating the Cloud: Policy for Computing Infrastructure* (MIT Press, 2015).

Caitlin Blanchfield is a writer, researcher, and editor who lives in New York City. Her work focuses on issues of infrastructure, territory, and political economy. She has a master of science in critical, curatorial, and conceptual practices in architecture from Columbia University, and is an editor in the Office of Publications at Columbia's Graduate School of Architecture, Planning and Preservation as well as of the *Avery Review*. Her writing appears in *San Rocco*, *Apogee*, *Artforum*, and elsewhere.

Benjamin H. Bratton is a theorist whose work spans philosophy, computer science, art, and design. He is associate professor of visual arts and director of the Center for Design and Geopolitics at the University of California, San Diego. He is also professor of digital design at the European Graduate School in Saas-Fee, Switzerland. His research is situated at the intersections of contemporary social and political theory, computational media and infrastructure, architectural and urban design problems, and the politics of synthetic ecologies and biologies. His next books are *The Stack: On Software and Sovereignty* (MIT Press, 2015) and *Dispute Plan to Prevent Future Luxury Constitution* (e-flux/Sternberg Press, 2015).

Ali Fard is a designer and a researcher. He is currently a lecturer at the University of Waterloo, a doctoral candidate at Harvard University Graduate School of Design, and an editor of the *New Geographies* journal. Ali is the cofounder of Op.N, a design and research office based in Toronto and Boston, and a research associate at the Urban Theory Lab at Harvard GSD. His current research deals with the operational landscapes of connectivity and the urban/spatial disposition of information and communication technologies. Ali's research and design work have appeared in *MONU*, *MAS Context*, *Bracket*, *Azure*, and *Harvard Design Magazine*. He holds a master of architecture from the University of Toronto.

Mark Graham is associate professor at the Oxford Internet Institute, University of Oxford. His research focuses on information geographies, and the differences that changing digital connectivities make at the world's economic margins. His current work looks at changing "knowledge economies" in sub-Saharan Africa, focusing on geographies of information production, virtual labor and microwork, and innovation hubs and the digital economy in fifteen African cities. Mark's recent books include *Society and the Internet: How Networks of Information and Communication Are Changing Our Lives* (with Bill Dutton; Oxford University Press, 2014) and *Research and Fieldwork in Development* (with Dan Hammett and Chasca Twyman; Routledge, 2014). His research has been featured in the *Economist*, the BBC, the *Washington Post*, CNN, the *Guardian*, and other international media. He is an editor or editorial board member of *Information, Communication, and Society*, *Geo*, *Environment and Planning A*, and *Big Data & Society*, and a member of the Department for International Development's Digital Advisory Panel.

Stephen Graham is professor of cities and society at Newcastle University's School of Architecture, Planning and Landscape. Graham has an interdisciplinary background linking human geography, urbanism, and the sociology of technology. He uses this to explore the political aspects of infrastructure, mobility, digital media, surveillance, security, and militarism, emphasizing, in particular, how these work to shape contemporary cities and urban life. His books include *Splintering Urbanism* (with Simon Marvin; Routledge, 2001), *Disrupted Cities: When Infrastructures Fail* (with Simon Marvin; Routledge, 2010), *Cities under Siege: The New Military Urbanism* (Verso, 2010), and *Infrastructural Lives* (with Colin McFarlane; Routledge, 2015). Graham's latest research—including a forthcoming Verso book—focuses on the political aspects of verticality.

Adam Greenfield is senior urban fellow at LSE Cities, managing director of design practice Urbanscale, and the author, most recently, of *Against the Smart City* (Do projects, 2013). His next book, *The City Is Here for You to Use*, is forthcoming from Verso in 2016.

Shuli Hallak is an award-winning professional photographer with ten years of experience documenting core infrastructure. In 2013, she founded Invisible Networks with the mission of making the Internet visible. Currently, she is developing web-based, data-driven interactive visuals. Her work has been published extensively in *Fortune*, *Fast Company*, the *Wall Street Journal*, the *New York Times Magazine*, *Bloomberg News*, *Slate*, *Orion*, and elsewhere. Shuli has a bachelor of arts in philosophy from Washington University in St. Louis, and a master of fine arts in photography from the School of Visual Arts in New York.

Rob Kitchin is European Research Council advanced investigator at the National University of Ireland Maynooth. He is a principal investigator on the Programmable City project, the All-Island Research Observatory, the Digital Repository of Ireland, and the Dublin Dashboard. He has authored or edited twenty-four academic books and written four crime novels. In 2013, Kitchin received the Royal Irish Academy's Gold Medal for the Social Sciences.

Evangelos Kotsioris is an architect and doctoral candidate in the history and theory program at the Princeton School of Architecture. His research focuses on the intersections of architecture with science, technology, and media. He has taught at Princeton University (School of Architecture and Department of Art and Archaeology), the Harvard Graduate School of Design (GSD), the Boston Architectural College, and The Cooper Union. He is a cocurator of the ongoing collaborative research project Radical Pedagogies, which was awarded a special mention at the 14th Venice Biennale of Architecture (2014). Kotsioris has presented his research in conferences and symposia of the Society of Architectural Historians, Harvard GSD, Columbia Graduate School of Architecture, Planning and Preservation, Princeton University, Boston University, and Georgetown University, among others. He has worked as a registered architect in Greece (2002–09) and at OMA/AMO in Rotterdam (2007–08). He has authored and coauthored chapters and articles for edited volumes, catalogs, and journals, such as *Conditions*, *On Site*, *Pidgin*, *Uncube*, and the *Architectural Review*.

Jennifer Light is professor of science, technology and society and professor of urban studies and planning at MIT, where she teaches courses on the histories of technology, computing, and technocracy. Her most recent book is *From Voice to Influence: Understanding Citizenship in a Digital Age* (University of Chicago Press, 2015), coedited with Danielle Allen. Light is currently working on a historical study of participatory virtual worlds.

Merlyna Lim is Canada research chair in digital media and global network society with the School of Journalism and Communication, Carleton University in Ontario. Lim has also held positions at Princeton University, Arizona State University, and the University of Southern California. Lim's research interests revolve around societal implications of digital media globally, especially the production, consumption, and exchange of information in cyberspace

and physical space. Much of her work explores how power relations are embedded in the production of spaces and how people continue to contest, create, and expand spaces of participation, engagement, and social movements.

Malcolm McCullough is professor of architecture at Taubman College, University of Michigan. Previously he served on the faculty at Carnegie Mellon (1998–2000) and at the Harvard Graduate School of Design (1988–98). His most recent book, *Ambient Commons: Attention in the Age of Embodied Information* (MIT Press, 2013), explores information environmentalism and attention to surroundings. *Digital Ground: Architecture, Pervasive Computing, and Environment Knowing* (MIT Press, 2004) became a widely read crossover between architecture and situated interaction design. *Abstracting Craft: The Practiced Digital Hand* (MIT Press, 1996) remains an early cult classic in digital form-giving. On the basis of these writings, McCullough has given nearly fifty invited talks in over a dozen countries. He is currently researching a book on responsive surfaces.

Taraneh Meshkani is an architect, urbanist, and educator. She is a doctoral candidate at Harvard Graduate School of Design, a doctoral fellow at the Graduate Consortium on Energy and Environment at Harvard, and an editor of the *New Geographies* journal. Her research examines the linkage of new information and communication technologies and their spatialities to the social and political processes of contemporary societies. She is currently writing her dissertation on the impact of social media on physical urban spaces as the issue relates to recent sociopolitical movements. She holds a master of architecture from the University of Toronto. Meshkani has worked in different architectural firms, including Morphosis Architects, organized many conferences and exhibitions, and taught as an instructor and a teaching fellow at Harvard Graduate School of Design. Her work has been published and presented in *Canadian Architect Magazine*, the *International Journal of Islamic Architecture*, *MediaCities*, and ACADIA.

Dimitris Papanikolaou is an architect, engineer, and a scholar of media arts and sciences. His research examines urban intelligence through the lens of design, information theory, communication, and social behavior. Currently a doctoral candidate at Harvard Graduate School of Design, he holds a MSc from the MIT Media Lab, a master of science in architecture studies in design and computation from the Massachusetts Institute of Technology's School of Architecture and Planning, and a diploma in architectural engineering from National Technical University of Athens. He has been a researcher in HCI at Microsoft

Research, and has taught at New York University, MIT, and Harvard. He has authored more than twenty articles and book chapters in peer-reviewed conference proceedings, academic journals, and edited volumes; he has organized conference panels and exhibitions and has served as a scientific committee member in conferences in areas of design, digital media, and computation.

Antoine Picon is the G. Ware Travelstead Professor of the History of Architecture and Technology at Harvard Graduate School of Design. His research addresses the complementary histories of urban and architectural space, technology, and society. Picon's *Digital Culture in Architecture* (Birkhäuser, 2010) proposes a comprehensive interpretation of the changes brought by the computer to the design professions. His recent book *Ornament: The Politics of Architecture and Subjectivity* (Wiley, 2013) deals with the relation between digital culture and the "return" of ornament in architecture. His next book, *Smart Cities: A Spatialized Intelligence* (Wiley), will be published in the fall of 2015.

Peter Del Tredici is associate professor in practice at the Harvard Graduate School of Design, where he has been teaching in the Landscape Architecture Department since 1992. He recently retired from the Arnold Arboretum of Harvard University, where he worked for thirty-five years as director of living collections and senior research scientist. His interests are wide-ranging and include such subjects as the root systems of woody plants, the ecology of hemlocks, and the natural and cultural history of the ginkgo tree. His recent work is focused on urban ecology and was published in the widely acclaimed *Wild Urban Plants of the Northeast: A Field Guide* (Cornell University Press, 2010) as well as a GPS-based mobile app, Other Order, which interprets the Bussey Brook Meadow section of the Arnold Arboretum (with Teri Rueb).

Erle Ellis directs the Laboratory for Anthropogenic Landscape Ecology (ecotope.org), is professor of geography and environmental systems at the University of Maryland, Baltimore County, and is visiting professor of landscape architecture at Harvard Graduate School of Design. His research investigates the ecology of human landscapes at local to global scales with the aim of informing sustainable stewardship of the biosphere in the Anthropocene. Recent projects include the global mapping of human ecology and its changes over the long term (anthromes), online tools for global synthesis of local knowledge (GLOBE), and inexpensive user-deployed tools for mapping landscapes in 3-D (Ecosynth).

Michalis Pirokka is a licensed architect in Europe and has a master of landscape architecture from Harvard Graduate School of Design and a bachelor of architecture from the University of Patras in Greece. During his studies, he received awards in a number of international competitions and was the recipient of the Penny White Project Fund at the GSD, a fund that is awarded annually to students in landscape architecture and allied design disciplines that promote creative research. He was a research assistant at the "Structures of Coastal Resilience" project, a design research project coordinated by a Princeton University team led by Guy Nordenson and Michael Oppenheimer. He is currently a landscape designer at MVVA.

Mark Shepard is associate professor of architecture and media study at the University at Buffalo, SUNY, where he directs the Media Arts and Architecture Program and codirects the Center for Architecture and Situated Technologies. He is an editor of the Situated Technologies Pamphlets Series and editor of *Sentient City: Ubiquitous Computing, Architecture and the Future of Urban Space* (Architectural League of New York and MIT Press, 2011). His work has been presented at the 2012 Venice International Architecture Biennial, the 2011 Prix Ars Electronica in Linz, Austria, and the 2009 International Architecture Biennial Rotterdam.

Molly Wright Steenson is associate professor at Carnegie Mellon School of Design. She is currently at work on a book, titled *Architectures of Interactivity*, about the architectural and design history of artificial intelligence and cybernetics. From 2013 to 2015, Steenson was assistant professor in the School of Journalism and Mass Communication at the University of Wisconsin-Madison. She holds a PhD in architecture from Princeton University and a master of environmental design from Yale University School of Architecture.

Kazys Varnelis is a historian and theorist of architecture as well as a designer and developer. He holds a PhD from Cornell University and is director of the Network Architecture Lab and codirector of AUDC. He teaches at the University of Limerick, Ireland, and has taught at SCI-Arc, Columbia, University of Pennsylvania, and MIT. His books include *Blue Monday* (Actar, 2007), *The Infrastructural City* (Actar, 2009), *The Philip Johnson Tapes* (Monacelli Press, 2008), and *Networked Publics* (MIT Press, 2008). He has exhibited his architectural work at venues such as MoMA, the New Museum, and High Desert Test Sites.

Mason White is Associate Professor at the University of Toronto and a partner at Lateral Office. His research, design work, and writing charts architecture's typological collisions with infrastructure and the environment. He is the coauthor of *Bracket 1: On Farming* (Actar, 2009), *Pamphlet Architecture 30: Coupling* (Princeton Architectural Press, 2010), and *Many Norths: Spatial Practice in a Polar Territory* (Actar, 2015).

Matthew W. Wilson, PhD, is associate professor of geography at the University of Kentucky and visiting scholar at the Center for Geographic Analysis at Harvard University. He cofounded and codirects the New Mappings Collaboratory, which studies and facilitates new engagements with geographic representation. His research in critical GIS draws upon STS and urban political geography to understand the development and proliferation of location-based technologies, with particular attention to the consumer electronic sector. He has previously taught at Harvard Graduate School of Design, and his current research examines mid-twentieth-century digital-mapping practices.

Eleonora Marinou holds a diploma in architecture from the University of Patras. Since 2008 she has participated in multiple international urban planning and research projects. As a researcher she worked on the development of a new model settlement of 25,000 inhabitants for the victims of the 2,008 wildfires in Peloponnese, Greece. She collaborated as consultant for Harvard research projects with the Zofnass Program for Sustainable Infrastructure on the development of the Zofnass Planning Guidelines for Sustainable Cities. She also contributed to the project Gulf Sustainable Urbanism for ten cities in the Persian Gulf, sponsored by the Qatar Foundation. As an urban planner she worked for the preparation of a detailed master plan for the new DCK City in Karachi, Pakistan, developing sustainable infrastructure solutions in the sectors of energy, waste, transportation, water, and landscape, giving emphasis on information as the core infrastructure system of the twenty-first century.

Spiro N. Pollalis is professor of design, technology and management at Harvard Graduate School of Design. He is director of the Zofnass Program for Sustainable Infrastructure, which has led to the Envision Rating System. He is the principal investigator of the project Gulf Sustainable Urbanism for ten cities in the Persian Gulf, sponsored by the Qatar Foundation. He has taught as visiting professor at the ETH Zurich, Switzerland; Delft University of Technology, Holland; University of Stuttgart, Germany; and University of Patras, Greece. He serves as the cochair of the Advisory Committee on Future Cities for the Singapore ETH-Zurich Center. Pollalis is the chief planner for the new DHA City Karachi for 600,000 people,

under construction, and the concept designer of the information infrastructure in the new administrative city in Korea. He served as the chairman of the public company for the redevelopment of the former Athens airport, and developed its base master plan and business plan. He currently serves as a member of the Athens Planning Committee. Pollalis received his first degree from the University in Athens (EMP) and his master's degree and PhD from MIT. His master of business administration in high technology is from Northeastern University. He has an honorary master's degree in architecture from Harvard.

Vicky Sagia holds a diploma in architecture from the University of Thessaly and a MSc in sustainable environmental design from the Architectural Association Graduate School, London. Since 2006, she has participated as a sustainability consultant in diverse international projects ranging from policy development, building design, and retrofitting to master planning for new cities with emphasis on sustainable infrastructure solutions. She is currently a consultant for research projects for the Zofnass Program for Sustainable Infrastructure at Harvard Graduate School of Design, working on the development of the Zofnass Planning Guidelines for Sustainable Cities.

Yannis Orfanos's work focuses on enhancing the sustainability of cities with information technology. It concerns the development of data-driven tools to better understand how urban environments work and address the existing or emerging challenges. He has a diploma in architectural engineering and master of philosophy in architecture from the National Technical University of Athens, and master of architecture in architecture and urbanism from the Design Research Lab at the Architectural Association. Yannis has professional experience as an architect and planner in Athens, London, and Barcelona. He is currently research associate at Harvard Graduate School of Design, where he is investigating sustainable infrastructure systems at the Zofnass Program for Sustainable Infrastructure and healthier cities at the Health and Places Initiative.

NEW GEOGRAPHIES

New Geographies 07: *Geographies of Information* is the second in a series of three volumes that question the dimensions and materialities associated with the geographical registration of the complex and multiscalar social, technical, and environmental processes that constitute contemporary urbanization. In volumes 0 to 5, the primary aim of the journal was to foreground the emergence of the geographic as a paradigm that would allow design to provide a broader, more engaged, and more dialectical response to context. This investigation revealed that as designers are increasingly compelled to shape larger scales and address complex urban and ecological issues, they depend increasingly on social, economic, and ecological interpretations of space. While these interpretations typically embrace the dynamism of processes, flows, and networks, they seem to have overlooked their material imprints on geographic space. This series addresses the apparent disjunction between verifiable as well as speculative relations among processes, flows, and networks (which has dominated contemporary debates on urbanization) and their geographical imprints, whether designed or simply inherited in the physical organization of territories.

New Geographies 06: *Grounding Metabolism*

Over the past decade, there have been widespread efforts to reposition design and its agency in relation to a changing, more fluid, and expanding context. Yet the redefinition of the context itself has proven to be a serious challenge—not only due to the increasing complexity of urban environments, but because their socio-environmental intensities and interdependencies are now expanding across the earth. As a metaphor derived from the physical sciences, the notion of urban metabolism offers a framework for understanding the production of space as well as its circulatory and functional dynamics. Bringing together contributions within and outside the design disciplines, *New Geographies* 06: *Grounding Metabolism* aims to trace alternative routes to design through a more elaborate understanding of the relation between concepts of urban metabolism and the formal and material engraving of metabolic processes across scales. This volume addresses the challenges associated with the planetary dimension of contemporary metabolic processes, it offers a critical examination of the long lineage of historical discussions and schemes on urban metabolism from the design disciplines, and it places them in parallel with a set of contemporary projects and interventions that open up new approaches for design.

New Geographies 08: *Island*

As a master metaphor, the island has been a fecund source of inspiration in multiple domains. From Thomas More's *Utopia* to Darwin's evolutionary theory to Ungers's archipelago, insights derived from "island thinking" are commonly extrapolated across scales and fields. The recurrence and appeal of the island metaphor lie in its capacity to simplify the complex and to frame the seemingly unbounded. Yet the island seems to confront current ontological mainstreams in the geographic and its articulation in the design fields. Globalization's motifs of openness and interconnection and ecology's privileging of environmental processes and flows over forms and objects challenge the pertinence of the island as a cognitive device for territorial description and intervention. *New Geographies* 08 proposes an epistemological pulse between the ultimate loss of the exterior implied in the planetary upscaling of territorial interpretations towards an idea of the world as a whole, and the need to rearrange new boundaries in an environment frequently explained through the process-oriented lens of ecology. As an "atlas" of islands, *New Geographies* 08 will explore the new limits of islandness, and will gather examples to reassert its relevance for the design disciplines.